INSIDE THE BRITANNIC

UNCOVERING THE WRECK OF THE TITANIC'S SISTER SHIP

SIMON MILLS

ADLARD COLES

ADLARD COLES
Bloomsbury Publishing Plc
50 Bedford Square, London, WC1B 3DP, UK
29 Earlsfort Terrace, Dublin 2, Ireland

BLOOMSBURY, ADLARD COLES and the Adlard Coles logo are trademarks of
Bloomsbury Publishing Plc

First published in Great Britain 2025

Copyright © Simon Mills, 2025

Simon Mills has asserted his right under the Copyright, Designs and Patents Act, 1988, to be
identified as Author of this work

For legal purposes the Acknowledgements on p. 284
constitute an extension of this copyright page

All rights reserved. No part of this publication may be reproduced or transmitted in any form or by
any means, electronic or mechanical, including photocopying, recording, or any information storage
or retrieval system, without prior permission in writing from the publishers

A catalogue record for this book is available from the British Library

Library of Congress Cataloguing-in-Publication data has been applied for

ISBN: HB: 978-1-3994-1450-0; ePub: 9781399414494; ePDF: 9781399414487

2 4 6 8 10 9 7 5 3 1

Designed by Nick Avery Design
Typeset in Garamond Premier Pro
Printed and bound in India by Replika Press Private Ltd.

To find out more about our authors and books visit www.bloomsbury.com and sign up
for our newsletters

CONTENTS

INTRODUCTION 4
1 Weathering the Storm 8
2 Aegean Prelude 23
3 The Secret History of the *Britannic* 34
4 Science and the Modern Shipwreck 48
5 CSI *Britannic* 63
6 What Lies Within 86
7 The Superstructure 103
8 The Bridge Deck 128
9 The Shelter and Saloon Decks 151
10 The Upper and Middle Decks 174
11 The Tank Top 197
12 The Stern 224
13 A Tale of Two Sisters 247
14 Taking Stock 264

APPENDIX I 275
APPENDIX II 277
APPENDIX III 279
BIBLIOGRAPHY AND SOURCES 282
ACKNOWLEDGEMENTS 284
INDEX 286

Left: One of the *Britannic*'s intact funnel casings, large enough to pilot a submersible into several parts of the superstructure. (Leigh Bishop)

INTRODUCTION

I stopped counting how many times I have visited Kea years ago. It must be at least a dozen occasions in the last 20 years, and in all that time it is curious to see how much has changed on the island, and yet how so much more remains the same. If you want glitzy nightclubs and noisy bars then Kea is probably not the destination for you, but if you're looking for a distinctive island with a more traditional Greek atmosphere, Kea ticks many boxes.

Kea is a mountainous, rocky island with a high central ridge rising to a height of some 1,800 feet (550m), its deep-cut barren valleys falling symmetrically away on either side to the coast. St Nikolo is the only harbour of any significance on the island, and was once of some importance as a coaling station for the smaller steamers plying between the west European ports and the Black Sea. Today those steamers are long gone, and the now sleepy harbour has become the more seasonal

Above: Port St Nikolo, with the distant island of Makronisos marking the northern side of the Kea Channel.

INTRODUCTION

reserve of yachtsmen keen to test their skills against the local etesian winds. The harbour itself has two arms, Vourkari Bay to the north, providing much the best shelter, while the smaller southern arm, formerly Livadi Bay but now better known as Korissia Harbour, serves the daily ferries from the Greek mainland. A road links these two villages, which are about a mile apart, with eucalyptus and almiriki trees – also known as salt cedars – comprising the wooded glade at Gialiskari Beach. This road, according to local lore, is haunted by the ghost of a British nurse lost on the *Britannic*. Another road from Korissia leads up the mountain to Ioulis, the island's capital. Beyond Ioulis lies Kea's oldest inhabitant – a friendly, smiling lion carved out of the island's rock, believed to date back to 600 BC.

Until after the First World War, Greek fishing vessels, known as *caïques*, had no motors and would usually take the direct open-water route to make their northing. When bound for Salonika, they would take advantage of the fact that the north-west wind blowing in from the Attica shoreline changes its direction further to the east; thus, sailing vessels were often favoured with an easterly slant that enabled them to fetch right up the Salonika Gulf. This would take vessels through the Kea and Doro channels.

My reason for being so intimately familiar with the Kea weather patterns has always had very little to do with sailing. On countless occasions – certainly more than I care to remember – I have stood in the graveyard of the church of Agia Triada in Korissia, staring out into the Kea Channel at the white horses

Above: The RV *Odyssey*, directly above the wreck of the *Britannic* and less than three miles from the island of Kea.

atop the waves when a northerly wind, known locally as the Meltemi, was passing through. The havoc that a particularly strong Meltemi can leave in its wake will usually force any passing yachtsmen to run for the shelter of the nearest safe harbour, or for any diving operations in the Kea Channel to be put on hold until the storm front has passed through, which can sometimes take several days.

And it is with the diving that this particular journey begins, as on 20 August 1996 I had become the proud owner of the UK government's legal title to the wreck of the hospital ship *Britannic*. The *Britannic* was no ordinary vessel, as she was then, and indeed still is, the largest liner on the seabed, although if you like your history to be quirky then it's interesting to think that the *Britannic* is the only vessel to have ever held that title twice. She lost it briefly on 13 January 2012, when the 114,147 GRT *Costa Concordia* capsized and sank off the Italian island of Giglio, and it

Above: The St Nikolo light, overlooking the Kea Channel since 1864.

was only after the *Costa* had been raised, in July 2014, that the *Britannic* regained this rather dubious distinction.

Without doubt, the *Britannic*'s real claim to fame is that she is the younger and larger sister ship of the legendary RMS *Titanic*, but although I have been investigating this wreck site across two millennia, this project has never been about building on the history of the earlier vessel. Like any shipwreck, the *Britannic* has her own mysteries and stories to tell, but while the legends of a clandestine name change and various post-*Titanic* design modifications are perhaps understandable, the numerous myths and conspiracy theories that subsequently became associated with the wreck, possibly in an attempt to further sensationalise the *Titanic* legend, have also made the subject that much more enticing. After all, why was the *Britannic* eventually located so far from her charted position? What was the source of the mysteriously large internal explosion? Was she really the victim of a mine or a torpedo?

When I first started out on my own particular Aegean odyssey, I had no concept whatsoever of the legal and political minefield I was about to enter, to say nothing of a total lack of diving or logistical experience. Back in 1996, the *Britannic* was also largely unknown to most of the inhabitants of Kea, even though she lay barely 3 miles (4.8km) from the island's harbour. Thirty years later, things are very different. The wreck is not only better documented and understood, but it is now also a protected monument and even a marine tourism attraction. All these developments combined should help to ensure that the *Britannic* will hopefully go on to enjoy a greater degree of protection than I could previously have imagined.

When *Exploring the Britannic* was first

INTRODUCTION

published, in March 2019, the story of our exploration of the wreck seemed to be complete, but while I had neatly summarised the work carried out on the *Britannic* up to the centenary of the ship's sinking, this didn't necessarily mean that the job was done. I recall ending that particular volume focusing on the numerous challenges that still lay ahead, because even though we had already achieved so much, there was no doubt in my mind that from that point onward the principal targets lay inside the *Britannic*. The Covid-19 pandemic did its best to thwart those plans, but by the summer of 2021 the project had gained so much momentum that nothing was going to stop us, and as a result the saga of the *Britannic* can, at long last, be seen in its more complete light.

As I put the finishing touches to this introduction, it occurs to me that I never for a moment imagined I was embarking on a project that would swallow up more than a quarter of a century of my time on this planet. It's also no exaggeration to say that it has taken the better part of 30 years of research, 14 diving expeditions and a likely overall expenditure of hundreds of thousands of dollars just to get to this point; but as with Homer's *Odyssey*, perhaps the important message in all this is that it is not so much a question of getting to the destination, but rather the journey itself. If this is true then all I can say is that it has been quite a voyage of discovery, if only to answer finally the questions as to how and why my ship sank. It was Oscar Wilde who once wrote 'the one duty we have to history is to rewrite it', and I hope that this book will help to do just that.

Above: The famous smiling lion of Kea.

1

WEATHERING THE STORM

The RMS *Britannic* is probably one of the great enigmas in the story of ocean-going vessels. Conceived as the largest British-built liner prior to the advent of the *Queen Mary*, she would have been the crowning glory of the White Star Line's North Atlantic mail service, or the safest liner in the world, or perhaps even the most luxurious vessel of her time. She could have been any or all of these things, but in the end her fate was, sadly, to be none of them.

When her keel was laid, on 30 November 1911, the *Britannic* was intended to be the third and largest of the White Star Line's Olympic class liners. But the first shadows over her intended life on the North Atlantic were cast long before she had even been launched, when, at 2.20am on Monday 15 April 1912, the RMS *Titanic* sank after hitting an iceberg on her maiden voyage from Southampton to New York. At this point, the *Britannic*'s hull, which had been progressing quietly on slip 2 at the Belfast shipyard of Harland & Wolff for less than 20 weeks, was barely framed to the height of the double bottom, and yet overnight the new vessel would be subjected to scrutiny, rumours, speculation and innuendo that, only days earlier, would have been unimaginable.

The legends of what had happened on the *Titanic* very quickly took hold on the public imagination, but despite the cloud hanging over the *Britannic*'s future, if indeed she had one, the task of separating the fact from the

Right: By April 1913 the *Britannic*'s framing had been completed. (Harland & Wolff)
Above: Launch booklet of the RMS *Britannic*, on 26 February 1914.

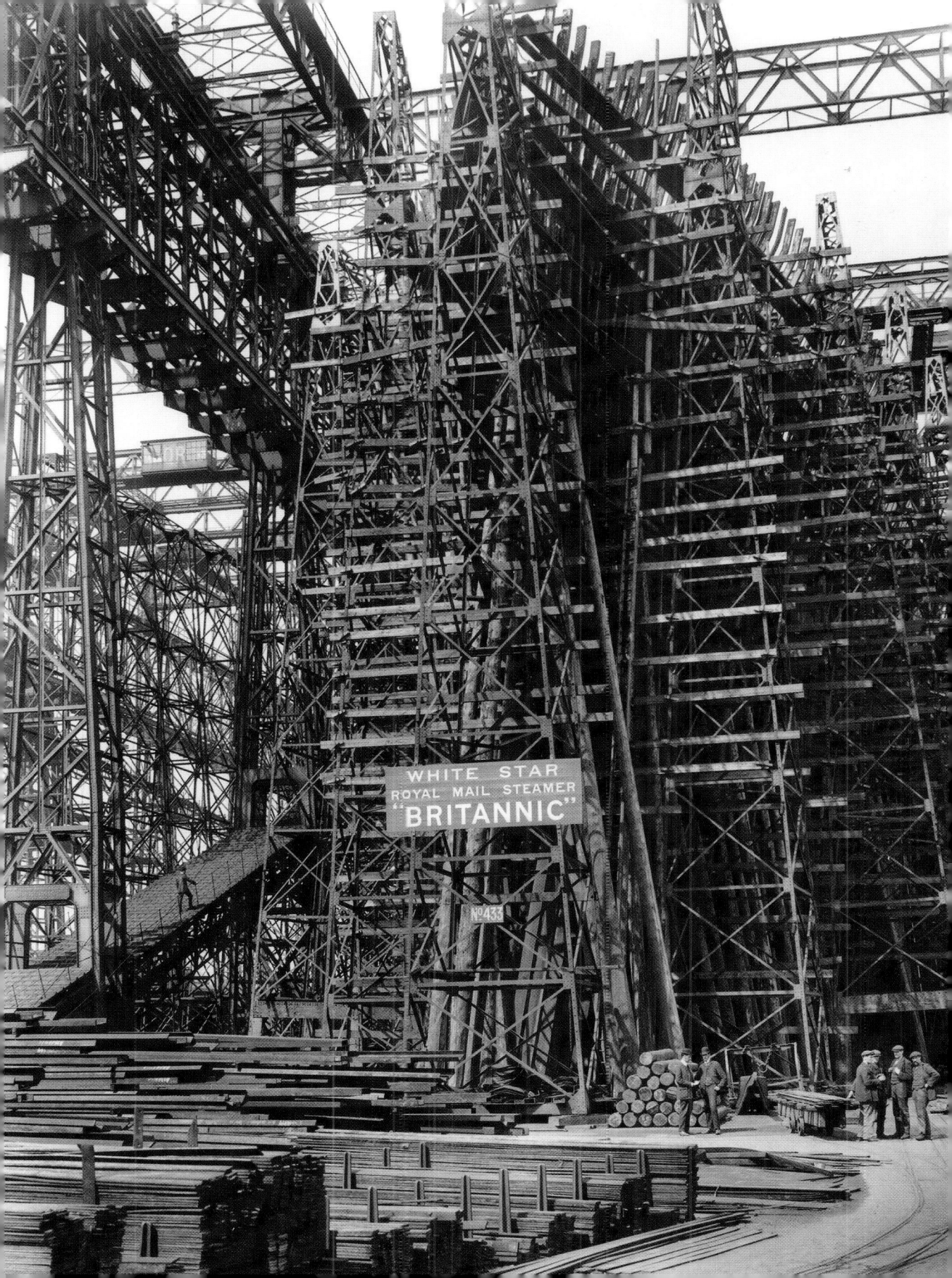

fiction would ultimately fall to Edward Wilding, who up until this point in the story of the Olympic class liners had enjoyed a reasonably low profile. Lord Pirrie, the chairman of Harland & Wolff and the man ultimately responsible for the design of the *Olympic* and *Titanic*, had been in the process of recovering from a prostate operation, which, according to legend, might even have prevented him from sailing on the *Titanic*, but in addition to his illness, Pirrie was totally devastated not only by the loss of the ship, but also by the death of Thomas Andrews, who was both his nephew and head of the company's design department. Alexander Montgomery Carlisle, Pirrie's brother-in-law and formerly the company's chief naval architect, had also been crucial to the original design of the Olympic class, but he had retired from the company at the end of June 1910, and it was into this unenviable vacuum that Wilding unexpectedly found himself taking on the mantle of head of the design department.

It would be Wilding's task to salvage the professional reputation not only of Harland & Wolff, but also of British shipbuilding as a whole. Looking back on it, it is difficult to comprehend the ordeal that Wilding would have faced in London in June 1912, as he fielded something in the order of 1,200 questions at Lord Mersey's *Titanic* wreck inquiry. Being cross-examined in a hostile environment, dealing with repetitive questions and trying to make crucial technological and scientific details even remotely comprehensible to the batteries of lawyers with little or no

Above: Edward Wilding, who would succeed Thomas Andrews as the head of the design department at Harland & Wolff and oversee the modifications in the *Britannic*'s original design.

understanding of the technical jargon would probably have tested any man, yet through it all he somehow retained his poise, patience and dignity, assisting the inquiry as much as he could, while at the same time protecting the reputation of Harland & Wolff. There was certainly no doubting his professional credentials, having attended both the Royal Naval Engineering College at Devonport and the Royal Naval College at Greenwich, before spending five years at the Royal Corps of Naval Constructors. During this time he undertook experimental work at Haslar, and by the time he joined Harland & Wolff as a naval architect in 1904, his experience in the world of marine and naval engineering would prove invaluable

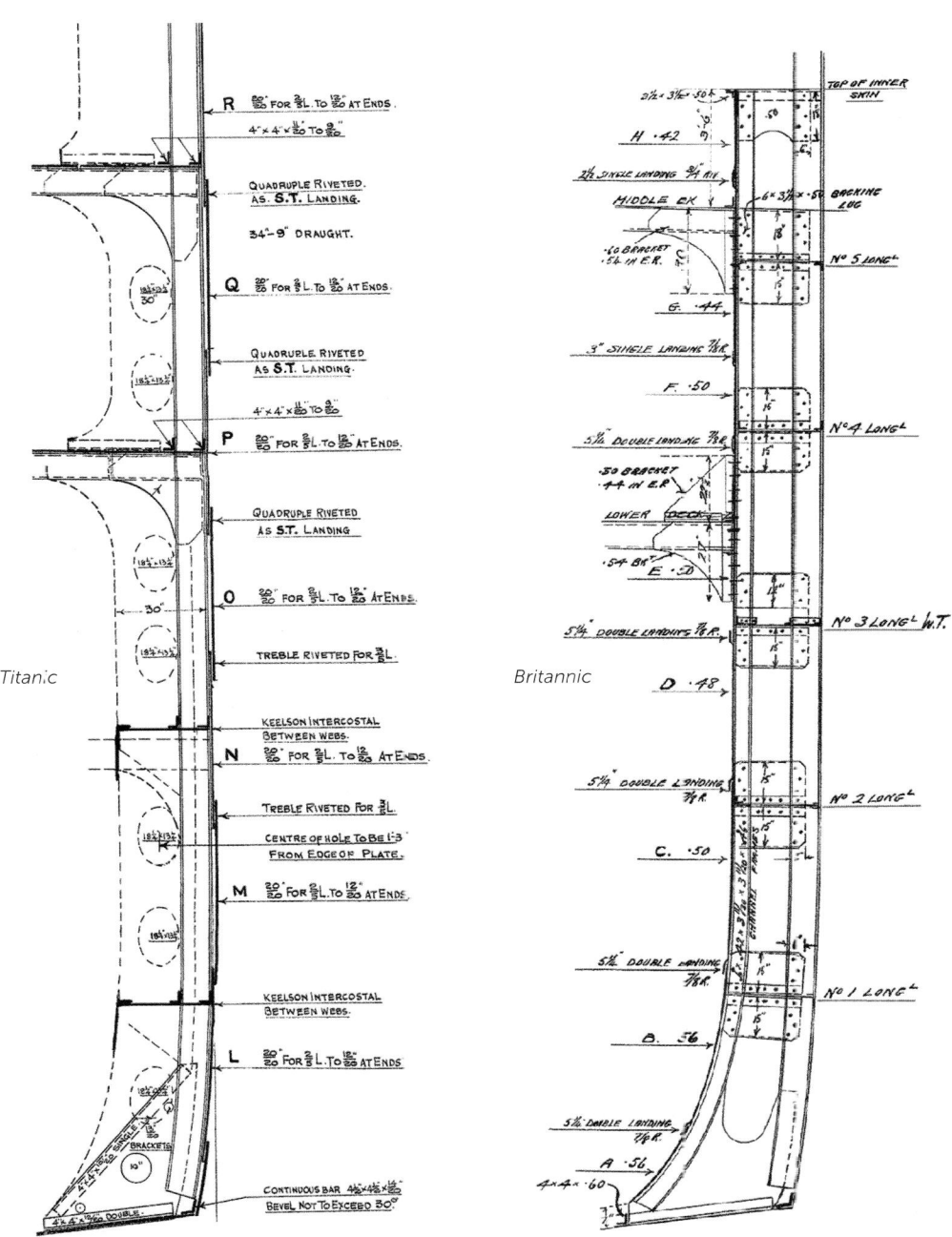

Above: *Britannic*'s double skin, compared to the original design in the *Olympic* and *Titanic*. (Harland & Wolff)

at a time when shipping companies were ordering ever larger and faster vessels. By this time the 24,541 GRT White Star liner *Adriatic* was already on the stocks, and with Cunard in the process of planning the even larger *Lusitania* and *Mauretania*, the trend in terms of ship construction, particularly for vessels destined for service on the North Atlantic, was not difficult to foresee. The *Olympic* and *Titanic* would be White Star's logical response to the Cunard sisters, and if Wilding's role would not be as crucial to the early development stages as that of Pirrie, Carlisle and Andrews, he would nevertheless have been closely involved in the discussions and various calculations as the plans took shape.

By the spring of 1912, however, those plans needed to be seriously rethought. In order to comply with the Board of Trade requirements, the Olympic class had been designed to float with any two contiguous compartments flooded; but while the *Titanic* could actually float with all four of her smaller forward compartments open to the sea, the moment the hull damage extended as far aft as boiler room 6, the fifth compartment from the bow, the ship was effectively doomed. Wilding's analysis of the data, however, enabled him to provide Lord Mersey with more than just the idle speculation that abounded in the national press, and based on the testimony of the survivors he was able to theorise that the scale of the damage to the *Titanic*'s hull did not result from a single continuous gash, but rather from a series of smaller wounds extending over an approximate length of 250 feet (75m). By the time his ordeal was over,

Wilding had not only earned the admiration and respect of the Wreck Commissioner himself, who even thanked him for his evidence, which had been of 'very great assistance' to the court, but he had also done enough to ensure that when the final report was published in July 1912, it acknowledged that the *Titanic* was 'efficiently designed and constructed to meet the contingencies which she was intended to meet'.

Even though the professional reputation of Harland & Wolff had been saved, along with that of British shipbuilding as a whole, there was still no denying that serious consideration needed to be given to the issues of internal subdivision and double sides in foreign-going passenger and emigrant ships. This thorny issue would ultimately be placed before the Board of Trade's Bulkheads Committee for consideration, but even before the conclusion of Lord Mersey's inquiry, Harland & Wolff had been giving serious consideration to the lessons learned in the loss of the *Titanic*, so much so that in October 1912 the *Olympic* would return to Belfast to undergo a six-month overhaul of the interior. By the time the work was completed, the ship would boast an additional watertight skin along the eight boiler and engine room compartments, higher and stronger watertight bulkheads, and even an additional aft bulkhead dividing the electric engine compartment in two. More noticeable to the passengers' eye, however, was the welcome sight of the additional lifeboats along the boat deck, providing reassurance that the lessons from the *Titanic*'s sinking had been well and truly learned.

Above: Colourised image of the builder's model of the RMS *Britannic*, after conversion from its original RMS *Olympic* configuration. (Harland & Wolff)

In the *Britannic*'s case the work would be even more extensive, although the builders did have the advantage of working on a largely incomplete hull, meaning that the modifications could be incorporated more easily; in fact, the extensive details of the proposed modifications in the *Britannic*'s specification book include several crucial passages relating to the revised watertight subdivision arrangements:

> 'Vessel to have sixteen watertight bulkheads extending to the Upper, Saloon, Bridge and Forecastle Decks, the bulkheads to be recessed where necessary to suit passenger and crew accommodation and machinery space. The collision bulkhead to extend to the Forecastle Deck, the bulkheads at the forward and after ends of the boiler space, the bulkhead between Nos. 2 & 3 Boiler Rooms, and the bulkhead between the two dynamo rooms abaft the Turbine Engine Room all to extend to the level of the Bridge Deck; the bulkhead between Nos. 1 & 2 Holds and also the after peak bulkhead to extend to the Saloon Deck; the remaining bulkheads to terminate at the Upper Deck.
>
> An inner skin to be fitted from f78 forward to f71 aft in way of Boiler and Engine rooms, extending in height from the tank top to 3'6" above Middle Deck.
>
> The cellular double bottom to extend from the Collision bulkhead forward to frame 125 aft.'

Based on the extensive modifications, it is clear that while the *Britannic*'s hull may have looked very similar to that of the *Titanic*, from a structural point of view they would actually be very different ships. The additional transverse bulkhead dividing the electric engine room not only increased the watertight compartmentalisation in the *Britannic*, but it also added considerably to the strength and stiffness in that area of the ship's hull. Combined with the fact that five of the existing bulkheads had been raised to the height of the bridge deck, along with the additional inner skin to protect the boiler and engine room compartments, the end result not only increased the hull's ability to survive the extent of the damage that ultimately overwhelmed the *Titanic*, but it added considerably to the overall strength of the entire structure, due to the extent of the additional stiffening members between the double bottoms and the double skin.

While the *Titanic* and *Britannic* may have differed considerably in their internal design, no one saw any great need to rethink the new ship's propulsion. White Star had long given up in their quest for speed on the North Atlantic, and by the early 20th century the company's emphasis had focused largely on slower and more luxurious vessels. This not only resulted in steadier and more comfortable ships, but it also brought the added benefit of greater economy, on account of the fact that they required less coal and smaller stokehold crews to power them. However, the advent of the Cunard Line's *Lusitania* and *Mauretania*, each with a gross tonnage of over 31,500 tons and capable of maintaining a service speed in excess of 25 knots, had ultimately forced the White Star Line to reconsider the maximum speed of their vessels, which would be crucial if the company was to maintain a credible express service on the North Atlantic.

In 1909 the White Star Line had experimented with two near-identical vessels destined for their Canadian service. The twin-screw SS *Megantic* was designed to be driven with conventional quadruple-expansion reciprocating engines, while the SS *Laurentic* was instead equipped with a novel combination of triple-expansion engines driving the two wing propellers, with the remaining steam exhausting into a low-pressure Parsons' marine turbine engine to drive a third propeller on the ship's centreline. The results were indisputable. At half power, the steam consumption for propulsion worked out at 15lb per indicated horsepower per hour on the *Megantic*, and 14lb for the *Laurentic*, whereas at full power the comparative figures were even more telling, being 14lb and 11½lb respectively. The *Laurentic*'s combination machinery not only made her the more economical and steadier vessel of the two, but the added bonus of the combination engine arrangement was that there was also no need to install reversing turbines. The turbine could be quickly deactivated simply by pulling a lever in the reciprocating engine room, which redirected the exhaust steam directly into the condensers. As the reciprocating engines could run just as well astern as they did when the ship was moving forward, all of the manoeuvring in port could therefore be carried out just by using the wing propellers.

Although there were still a number of small improvements in the *Britannic*'s power plant, the engine room arrangement was practically

Above: The July 1914 cover of *Popular Mechanics* provides one of the few colourful views of the *Britannic*'s planned interiors.

identical to those in the *Olympic* and *Titanic*. The main reciprocating engines were of the four-cylinder triple expansion type, balanced on the Yarrow-Schlick-Tweedy system, in order to minimise the vibration of the main crankshafts during rotation. The diameters of the individual cylinders were also identical, the high-pressure cylinder being 54 inches (1.37m), the intermediate-pressure cylinder being 84 inches (2.13m) and the two low-pressure cylinders each being 97 inches (2.46m). The length of stroke was also unchanged at 75 inches (1.9m), the only real difference being that the cylinders in the *Britannic*'s engines were fitted with piston valves, whereas in the two earlier vessels the low-pressure cylinders had flat slide valves with relief rings at the back. This change in design was specifically intended to help increase the pressure in the low-pressure chest, in order to exhaust into the turbine engine at a slightly increased pressure – about 10lb absolute, instead of 9lb under the same conditions in the two earlier ships.

The reason for the higher exhaust pressure related largely to the modified turbine engine. As in the *Olympic* and *Titanic*, the *Britannic*'s marine turbine was also of the Parsons' exhaust type, taking steam from the two reciprocating engines before exhausting into two condensers at either side. In terms of scale, however, the *Britannic*'s engine was somewhat larger, the overall length of the turbine being about 50 feet (15m), with the bladed rotor alone weighing 150 tons. All told, the total weight of the turbine engine – then the largest marine turbine afloat – was 490 tons, with the modified design capable of developing some 18,000-shaft horsepower when running at about 170 revolutions per minute, as opposed to the 16,000-shaft horsepower at 165 revolutions in the two earlier ships. Other than that, the shaft arrangement was practically identical. The two wing propellers each consisted of three manganese bronze blades bolted onto a cast-steel boss, the diameter being 23 feet 9 inches (7.2m), with the screws designed to run at 77 revolutions per minute when the two engines were indicating collectively 32,000 horsepower. As in the original design, the *Britannic*'s centre propeller, cast in solid manganese bronze and with a diameter of 16 feet 6 inches (5m), had four blades, although an early elevation plan suggests that at one stage Harland & Wolff may have been contemplating installing a triple-bladed screw.

To help generate the additional power required for the larger turbine, while the general layout of the boiler rooms was practically identical to the original design, the *Britannic*'s double-ended boilers would also be slightly larger. They would still retain the original diameter of 15 feet 9 inches (4.8m), but at 21 feet (6.4m) in length they would be slightly longer; this would result in a total of 159 furnaces, 3,461 square feet (321.5 sq m) of grate area and 150,958 square feet (14,024 sq m) of heating surface.

In one important respect, however, the most noticeable design modification would have been unmistakeable to even the most casual observer. The 1894 Board of Trade lifeboat regulations, which had been in force since April 1912, had been based on vessels with a gross tonnage of up to 10,000 tons, but with the Olympic class vessels each boasting a GRT well in excess of 45,000 tons, the legal requirements had become hopelessly out of date long before the 31,550 GRT *Lusitania* had even sailed on her maiden voyage in September 1907. The 1,500 souls lost when the *Titanic* sank bitterly proved the point that the existing lifeboat requirements were wholly inadequate, but while the 1913 *Olympic* lifeboat arrangements more than satisfied the updated legal requirements, the increased lifeboat capacity had only been achieved at the cost of the open deck space that had previously been one of the ship's main selling points. If that lost space was to be regained in the new *Britannic*, then it called for a completely different approach.

The engineer tasked with finding a solution to this problem was William Edward Armstrong, and his vision was certainly unique. The final design was submitted to the Patent Office as early as 21 November 1912, which in itself is an interesting coincidence as exactly four years later, his design would be put to the ultimate test. The concept was largely based on davits that were designed to turn on horizontal pivots, like sheerlegs, each placed sufficiently far apart so that the lifeboats could pass between them. The davit arms were made of considerable length and the gearing for operating them was arranged so that they could be turned in both directions through a large angle from the vertical, making it possible to lower a boat into the water at a considerable distance from the side of the ship. The scale of the tier support structure also made it possible for one pair of davits to handle multiple lifeboats in one location.

The motive power for these immense structures operated through a deck-mounted drive gear shaft between the two davits; this ensured that the movement of the two davit arms, which were operated by means of a horizontal screw, were properly synchronised. Even now, a complete description of the mechanical system can be found in the UK Patent Office records:

Figure 1 is a side elevation, Figure 2 an end elevation and Figure 3 a plan of a pair of davits constructed according to this invention. Figure 4 is a plan of the gearing to a larger scale and Figure 5 is a part right hand end elevation of Figure 4.

Each davit consists of a lattice work girder (1), the lower end of which is pivoted at (2) and which has an overhanging upper end (3). Each davit (1) is connected by a lattice work link (4) to a nut (5) working on a horizontal screw (6). (7) is a bevel wheel fixed to the screw (6) and gearing with a bevel wheel (8) fixed to the longitudinal shaft (9). This shaft has fixed to it a spur wheel (10) gearing with a pinion (11) fixed to a countershaft (12), to which is also fixed a wheel (13) gearing with a pinion (14) fixed to the shaft of an electric motor (15). (16) is a brake drum fixed to the shaft (12).

The boats are lifted and lowered by ropes (17) which pass over pulleys (18) and (19) on the top of the davits and pulleys (20) at their feet and are led to drums (21) and (22). The drum (21) is fixed to a shaft (23) to which is also fixed a spur wheel (24) gearing with a pinion (25) on a shaft (26) to which is also fixed a wheel (27) gearing with a pinion (28) on a countershaft (29) to which is also fixed a wheel (30) gearing with a pinion (31) on the shaft of an electric motor (32). (33) is a brake drum fixed to the shaft (29).

The drum (22) is fixed to a sleeve (34) on the shaft (23). This sleeve has fixed to it a bracket (35) carrying a worm (36) gearing with a worm wheel (37) keyed to the shaft (23). By turning the worm (36) the sleeve can be rotated relatively to the shaft. The object of this arrangement is to allow rope to be let out from or wound up on the drum (22) to enable the boat to be lowered on an even keel, in spite of the ship being down by the head or stern.

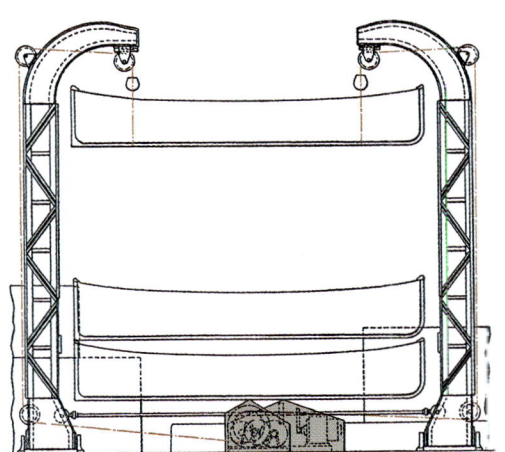
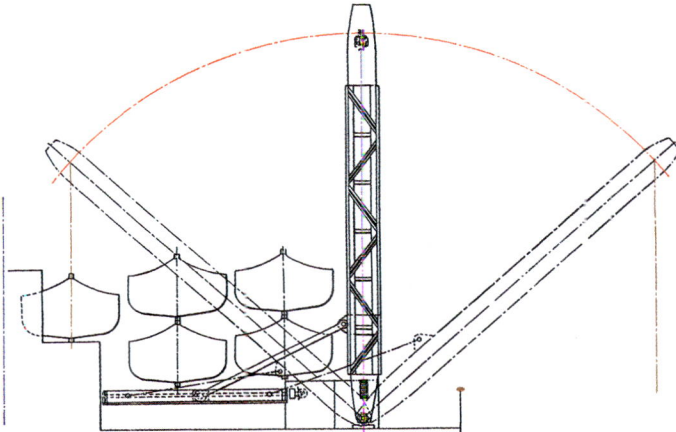

Above: Schematic of the Armstrong davit design.

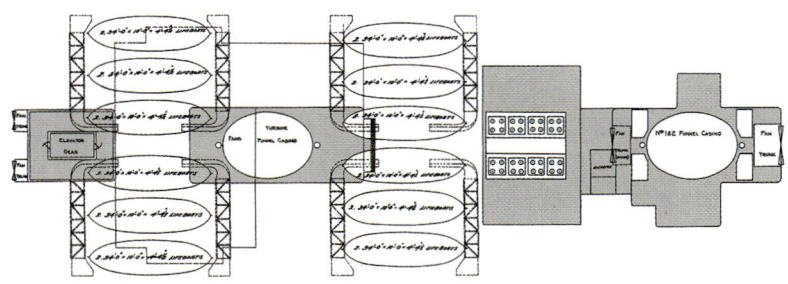
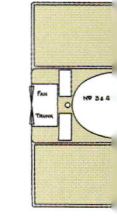
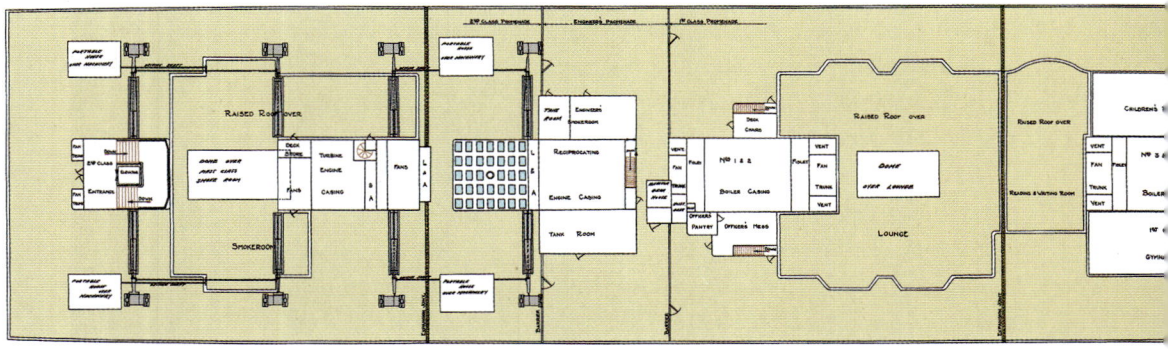

Above: General arrangement of the *Britannic*'s boat deck layout and deck houses. (Harland & Wolff)

With all this additional work, it would be another 15 months before the great ship would be ready for launching, but on 26 February 1914, at precisely 11.15am, the *Britannic* finally took to the water. The launch, carried out on a calm but typically wet Belfast day, was greeted with the customary hyperbole in the press, but the less sensationalist reporter of *Engineering* magazine was on hand to record the pertinent technical minutiae of the day:

> **Duration of Launch:** 81 seconds
> **Maximum Speed:** 9½ knots
> **Stern dip:** 31 feet
> **Stem dip:** 17 feet
> **Draught when afloat:** 15 ft 4½ inch forward, 25 feet 7 inches aft
> **Launch Displacement:** 24,800 tons

Despite the *Britannic*'s increased beam and stronger hull, the launch displacement figure is actually only 200 tons greater than that of the *Olympic*, but her projected gross tonnage of 47,500 tons would ultimately make her the largest British vessel by a long margin – a title that would not be lost until the advent of the *Queen Mary* over 20 years later. The outfitting, alas, would eventually proceed at a much slower pace than the White Star Line would have wished. Press reports initially suggested that the ship would be ready for her maiden voyage during the autumn of 1914, and in that

WEATHERING THE STORM

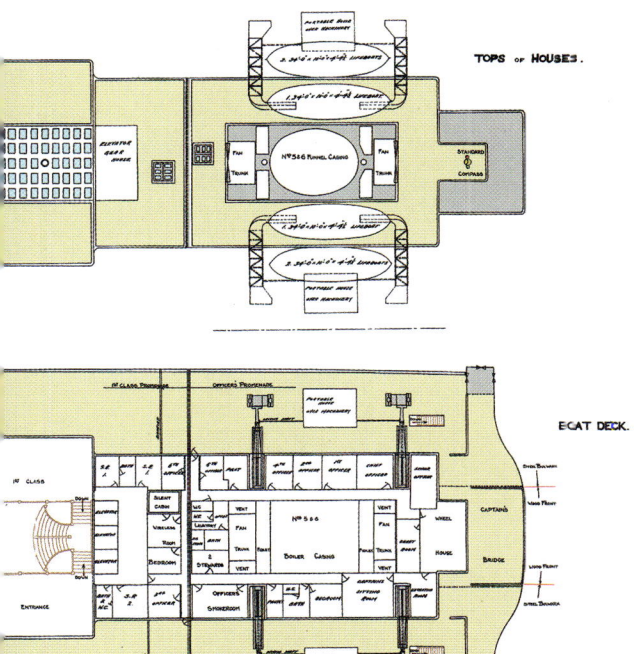

it had taken only seven months to fit out the *Olympic*, this was by no means wishful thinking, although the situation facing the White Star Line in 1914 was very different from that which had existed four years earlier. A combination of supply issues and declining industrial relations at Belfast was not helped by the fact that International Mercantile Marine (IMM), the American shipping conglomerate and ultimate owner of the White Star Line, still owed Harland & Wolff £585,000, all of which combined to ensure that progress on the *Britannic*'s outfitting was slower than planned. As a result, it was subsequently announced on 2 July 1914 that the maiden voyage would be postponed until the spring of 1915, by which time the quieter winter season would be over and the passenger figures would begin to rise.

Sadly, it was not to be. On 4 August 1914 Harland & Wolff's revised schedule was abruptly interrupted by Great Britain's declaration of war on the Central Powers of Germany and Austria-Hungary. The outbreak of hostilities would result in massive upheaval in the world of shipbuilding, with the majority of raw materials suddenly being prioritised to shipyards with existing Admiralty contracts, meaning that any work on existing civil contracts would have to be dramatically scaled back. The lack of resources also meant that before long more than six thousand skilled workers had been laid off, and as if that did not complicate matters enough, many of these men immediately rushed to enlist before the show was over. It was only when it became apparent that the hostilities were going to continue for a lot longer than previously expected that the loss of so much skilled labour would prove problematic. In the meantime, some limited work on civilian contracts could still continue, and in early September the *Britannic* was finally placed in the Thompson graving dock to have her propellers fitted; but as soon as the first Admiralty contracts began to arrive at Belfast the following month, any work on the incomplete merchant hulls once again became of secondary importance.

The reduced passenger traffic on the North Atlantic meant that IMM could just about maintain a makeshift service using the *Baltic*, *Adriatic* and Red Star liner *Lapland*, but with the larger vessels considered totally unsuitable for commercial or military service, it was only a matter of time before the *Olympic* would be considered surplus to requirements. Sure enough, she eventually arrived back at Belfast on 3 November 1914, where White Star's two largest vessels looked set to remain tied up for the foreseeable future. It would be another ten months before the *Olympic* was finally requisitioned for service as a troopship, a change of attitude at the Admiralty largely brought on by the urgent need to transport large numbers of troops to the Gallipoli front in the eastern Mediterranean, although in truth the White Star Line probably had little option. Based on their gross tonnages, the *Mauretania*, *Aquitania*, *Olympic* and *Britannic* would have been prohibitively expensive for the Admiralty to charter, so in the end the Transport Division had made Cunard an offer they couldn't refuse: either they chartered the *Mauretania* and *Aquitania* at a more advantageous rate, or they risked losing a larger number of smaller and infinitely more useful vessels to government service. In the end, Alfred Booth, chairman of the Cunard Line, reluctantly acceded to the Admiralty's proposal, and by the summer of 1915 both vessels were in the service of the British government.

It was a classic example of the thin end of the wedge: once Cunard had accepted the terms, there was no way the White Star Line could be offered anything more advantageous and, sure enough, on 1 September 1915 the *Olympic* was finally requisitioned for trooping duties. After a hurried fitting out, she was moved to Liverpool and placed in the Gladstone graving dock on 11 September to complete the process, departing from that port on 24 September 1915, in the

guise of Transport 2810, for her first trooping run to Mudros, on the Greek island of Lemnos.

The *Britannic*, meanwhile, remained safe and secure alongside Belfast's deep-water wharf. Despite their Admiralty contracts, Harland & Wolff had at least been able to successfully carry out the mooring trials of the ship's engines in May 1915, so in that respect the *Britannic* was at least seaworthy, but it would still need a further month's work before she could be made ready for service, provided that the Admiralty gave the vessel priority. For a while there seemed to be no further movement at the Transport Division, but by the autumn of 1915 the casualty figures from the Dardanelles campaign were on the verge of overwhelming the hospital ships already serving in the Mediterranean, and on 13 November 1915 Britain's largest liner was finally requisitioned for service as a military hospital ship.

By 8 December the *Britannic* was finally ready for sea, and with the German authorities already advised of the ship's protected status as a hospital ship, the sea trials, under the command of Captain Joseph Ranson, were safely completed in calm but foggy weather in the Irish Sea. However, any thoughts of an immediate departure for Liverpool, where the outfitting would be completed, were dashed by the fact that the battleship HMS *Barham* was still occupying Liverpool's Gladstone graving dock. As a result, it would be several more days before the ship was cleared to leave Belfast, but finally, on the evening of 11 December 1915, after four weeks' work and an overall expenditure in the region of £90,000, the *Britannic* headed into Belfast Lough, before assuming a south-easterly course for Liverpool, arriving safely the following morning. Two days later, Captain Charles Bartlett, the White Star Line's pre-war marine superintendent, arrived back in Liverpool fresh from patrolling duties in the North Sea, leaving him with only nine days to familiarise himself with his new command and, more importantly, the unfamiliar onboard procedures as the medical staff and supplies were taken on board. Even then, the scheduled departure would be delayed by the late arrival of the Royal Army Medical Corps (RAMC) orderlies from Aldershot, but by the early hours of 23 December the *Britannic* was finally outward bound for the eastern Mediterranean.

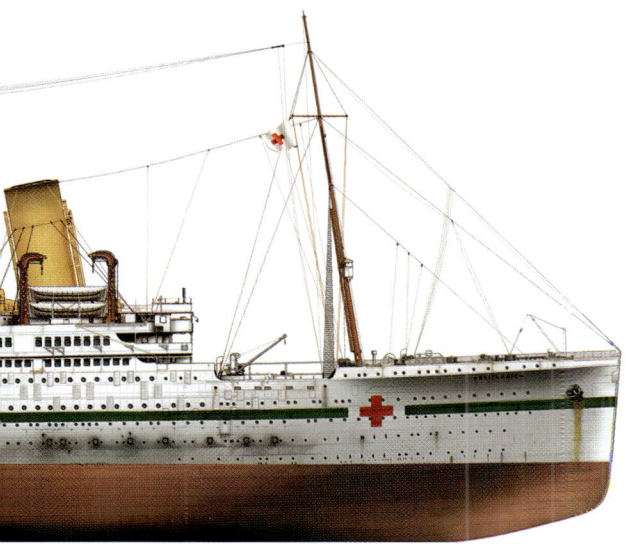

Left: *Britannic*'s starboard profile as a completed hospital ship. (Cyril Codus)

2

AEGEAN PRELUDE

The *Britannic*'s terminal in the eastern Mediterranean would be the port of Mudros, on the Greek island of Lemnos, but despite being designed to comfortably cross the North Atlantic with fuel to spare, the 4,000-mile (6,450km) round trip to the northern Aegean Sea was too great even for an Olympic class liner. At best the ship might get as far as Gibraltar, but facilities at that port were limited, and any coal supplies that did exist were reserved for use by naval vessels. The *Olympic* solved the problem by calling at the northern Italian port of La Spezia on the homeward journey to refuel, but as the *Britannic* was largely empty on the outward voyage, she would instead call at Naples while en route to Mudros, in order to take on the necessary coal and water to complete the homeward journey without stopping.

Between 22 December 1915 and 4 April 1916, the *Britannic*, working in rotation with the *Mauretania* and *Aquitania*, completed three round trips to the Mediterranean, before the welcome drop in casualties following the Allies' abandonment of the Gallipoli peninsula resulted in the ship being paid off on 21 May 1916. The hiatus, however, would only be temporary; three months later the *Britannic* would once again be recalled for military service, and between 24 September and 6 November Captain Bartlett would complete two further voyages in his ship to Mudros.

Left: HMHS *Britannic* at sea. (Ken Marschall)

Following an unusually quick one-week turnaround after the second of these voyages, largely due to storm damage suffered by the *Aquitania*, by the afternoon of 12 November 1916 the *Britannic* was once again outward bound, arriving at Naples on 17 November to take on coal and fresh water as usual.

Unbeknown to anyone on board, however, the seeds of the *Britannic*'s demise had, quite literally, already been sown. Lurking in the darkness of the tranquil waters of the Kea Channel in the early hours of Saturday 28 October 1916, the German submarine *U73* was six days out of her base at Cattaro, in the southern Adriatic. Commanded by 32-year-

Above: Kapitänleutnant Gustav Johannes Siess, commander of the *U73* and the *Britannic*'s ultimate nemesis. (Michail Michailakis)

old Kapitänleutnant Gustav Johannes Siess, *U73* was not exactly what you might call a fighting submarine. Launched at the Kaiserliche Werfte shipyard in Danzig on 16 June 1915, she was actually designed to complement the smaller UC mine-laying U-boats, although with an overall length of 186 feet 4 inches (56.8m) and a surface displacement of 745 tons (890 tons submerged), she was somewhat larger and could operate at considerably longer ranges. The two 800 HP Körting diesel engines were sufficient for a maximum surface speed of 9.6 knots, while a cruising speed of 7–8 knots provided an operational range of up to 7,500 nautical miles (13,900km), although this particular U-boat was not designed for speed. The *U73* may have mounted two external 20-inch (50cm) torpedo tubes and a single 3.5-inch (9cm) gun, but these accessories were really of secondary importance, as this submarine was designed with a more clandestine role in mind. Far more insidious was her cargo of 34 mines, which could be laid through two tubes mounted aft.

By this stage of the war the *U73* had been in the Mediterranean for six months, having departed Cuxhaven on 1 April 1916 for the long and hazardous voyage via the north of Scotland. The stormy waters of the North Sea and the Bay of Biscay provided more than adequate evidence to her crew, if it were needed, of why the submarine was referred to as the 'floating coffin', as the modified saddle tanks, specifically incorporated into the design to increase the range, also had the unfortunate effect of forcing the submarine to pitch rather heavily. Nevertheless, Siess was able to lay his first barrage of mines off Lisbon, before slipping through the Strait of Gibraltar on the night of 19 April, although an attempt to lay another mine barrage off the French naval base at Bizerte, Tunisia, had to be abandoned due to a combination of poor weather and technical issues. That disappointment, however, would be more than offset when Siess proceeded to his secondary target at Valletta, where his mines would later account for no fewer than three British ships: the sloop HMS *Nasturtium*, the Admiralty yacht *Aegusa* and, the biggest prize of all, the 14,000-ton pre-dreadnought HMS *Russell*. One week later, a mine credited to Siess also sank the navy trawler *Crownsin*, so while the *U73* may not have been an overly glamorous command, this particular voyage, having accounted for four vessels with an aggregate tonnage of 16,629 tons, had by any measure been an unqualified success.

The second voyage was less productive, but by 22 October the *U73* was headed into the war zone for the third time, tasked with disrupting the movement of Allied transport vessels in the eastern Mediterranean. Stage one of the voyage involved the laying of a mine barrage in the Saronic Gulf, specifically to the south of the Greek island of Phleva, but while two barriers of six mines were successfully deployed on the afternoon of 27 October 1916, it was by no means a straightforward operation. Due to the combination of heavy seas and the lightened condition of the submarine after laying the mines, the *U73*'s excess buoyancy forced the U-boat to the surface on several occasions, and it was not until the ballast tanks could be sufficiently flooded that the vessel was once again able to return to the invisible safety of the depths. It was probably only the poor weather that enabled Siess to remain undetected by the nearby French patrol ships, but with little chance of being able to observe any immediate success in the rough conditions, he concluded that discretion was the better part of valour and by 3.10pm the U-boat was headed for the more open waters to the south.

It proved to be a fortuitous decision, with the *U73*'s war diary recording vastly better conditions in the Kea Channel the following morning, enabling Siess to surface at 3.25am to recharge his batteries and load the first mines

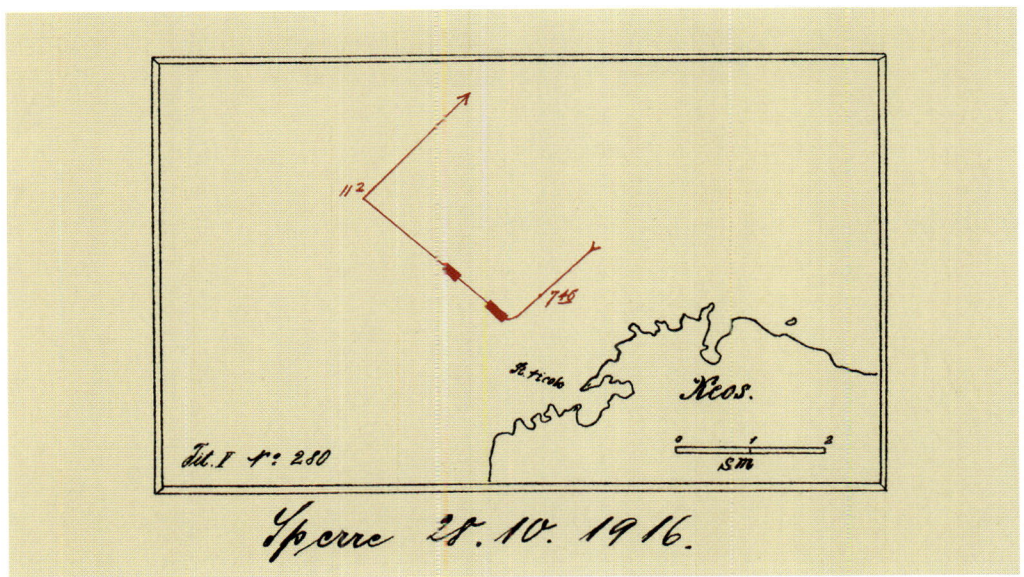

Above: *U73*'s war diary, charting the location of what the German naval records would refer to as 'Barrage 32', which would claim both the SS *Burdigala* and HMHS *Britannic*. (Titanic Historical Society)

under the cover of darkness. By 5.10am the work was complete; as dawn broke to the east, the *U73* submerged and steered further into the Kea Channel to scout an appropriate location for the next barrier. As he observed the activities in the channel through his periscope, Siess noted that the steamers – and there were many – seemed to pass closer to Kea as they passed through the channel. So, taking a north-westerly course off Port St Nikolo, two barriers, each consisting of six mines, were stealthily deposited on the bottom of the Kea Channel, while numerous steamers, fishing boats and even a destroyer passed overhead, oblivious to the danger unfolding below.

By 8.27am the second barrier had been laid, and Siess withdrew to the north-east to await developments, in the hope that he would be able to observe the results of the mischief he had wrought. He would be disappointed. At 10.45 a large two-funnelled steamer had stopped near the barrier, and through the periscope it did appear to be listing, but a detonation was not detected and 15 minutes later the vessel resumed its south-westerly course. Several more vessels passed close to the barriers without result, so at 1pm Siess took up a waiting position to the north of the barrier, where he planned to torpedo any passing vessels. Before long, the smoke of a large steamer appeared obligingly on the horizon, headed north towards the Doro Passage, but the attack was quickly aborted when Siess spotted the unmistakeable markings of a hospital ship. By 2pm the activity in the Kea Channel had died down, so much so that the *U73* headed north-east to the Doro Passage, between the islands of Euboea and Andros, before surfacing to recharge the batteries while making a surface run to the south. The following day, the third and final mine barrier of the voyage would be laid in the Mykoni Channel, between the islands of Mykonos and Tenos.

Although the Kea Channel mine barrier had not yielded any immediate results, by setting his hydrostatic depth controls at a greater depth an experienced commander like Siess was clearly prepared to be patient, bide his time and wait until a larger and more important vessel came along. Sure enough, his patience eventually paid off when, a little over two weeks later, on the morning of 14 November 1916, the French transport SS *Burdigala* was suddenly wracked by an explosion while on route from Salonika to Toulon. Without realising it, the ship had steamed directly into the *U73*'s minefield. The mines had been silently waiting for their victim for over two weeks and the *U73* had actually returned to Cattaro a full week earlier, but this did not stop someone from reporting what they took to be the periscope of a German submarine at the scene; nor did it prevent one of the *Burdigala*'s gun crews from firing at the mysterious object. To further complicate matters, at 10.24am the British destroyer HMS *Rattlesnake* sighted the sinking *Burdigala* and immediately rushed to her assistance, while Captain Richard Farquharson noted in his logbook that he searched for a submarine in the vicinity in which the French ship had been "torpedoed." The *Burdigala* eventually sank at 11.19am, at

Above: Captain Charles Alfred Bartlett (1868-1945), one of the very few captains to see his ship being built, launched and sunk. (Alasdair Fairbairn)

which point HMS *Rattlesnake* set course for Piraeus with 380 French survivors on board, practically all of them convinced that their ship had been the victim of a deliberate torpedo attack. As a direct consequence of this fatal assumption no systematic sweep for mines in the area would ever take place, and exactly one week later, on the morning of Tuesday 21 November 1916, the *Britannic* would find herself steaming into the same perilous waters in which the *Burdigala* had been lost.

This particular Tuesday morning would find the *Britannic* in sunny and calm waters, although the journey up to that point had been far from tranquil. The weather on the departure day from Southampton had been bitterly cold, and when arriving at Naples it was so stormy that the ship's departure even had to be delayed until the Sunday afternoon; but by the Monday morning, just as the *Britannic* was passing through the Messina Strait, the storms had abated and the conditions were much improved. By 7.52am on 21 November the ship was making a steady 20 knots, 4 miles (6.4km) south of Angalistros Point, on the south-west tip of the island of Makronisos, which marked the northern extent of the Kea Channel. The senior officer of the watch, Chief Officer Robert Hume, altered course to N 48° E (magnetic) in order to pass through the Kea Channel and the Doro Passage. Below deck, everything was equally calm as the medical staff were just sitting down to breakfast, with no one anticipating anything untoward for the last 200 miles (322km) of the voyage to Mudros, when, at 8.12am, a massive explosion low down on the forward starboard side suddenly rocked the ship.

Like many of the survivors that day, Reverend John Fleming, the ship's Presbyterian chaplain, later wrote that 'the great ship shuddered for a moment from end to end', while 15-year-old boy scout George Perman, operating one of the aft lifts, recalled that the shaking along the entire length of the ship lasted for anything up to 30 seconds. Immediately rushing onto his bridge, Captain Bartlett, still dressed in his pyjamas, set about assessing the situation and the scale of the damage. The explosion had occurred on the starboard side near the bulkhead between holds 2 and 3, and with only two compartments open to the sea, the damage should have been well within the *Britannic*'s margin of safety, but inevitably it wasn't going to be that straightforward. The *Britannic*'s watertight skin, a major safety feature incorporated into the design following the loss of the *Titanic*, extended as far forward as boiler room 6, but while the main damage seemed to be limited to the bulkhead between holds 2 and 3, with possible damage to the bulkhead between holds 1 and 2, the three forward watertight doors sealing off the forward pipe tunnel and boiler rooms 6 and 5 had, for reasons unknown, failed to close. Even so, despite the scale of the internal flooding, the *Britannic* was designed to float with anything up to six of her forward compartments open to the sea, and with calm waters and land barely 3 miles (4.8km) distant, Captain Bartlett would have felt moderately confident that he could make land.

That confidence, however, would be sadly misplaced. Following the explosion, the *Britannic*'s engines, in line with established naval procedure, had been stopped while the scale of the damage was assessed. As the first distress signals went out to call for help, advising that the *Britannic* had struck a mine off Port St Nikolo, Captain Bartlett quickly weighed up the various options available to him, before ordering a course toward the island of Kea, only to be told that the ship's helm was not responding. It was only through using the propellers that he could manoeuvre his ship towards Kea, while the ship's crew set about uncovering and loading the lifeboats. Crucially, at this stage there was still no order to actually release the lifeboats, which, after being lowered over the side, remained suspended some 6 feet (1.8m) above the water along each side of the vessel. Both Captain Harry Dyke, the *Britannic*'s assistant commander, and Fifth Officer Gordon Fielding were unwilling to release the boats until receiving definite orders from the bridge to do so, and as long as the ship's engines were still turning it was all they could do to endure the annoyed curses of the occupants hanging over the side of the ship, as their lifeboats swung precariously above the water.

There is no detailed record as to the *Britannic*'s precise speed and movements during this time. The only surviving indication

Above: Captain Harry Dyke, the *Britannic*'s assistant commander. (Harold Roberts)

of the ship's course, courtesy of Lieutenant Colonel Henry Stewart Anderson, the ship's senior medical officer, notes that the ship seemed to be moving in a large circle to the right, but before long it was becoming clear that the *Britannic* was also taking on an increasingly alarming list to starboard. Barely 15 minutes after the explosion, the portholes on E deck, which would normally be some 25 feet (7.6m) above the waterline, were awash, and with the forward motion of the ship apparently causing the forward compartments to fill more rapidly, at 8.35am Captain Bartlett finally gave the order for the engines to be stopped, and for the lifeboats to be released.

Despite the increasing list to starboard, for the most part the evacuation of the *Britannic* largely appears to have been a well-organised and controlled procedure. No doubt the combination of daylight and the calm conditions helped no end – certainly when compared to the icy cold dark and uncertainty that existed on the night the *Titanic* sank – while the RAMC medical orderlies lined up patiently on the aft promenade before being sent up to the boat deck in groups of 50. Not surprisingly, the ladies were given priority, as the nurses calmly waited to be counted into two of the lifeboats by Elizabeth Dowse, the *Britannic*'s formidable matron; it was only when the last of the nurses had entered the boats that Miss Dowse, later recalled by nurse Vera Brittain as a '…sixty-year-old "dug-out" with a red cape and a row of South African medals', finally took her own place in the lifeboat, before being lowered over the side.

The raw data with regard to the lifeboat-

Above: Lieutenant Henry Stewart Anderson, the ship's senior medical officer during both tours of duty. (John Fleming Jr.)

lowering arrangements leaves little room for doubt that the system on the *Britannic* worked well. In April 1912, the *Titanic*'s conventional Welin davits had lowered a total of 18 lifeboats in an approximate time span of 85 minutes, whereas the *Britannic*'s combination of Welin and Armstrong girder davits succeeded in lowering some 35 boats over the side, all of them in the 20 or so minutes that the ship lay stopped. The lowering of the *Britannic*'s lifeboats might even have been looked upon as a textbook success, especially when you take into account the heavy list to starboard, but inevitably disaster was just around the corner, and the events that were about to occur would lead to the greatest tragedy of the day.

More than a century after the sinking of the *Britannic*, opinion remains divided about what came next. In a diary entry attributed to Fifth Officer Fielding, he recalled that two of the lifeboats in the charge of the third officer, Francis Laws, were lowered early and without his knowledge into the water, whereas stewardess Violet Jessop, herself a *Titanic* survivor, recalled in her memoirs that when she reached the boat deck, not only had the boats with the nurses already left, but that she could also see a number of other boats pulling away from the ship. Stepping into lifeboat number 4 – the second boat along the higher port side – she recalled the boat hooking itself onto an open porthole, causing it to tilt considerably as it scraped down the listing side of the ship, in the process splintering the glass faces of the green electric light boxes that would be illuminated at night to identify the *Britannic* as a hospital ship. The lowering of lifeboat 4 may not have been a textbook operation, but based on Violet's memoir it is reasonably clear that it was not launched without the officer's knowledge.

On the other hand, it does seem to be clear that by the time lifeboat 4 touched the water, the *Britannic* was still moving forward. We can only speculate on whether this was before Captain Bartlett had given the order to stop the ship, or after he had given the order to resume a course towards Kea, but either way the results were the same. As the 53,000-ton *Britannic* continued to surge forward, the lifeboat, tiny by comparison, found itself trapped by the hydrodynamic forces as it bounced along the side of the ship and towards the stern. Before long, Violet realised that everyone was suddenly jumping overboard and

Above: Stewardess Violet Jessop, who would serve in all three of the White Star Line's Olympic class liners. (Margaret Meehan)

into the water, and within a few seconds she found herself almost alone in the boat, save for one RAMC officer. It was only when she turned around to see what was happening that, to her horror, she finally became aware of the *Britannic*'s huge 23-foot (7m) port propeller, slicing into another unfortunate lifeboat and turning it to matchwood, while the splintered fragments of the boat and mangled bodies of its former occupants were tossed in every direction. With seconds to spare, Violet also jumped into the water, but it was too late. After being spun around by the propeller, sustaining a serious gash to her thigh in the process, the weight of her coat seemed to be dragging her down into the depths before she finally began to feel herself rising through the water column. She recalled banging her head on the shattered fragment of one of the lifeboats as she struggled to reach the surface, before finally being able to breathe in fresh air once more, only to be greeted by the gruesome sight of the body of a young medical orderly floating in the water, his head completely split open and his brains spilling onto his khaki tunic.

Young George Perman had also been in lifeboat 4, but somehow he had managed to grab hold of a lifeboat fall hanging down from the poop, saving him from an even worse experience. Nevertheless, he would never forget the sight of red blood being splattered along the ship's white flanks as he hung precariously above the maelstrom below, nor the sight of the dead bodies and severed limbs and the cries of the wounded. However, even though the injuries sustained by the occupants of the two lifeboats were horrific, it could have been worse, as all of a sudden, the propellers stopped turning. The timing certainly could not have been better for the occupants of a third lifeboat, which was about to suffer the same grisly fate, as it allowed Captain T. Fearnhead to finally get his boat clear of the ship's side by pushing against the now motionless blades.

Over the 20 or so minutes that the *Britannic* lay stopped, William Armstrong's davit design proved its worth, although by no means flawlessly. One of the first boats lowered by Fifth Officer Fielding, despite the increasing list to starboard, was the port-side motor launch – boat 16A – under the command of First Officer George Oliver, who had been tasked with co-ordinating the rescue of any swimmers in the water. Unfortunately, no sooner had Fielding lowered his first two boats into the water than the forward set of davits, servicing lifeboats 14A to 14F, jammed inboard. With the aft set of davits still operational, he continued to lower the other boats as best he could, but by the time he was launching his fourth boat the task was becoming increasingly difficult on account of the ever-increasing list to starboard. Even with the greater outreach of the Armstrong davits, on several occasions the last boat to be lowered had practically bounced down the side of the ship, nearly tipping its 75 occupants into the water, after which Fielding concluded that it would no longer be safe to lower any more boats on the higher port side. Moving forward to the raised roof above the lounge, he decided instead to spend his time more productively by throwing any deck chairs and life rafts he could find over the side, fully aware that he might well be utilising one of them himself before long. After a while, Fielding was just about ready to order his remaining men over the side when he noticed one of the smaller boats on the lower starboard side, where Sixth Officer John Chapman, who had apparently been able to safely launch ten boats from amidships, was contemplating going overboard with his remaining two or three seamen. Seeing the chance of launching one more lifeboat, after much manhandling they managed to get the boat over the side. No sooner was it in the water than Fielding, who had remained on deck with two seamen to steady the falls as it was lowered, finally

Above: Major Harold Priestley, a survivor of the Wittenberg prisoner of war camp typhus epidemic, posted to the *Britannic* after his repatriation.

slithered down the ropes and into the boat himself, burning his fingers with the running rope in the process.

By now time was almost up, yet even at this late stage Captain Bartlett still felt that there was hope. Noticing that the ship seemed to be settling more slowly, he had passed word to stop lowering the lifeboats as the *Britannic* slowly began to move forward one last time. The Kea shoreline was now less than 3 miles (4.8km) distant, but it was a forlorn hope. As the ship slowly inched forward, the propellers were by now working so high above the surface that they were of little practical use, and yet there still seemed to be just enough momentum for the vessel to once again start to settle more rapidly. It was only when word reached the bridge that water had been reported to have risen to the level of D deck that Captain Bartlett, accepting the inevitable, gave the order for the ship's engineers to come topside, signalling the final order to abandon ship on the ship's whistle.

The last few moments aboard the now fast-sinking *Britannic* were focused almost completely on the lower starboard side of the boat deck. Private Percy Tyler later wrote of having to place one of the sea scouts 'rather forcibly' into a lifeboat – the third last to be lowered; Reverend John Fleming wrote of leaving the ship in the second-to-last boat to be lowered, while Major Harold Priestley even took one last look around the boat deck to make sure that everyone was safe, before escaping moments later in the last boat to be lowered. Claude Lancaster, the *Britannic*'s purser, would be in that very same lifeboat, carrying not only the ship's log and papers with him, but also a spare uniform, while Fifth Officer Fielding, already safely in his lifeboat, recalled watching Captain Bartlett, Captain Dyke and Chief Engineer Robert Fleming swim off the starboard wing of the bridge, before moving aft to rescue the engineering officers who were leaping into the water from the stern, which still towered high above the surface.

In her remaining moments above the surface, the *Britannic* continued to heel increasingly to starboard as, one by one, the funnels finally gave way under the strain. Some survivors later claimed to have heard the noise of explosions inside the hull, said to be the boilers exploding as the cold seawater poured down the open funnel casings. The *Britannic*, with the last vestiges of stability all but gone, finally completed her roll to starboard as the stern slipped below the surface at 9.07am.

As the last of the smoke cleared, all that could be seen was a flotilla of 35 lifeboats scattered around the Kea Channel, with countless survivors floundering in the water. Francesco Psilas, a local fisherman from St Nikolo, was quickly on the scene to give what assistance he could with his small fishing boat, but by now the British were not far behind. At 8.15am the destroyer HMS *Scourge*, while arranging for the beached Greek steamer *Sparti* to be towed after having struck another of the *U73*'s mines off Phleva island the previous day, had picked up the *Britannic*'s SOS and headed at once for the Kea Channel, closely followed by the tugs *Goliath*, *Polyphemus* and a trawler. Twenty minutes later the destroyer HMS *Foxhound* was also signalled by *Scourge* to proceed at once to the Kea Channel. The auxiliary cruiser HMT *Heroic*, which had actually passed the *Britannic* earlier that morning while en route from Mudros to Salamis with mail, had also picked up the ship's distress signal at 8.28am, before immediately turning back and heading to the stricken hospital ship's aid.

By the early evening the *Britannic*'s surviving crew had been safely landed at Piraeus, where a roll call was taken as Captain Bartlett undertook the painful task of identifying the casualties. By the time the final list was completed, of the 1,065 crew and medical staff on board at the time of the explosion, 1,035 were accounted for. Of the 30 missing (21 crew and 9 officers and men of the RAMC), only five bodies were known to have been recovered. The log entry recalls that Serjeant William Sharpe had died of his injuries after being landed at Port St Nikolo, while Private Arthur Binks, fireman Joseph Brown, lookout George Honeycott and trimmer Charles Phillips would be interred in the Paramo Cemetery at Piraeus the following day. William Sharpe's body would remain in the church of Agia Triada graveyard on Kea until after the war, before being moved to the Imperial War Graves cemetery on Syra in 1921.

Of the remaining 25 casualties, no trace would ever be found.

Above: Private Percy D. Tyler, photographed aboard the French cruiser Ernest Renan after being rescued from the Kea Channel by the HMS *Scourge*.

3

THE SECRET HISTORY OF THE *BRITANNIC*

For the better part of 60 years the *Britannic* remained quietly at the bottom of the Kea Channel, all but forgotten, until, on 15 November 1975, the first distinct images appeared on the sonar of the RV *Calypso*, the famed vessel of the French oceanographic researcher Jacques Cousteau. In this case, the name of the vessel, *Calypso*, seems to be curiously appropriate. *Calypso*, according to the ancient Greek poet Homer, was the nymph who had held Odysseus captive on the island of Ogygia for seven years, while he was returning home to Ithaca at the end of the Trojan war. The *Britannic* had also been seemingly lost for decades, but if anyone thought the wreck's rediscovery would draw a line under the controversies once and for all, they were in for a bit of a shock. If anything, Cousteau's discovery was only going to stir up the troubled waters of an almost completely forgotten allegation, which persists even to this day.

In truth, the *Britannic* has never been a stranger to controversy. Serious wartime allegations of the ship being used for the illegal transportation of combat soldiers dated back to January 1917, but even when looking back to the very earliest days at Harland & Wolff, a number of less significant but undoubtedly curious stories have also added to the ship's air of mystery. In that there have been so many dubious theories surrounding the fate of the *Titanic*, it is probably naïve to believe that the *Britannic* would not in some way have been drawn into the fracas. Interestingly two of the oldest legends had began to circulate before Yard No 433 had even taken to the water.

For decades, there has been a firmly held belief that Harland & Wolff made the *Britannic*'s hull 18 inches (46cm) wider in order to incorporate a watertight double skin

Right: The RV *Calypso* at Korissia, in Port St Nikolo, in 1976. (Peter Nicolaides)

Above: One of the original Belfast engineering notebooks, detailing the *Britannic*'s construction schedule. (Harland & Wolff)

into the design following the *Titanic* disaster, but more sensational is the perennial anecdote that the White Star Line originally intended to name their third Olympic class vessel *Gigantic*, further emphasising the size and power of the three behemoths constructed at Belfast. Following the loss of the *Titanic*, however, the company allegedly began to reconsider the wisdom of naming the ship *Gigantic*, before quietly changing it to *Britannic*, a name with an honourable and established heritage in the company. Both of these theories are undeniably attractive, and although there is an almost total lack of credible evidence, the question as to either theory being even remotely plausible has never really gone away.

The reality, however, is rather more prosaic. A table of particulars prepared for Lord Pirrie in October 1911, less than a week before the White Star Line confirmed their order for construction to begin on the *Britannic*, leaves little room for doubt that the vessel's beam had been increased long before the *Titanic* even left the shipyard. This was most likely following observations made in the *Olympic* during her first four voyages, as well as following a more detailed survey of the *Olympic*'s hull during the autumn of 1911 while being repaired following the collision in the Solent with the armoured cruiser HMS *Hawke*. The *Gigantic* legend, however, has always been more difficult to dismiss, most likely because it is the sort of myth that people genuinely – and perhaps understandably – want to believe. The fact that it was not at all unusual for a ship's name to be changed during the construction phase certainly makes the notion feasible, but when a number of Harland & Wolff engineering records were unearthed at the Public Record Office of Northern Ireland in 2007, historians finally had the source documentation necessary to settle the debate once and for all. Contained within the pages of each battered notebook were the details and construction schedules of numerous vessels, all listed in the correct numerical sequence of the vessel's official yard number, and in all these books are included the construction records pertaining to the *Britannic*. The earliest reference to the name *Britannic* is dated 28 June 1911, and the fact that not one of the surviving notebooks shows any indication of a name change is surely positive proof that the White Star Line had already settled on the third vessel's name within a month of the *Titanic*'s launch. Perhaps one small crumb of comfort to those who had been so determined to believe the name change theory is that in one of the books, the page including the *Britannic*'s entry includes references to another 20 vessels, of which no fewer than five had undergone a name change at one stage. In each case, the original names have been scrubbed out and replaced with an alternative, but, crucially, the *Britannic* is not one of them.

In the overall scheme of things, the legends surrounding the *Britannic*'s increased beam and nomenclature are reasonably inconsequential, whereas the allegations surrounding the use to which the vessel was put, and indeed the eventual means of her destruction, are considerably more significant to this story. It probably comes as no great surprise to learn that it all stems from German wartime propaganda, issued at a time when truth may have been a particularly rare commodity on both sides, but what is interesting is that 60 years later, the controversy would also provide Jacques Cousteau with exactly the information he needed to further his own objectives.

This part of the *Britannic* saga actually begins some 50 years ago, when Cousteau was working in the Aegean on behalf of the Greek Ministry of Culture during the autumn of 1975. Cousteau was conducting a number of sonar surveys in Greek waters for his memorable *Cousteau Odyssey* television series, and while one of the more questionable targets was the legendary lost civilisation of Atlantis, among the list of wrecks shortlisted for exploration was the *Britannic*. In theory, it should have been a relatively straightforward search, as the *Britannic* had sunk less than 60 years earlier and they also had a reasonably accurate location marked on the charts. The expectation had not been whether they would locate the *Britannic*, but, rather, how quickly

Above: Jacques Cousteau with Sheila Macbeth Mitchell aboard the *Calypso*. (Peter Nicolaides)

they would find the wreck. The only problem was that when they eventually arrived on site, the *Calypso*'s sonar could find no evidence whatsoever of what was supposed to be the largest liner on the seabed.

To be fair to Cousteau, the existing hydrographic data should have been reasonably sound, as it was apparently based on sonar surveys carried out in the Kea Channel in May 1947 and January 1960, but while the *Britannic* was known to be somewhere in the area, it is curious that at that time three other wartime wrecks located nearby were completely overlooked. There was of course the SS *Burdigala*, which sank after hitting another of the *U73*'s mines one week prior to the loss of the *Britannic*, but there was also the wreck of the armed merchant cruiser HMS *Louvain*, torpedoed in the same waters by the *UC22* on 20 January 1918, with the loss of over two hundred lives. Finally, there was the Italian steamer *Città di Tripoli*, torpedoed on 2 July 1941 by the British submarine HMS *Torbay*. Over the years, all these other vessels have also been found, with the wreck of the *Burdigala* located in 2008 during a marine biological survey being carried out by the University of Patras, while the *Città di Tripoli* was also pinpointed that same year. The location of the last missing piece in this particular jigsaw, HMS *Louvain*, was only finally confirmed on 7 August 2022, but as a result all four wartime wrecks in the Kea Channel have now been located, yet crucially *none* of them were found in the position indicated by the 1947 and 1960 surveys. The HMS *Louvain* is the closest of these wrecks to both the 1947 and 1960 positions – in fact, all three of these wrecks lie closer to the original charted symbol than the *Britannic* – and yet for some reason the original charted position had only been associated with the former White Star liner in the British hydrographic records.

On 15 November 1975, Cousteau's patience finally paid off, when Dr Harold Edgerton's side-scan sonar detected the first images of a wreck presumed to be the *Britannic*. Unfortunately, the prevailing weather conditions meant that it would not be possible to officially confirm the wreck's identity with divers until the following summer, but nonetheless, Cousteau was confident enough in his discovery to inform the British Hydrographic Office of the *Britannic*'s revised position on 7 December 1975. The revised position, however, raised more questions than answers, as people immediately began to ask themselves why the *Britannic* was 6.75 nautical miles 12.5 kilometres) from the position marked on the charts. In itself, that question was certainly fair enough, although in many ways the issue of the wreck's location should have been resolved long before the *Calypso* had even arrived in the Kea Channel, as even a cursory examination of the *Britannic*'s log – an open document in the British National Archives since the late 1960s – would have provided a much more accurate starting point some 3 miles (4.8km) north-west of the Port St Nikolo lighthouse.

The new Cousteau/Edgerton coordinates gave the revised position as 37° 42' 05" N, 24°

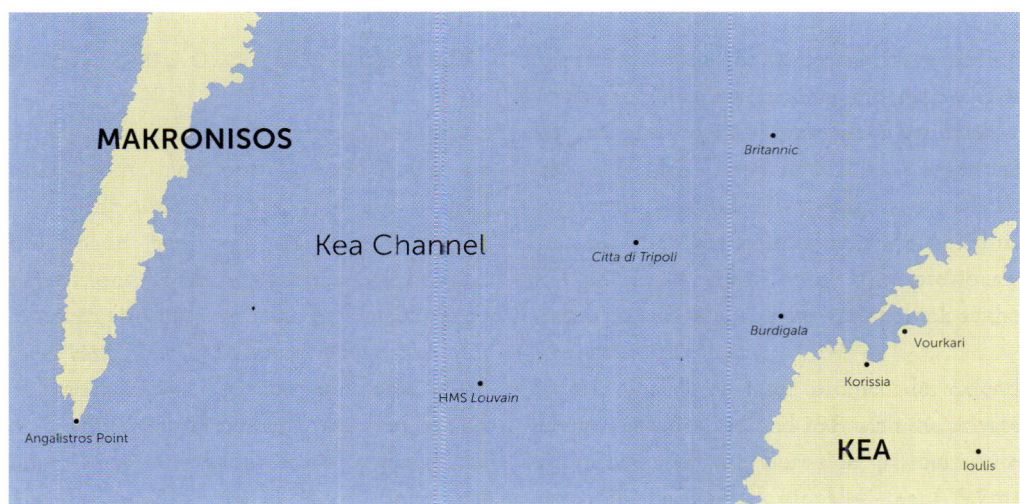

Above: The wrecks of the Kea Channel.

17' 02" E, well within the area indicated in the *Britannic*'s log, and it was at this point that the first of the conspiracy theories started to creep into our story, as people began to ponder the notion that the incorrect position was in fact no coincidence, and that the British Admiralty may have connived to deliberately misplace the wreck in order to conceal a hidden cache of munitions in the *Britannic*'s holds. If the wartime allegations were true then they would certainly have had a genuine reason to cover up the truth, as such a breach of the rules regarding the use of hospital ships would have been a major embarrassment for the British, although the less charitable observer might have pointed out that such speculation, despite a total lack of evidence, also provided Cousteau with useful publicity for his broadcasting partners. Exactly where Cousteau came up with his illicit munitions cargo theory remains uncertain, although there were undeniably grounds for him to investigate the possibility that things may not have been quite as above board as the British authorities would have liked everyone to believe.

The source of the *Britannic*'s tarnished reputation originated in January 1917, and it came from a surprisingly innocuous source. Adalbert Franz Messany, an Austrian opera singer, had been interned in Luxor following the outbreak of the war, before being transferred to Malta in December 1914. He would subsequently remain on the island for nearly two years, until, after contracting tuberculosis, the British medical authorities finally approved his repatriation to Austria. Messany's journey home began on 24 October 1916, when he went aboard the hospital ship *Wandilla* for the four-day voyage to Mudros, at which point he then had several days to observe the transfer of men and matériel between the various ships anchored in the bay. One of the activities he later reported observing was the transfer of uniformed personnel and unidentified crates to and from the *Britannic*. But what was more surprising was the fact that after going aboard the *Britannic* for the return voyage to Southampton, Messany also seemed to enjoy a surprising amount of freedom as he moved about the ship, observing the onboard activities and speaking freely with his fellow patients. Messany's eventual repatriation in December 1916, via neutral Holland, should have been the end of this particular odyssey, at least as far as the British were concerned; but, without realising it, for the Central Powers the timing was practically heaven-sent.

On 29 January 1917, Germany published details of 22 alleged misuses of hospital ships by the Allies, as a precursor to their decision to reinstate their campaign of unrestricted submarine warfare. Included in the 'evidence' were details from a statement given by Messany to the Austrian authorities in Vienna on 5 January, detailing his observations on the voyage between Mudros and Southampton, which at first sight appeared to be very concerning for the British. Among the allegations, Messany claimed to have seen men in military uniform and equipment being transferred to the *Britannic* at Mudros, that two servicemen, with whom he had spoken, had told him they were translators being transferred to France, and that there were 2,500 men below deck who had been ordered to stay out of sight and were on different rations to the other patients. Messany even noted that when the *Britannic* reached Southampton, these men were openly paraded on the quayside and marched away in military formation, although the German document did acknowledge that they were not carrying any weapons. Unfortunately, the same could not be said in regard to the wounded officers, some of whom had been allowed to retain their side arms for the voyage home. The evidence was hardly conclusive, but coming at a time when Germany was looking for any possible justification to reintroduce their policy of unrestricted submarine warfare, it seemed an ideal opportunity to provide a suspiciously convenient validation for the reckless course upon which they were about to embark. The following day, the Germans announced that from 1 February 1917 they would be resuming their campaign of unrestricted submarine warfare.

Ultimately, the German unrestricted submarine warfare campaign failed. Once the war had ended, even the propaganda faded into the mists of time, but when seen together, Messany's evidence combined with the *Britannic's* curiously inaccurate hydrographic data seemed to be more than enough to rekindle the old whiff of suspicion. The following summer, Cousteau returned to the Kea Channel to conduct a more detailed survey with manned divers, but while the resulting programme, *Calypso's Search for the Britannic*, would provide the world with its first glimpse in 60 years of the *Titanic's* lost sister, Cousteau's physical exploration of the wreck did little to resolve the issues regarding the *Britannic's* bona fides. True enough, the programme would eventually reveal no direct evidence of any munitions in the cargo holds, but the post-expedition publicity in the press, doubtless in an attempt to generate interest in the viewing public, speculating that a mysterious 150-foot (46m) hole on the wreck could not have been caused by a single weapon, therefore cast doubt on the official report that the *Britannic* had been sunk by a mine. It certainly added fuel to the proverbial fire, with the combination of the incorrect position, the wartime allegations and a mysteriously large hole in the hull being little short of a conspiracy theorist's dream.

Nor were the Germans completely off the hook. Just as the Central Powers had alleged that the *Britannic* was being used illegally to transport combatants, the Allies were equally keen to emphasise their belief that a British hospital ship, supposedly protected by the Hague Convention, had in fact been deliberately torpedoed by a German U-boat. Such a claim would certainly have helped to generate sympathy for the Allied cause in America, which at that time was still neutral, but once again the evidence is conflicting. Two of the *Britannic*'s crew, steward Thomas Walters and baker Henry Etches, had certainly claimed to have seen the wake of a torpedo, and indeed Walters' evidence was given particular credence on account of the fact that at the time he was standing on the forward starboard side of the ship, particularly close to the location where the explosion occurred. The inconsistency, however, is that Etches reported seeing his torpedo passing beneath the stern and on the port side. An engineers' writer named Thomas Eckett also wrote of seeing what looked like a periscope while seated in one of the lifeboats, so there was certainly enough evidence to suggest that the *Britannic* might have been the victim of a deliberate attack.

Not surprisingly, the Germans denied that the hospital ship had been deliberately torpedoed. After the war, the war diary of the *U73* would confirm that mines had indeed been laid in the Kea Channel on 28 October 1916, in the exact location where both the *Burdigala* and the *Britannic* had come to grief. The war diary even contained very specific information on the laying of this particular mine barrier (see page 43).

Although this document was unavailable to the British in 1916, the subsequent naval investigation in Athens eventually concluded that the initial damage to the *Britannic* was

Hole in hull of liner casts doubts on official report

**From Our Correspondent
Athens, Oct 11**

The discovery of a 150ft hole in the hull of the British liner Britannic which sank in the Aegean during the 1914-18 War, seems to cast doubt on the official report at the time that the 46,000-ton vessel, converted into a hospital ship, was sunk by a German mine.

The wreck of the Britannic, sister-ship of the Titanic, was found by Commander Jacques-Yves Cousteau, the French underwater explorer, in 330ft of water off the island of Kea, 40 miles south-east of Athens.

The hole apparently explains why the ship sank immediately, but experts assert that it is too big to have been caused by a First World War mine.

The Britannic carried no wounded at the time, and all but 21 of its 1,061 crew and medical staff survived. Some old people on Kea remember helping the survivors ashore on November 21, 1916.

M Cousteau said he was determined to investigate a theory that the ship had been carrying ammunition and explosives for the Allies fighting in Gallipoli, under cover of being a hospital ship, and was in fact torpedoed by a German submarine.

Mr William Tantum, vice-president of the Titanic Historical Society of Massachusetts, is now with M Cousteau in Kea, as his detailed knowledge of the Titanic might help in the exploration of its sister-ship.

An offer by M Cousteau to fly to Greece any Britannic survivors still living has been accepted by a former nurse on the ship, now aged 86. She says she hopes to retrieve an alarm clock she left in cabin 237, which has sentimental value for her.

Above: The October 1976 article in *The Times*, that has done so much to fuel the various conspiracy theories.

probably caused by a mine. Not surprisingly, this rather important piece of information was never passed to the British press, who wasted no time in highlighting alleged German attacks not only on the *Britannic*, but also on another hospital ship, the 6,266 GRT *Braemar Castle*, which they claimed had been damaged during another torpedo attack in the Mykoni Channel two days later on 23 November.

Had they but known it, once again it was one of the *U73*'s mines that had in fact inflicted the damage to the *Braemar Castle*, but while Captain Ernest Mais was credited with being able to save his command by beaching the ship on the island of Tenos, his actions in the run-up to the explosion were less inspiring. The mining and subsequent beaching of the *Braemar Castle* appears to have been a completely avoidable loss, with the possible presence of mines in the Mykoni Channel having already been communicated to the local naval authorities days earlier. We know this because the sailing orders given to Captain Mais for his voyage from Salonika to Malta specifically instructed him to pass through the channel between the islands of Mykonos and Naxos; unfortunately, he misread his paperwork, the consequence being that at 11.15 that morning, just as the ship was 1 mile (1.6km) off Ioannis Point on the island of Tenos, a large explosion occurred on the ship's port side in the area of hold 3, resulting in the death of three personnel in one of the wards, and two crewmen badly injured during the evacuation. Fortunately, there were several vessels close by to offer assistance, as the destroyers HMS *Honeysuckle* and HMS *Jonquil* were already in the area sweeping for mines; the French trawler *Marie Rose* also managed to go alongside the *Braemar Castle* to evacuate some of the survivors, before Captain Mais grounded his ship on the nearby Blabe rocks.

The inquiry into the grounding of the *Braemar Castle* was held at Mudros on Monday 27 November 1916, although curiously enough the cause of the explosion was never determined officially. It was thought to have been a mine, but, conveniently for Captain Mais, Quartermaster Thomas Hillier did report seeing what he took to be a submarine periscope about a quarter of a mile from the ship when he was in one of the lifeboats. No one else reported seeing anything, but evidently it was just enough to cast a shadow of doubt. Even so, Vice-Admiral Cecil Thursby, the commander of the British naval forces in the Mediterranean, advised that Captain Mais' actions in entering an area already known to be hazardous should be looked into once the crew had been returned to England. Sure enough, on 5 February 1917 the Admiralty duly wrote to the Union Castle Line, advising them that not only should Mais lose his gratuity for the period between 1 October and 23 November 1916, but that in future he would not be allowed to command any of their vessels in government service. But for Thomas Hillier's evidence, he may not have got off quite so lightly.

With both the British and Germans equally determined to peddle their versions of the truth, perhaps it is not surprising that the old rumours and innuendo would have such an influence on Cousteau's conclusions. Then

DATE/TIME	Location, Wind, Weather, Swell, Light, Visibility, Moonlight	OCCURRENCES
28.10.16.	Kea Strait Wind SE 2, Swell 1, clear, visible	
2h 23 a.m.		Vessel with high mast light (destroyer) starboard ahead, on course for U73. Alarm, submerged to 20 metres.
3h 25 a.m.		Surfaced for loading.
3h 50 a.m.	Petalioi Gulf	Destroyer in sight in gulf; hospital ship in the Keos Strait on southerly course.
5h 10 a.m.		Submerged at dawn and steered to location for mine laying. The steamers all sail on the Keos side of the strait. After it gets light many steamers are in sight.
8h 07 a.m. until 8h 27 a.m.		Laid two barriers of 6 mines each. During the mine laying more steamers and a destroyer are nearby.
10h 00 a.m.		On the steamer strait at Keos 2 fishing vessels in search formation.
8h 35 a.m. until 3h 30 p.m.		Cruising near barrier for observation.
10h 45 a.m.		A large passenger steamer with 2 funnels (about 10,000 tons) is stopped, listing to starboard, with signal flags in the vicinity of the minefield across the Keos Strait.
11h 00 a.m.		The steamer leaves on a south-westerly course. A detonation was not detected, although it appeared as if the steamer had struck a mine. Distance from U73 to steamer was about 3 nautical miles. A short time later another steamer runs over the barrier without hitting a mine.
12h midday until 1h 00 p.m.		Several steamers pass near the barrier. I now take up a waiting position north of the barrier in order to torpedo steamers that have passed the barrier.
2h 00 p.m.		A large steamer goes through the strait on a northerly course; attack scheduled. After identifying the ship as a hospital ship, attack aborted. The time for traffic seems to be over.
4h 00 p.m.		Leaving through Doro Passage; tomorrow the barrier in the Mykonos strait will be laid.
5h 15 p.m.		A barque with south-westerly course sighted ahead.
7h 00 p.m.		Surfaced. Hospital ship heading north-east sighted astern. (The fifth hospital ship in three days).

Above: *U73*'s war diary.

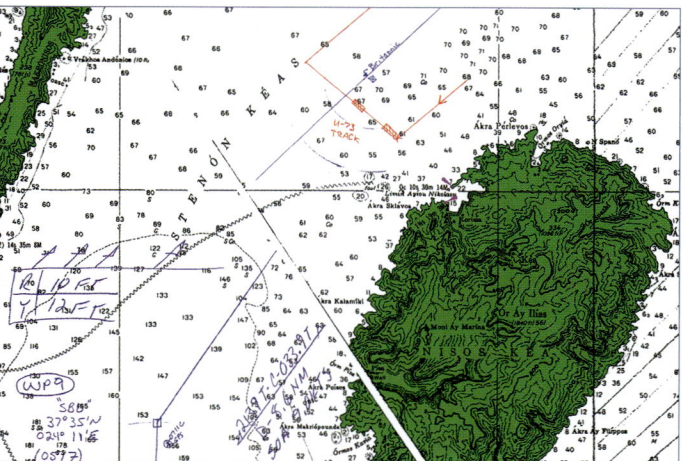

Above: Chart detailing the 1995 expedition operations.

advocate of unmanned technology, preferring instead to rely on the use of underwater Remotely Operated Vehicles (ROVs) as opposed to manned divers. The technology had certainly proved to be successful in obtaining the first internal images of the *Titanic* in the summer of 1986, but while the intention was to repeat the process on her sister ship, unfortunately it would not turn out to be quite as straightforward as planned.

Despite his state-of-the-art ROVs, not to mention the *NR-1*, a nuclear-powered research submarine operated by the US Navy, all of this effort would very nearly come to naught, with the Hellenic Navy reluctant to grant access to the wreck due to the possibility that contained within the *Britannic*'s hull was a hazardous cargo of illicit munitions. Clearly, the findings of Cousteau's exploration 19 years earlier were still enough to cast a shadow of doubt, and the fact that there was very little existing data on the *Britannic* at the time did not help the case for the project to go ahead. Fortunately, Ballard's expedition included a core team of historical advisers – Ken Marschall and Eric Sauder in America, along with yours truly in the UK – and following a check of every available crew list and cargo manifest held in the UK National Archives, one last official letter was sent to the Hellenic Navy's chief of staff, in the hope that it would bring about a change of heart in Athens. At the last minute the Greeks relented and the exploration was allowed to proceed, but only on the proviso that all activities were restricted to the exterior of the wreck.

The refusal of permission to go inside the

again, Cousteau's own findings did little to settle the controversy; in fact, they may even have made matters a lot worse, as the implication of the transportation of illegal war contraband, a huge internal explosion and the wreck then being deliberately misplaced in order to cover up the nefarious activities were subsequently woven together into the mother of all conspiracy theories. To be fair, with only the evidence of the Cousteau expedition to go on, for the next 20 years maritime historians really had no other evidence to hand, effectively giving them free rein to openly speculate on what would become an increasingly fantastic and, at times, lurid hypothesis.

It was not until the summer of 1995 that Dr Robert Ballard, the man who co-led the expedition that had located the wreck of the *Titanic* ten years earlier, decided to pick up where Cousteau had left off on the *Britannic*. Unlike Cousteau, however, Ballard was an wreck was a disappointment, for it effectively meant that we could not enter the *Britannic*'s cargo holds to look for any signs of the alleged munitions. Even when we were over the wreck, numerous technical glitches with the ROVs also cut short the planned operations on the first couple of days. Fortunately, the *NR-1* functioned flawlessly, and before long the submersible's high tech military sonar equipment had scanned the entire wreck site in the sort of detail that Cousteau would have found to be inconceivable. The 1995 satnav data also detected a slight discrepancy with the *Calypso*'s 1975 coordinates, revising the position slightly to 37° 42.37' N, 24° 16.74' E. Another interesting revelation was that the wreck lay on a heading of 253 degrees, which would have put the *Britannic*'s final heading on a south-westerly course, taking her back in the direction from which she originally came.

While the lack of any internal imagery was a disappointment, at least our closer examination of the forward part of the wreck settled once and for all the myth of an internal explosion. The British report into the sinking had always stated categorically that there was one explosion only, yet for 20 years the visions of Cousteau's huge 150-foot (46m) hole on the wreck had been used to support evidence of a secondary explosion of the illicit munitions cargo. The 1995 survey conclusively proves that no such feature ever existed on the wreck, the visible evidence instead indicating that the hull structure beneath the forward well deck, already weakened by the explosion of the mine, had actually collapsed due to the weight of the ship being concentrated in this area as the bow

was forced deeper into the seabed. Practically all of the hull structure beneath the forward well deck had totally collapsed, with the twisted bow subsequently tilting forward at such an angle that a chasm had opened up between the two intact sections. The breach is probably no more than about 50 feet wide (15m), while the jagged pieces of hull plating that resulted from an alleged internal explosion are in reality nothing more than fractured steel plates, twisted in every conceivable direction during the sinking process. This in itself was a huge step forward in the field of *Britannic*

Above: The US Navy's *NR-1* submarine alongside the support vessel *Carolyn Chouest*.

research. By the time our operations in the Kea Channel eventually concluded, on 4 September 1995, it was clear that the wreck of the *Britannic* had only just begun to give up its secrets.

When NOVA's *Titanic's Lost Sister* broadcast, on 28 January 1996, the fact that it had not been possible to film key internal areas of the wreck left me with a feeling of unfinished business. While there were hopes that this might one day be rectified when Ballard returned to the *Britannic* to carry out his 'Telepresence' project – a combination of permanently mounted cameras and satellite technology allowing shore-based scientists, teachers and students to access data and images from a shipwreck in real time – sadly, this concept would not come to pass. In the end, perhaps it didn't really matter, when, seven months later, I unexpectedly found myself in the curious position of having officially acquired the UK government's former legal title to the wreck. Suddenly, the responsibility for solving the host of mysteries surrounding the loss of the *Britannic* was no longer someone else's problem; it was now very much my problem, even if at that time I didn't have the faintest notion as to the scale of the task I had taken on, and exactly how I would go about resolving the questions that, up to that point, I had been happy to work on from behind the scenes.

It would not be until the spring of 1997 that I was even remotely in a position to start thinking of planning a way forward on the *Britannic*. As I pondered on the reality of following in the footsteps of luminaries like Jacques Cousteau and Bob Ballard, I instinctively knew that I was totally out of my depth. Not only that, but the financial considerations alone were daunting. Never mind contemplating whether or not it would be better to take the more physical manned approach to wreck exploration à la Cousteau, or instead pursue the safer but more detached use of ROVs as advocated by Ballard; if I was going to be able to realise my plans then not only was it going to cost a ton of money, but I had to face up to the fact that I had absolutely no diving experience, not even the slightest idea about how to go about generating the necessary funding, or even the faintest clue about arranging the underwater logistics that would be required. Apart from that, I was perfect for the job.

Above: Sonar scan of the bow damage in 2003. (Bill Smith)

It was the world of technical diving that finally solved my dilemma, which is curious considering that one of the reasons I had bought the wreck in the first place had been to protect it from unwanted interference by divers. Initially, I had little thought of cooperating with 'the enemy', and my philanthropic cause was not helped one iota when, no sooner had *Titanic's Lost Sister* been transmitted on TV, I learned that two teams of British technical divers were already planning expeditions to the Kea Channel. My first instinct was to put a stop to it, when it suddenly dawned on me that if I was going to be the one to unlock the *Britannic*'s secrets, rather than fighting the diving world, perhaps I should actually be working with it. The two dive team leaders, Kevin Gurr and Nick Hope, were also not at all what I had expected. They had not been at all combative in their approach; in fact, I recall receiving two very polite letters asking for permission to access the wreck, courtesy of the maritime attaché at the Greek embassy in Holland Park. On the face of it, I had absolutely nothing to lose…

The 1997 and 1998 expeditions have never really been given the credit they deserve, most likely due to the fact that, apart from some interesting imagery, they didn't really reveal very much about the wreck that we didn't already know. This is not intended as a criticism of the dive teams, as in the late nineties deep technical diving on a recreational basis was still very much in its infancy, but none of that seemed particularly important to me at that time. The divers still had much to learn about gas mixes and decompression tables at such

Above: The helm of the *NR-1*.

depths, while my primary goal had simply been to get a better understanding of the complexities of working at depths of up to 374ft (114m) and putting the building blocks in place for a more comprehensive survey of the wreck when the time was right. More importantly, the dive teams seemed more than happy to investigate the comprehensive individual targets that I set for them, content that they were gaining access to the largest liner on the seabed, so everyone seemed to be getting exactly what they wanted.

It was only after a third manned expedition in the autumn of 1999 by Jarrod Jablonski's Global Underwater Explorers team – the first to make more widespread use of the rebreather technology that was on the verge of changing everything – that I finally felt I knew enough about my wreck to take a more hands-on approach. At long last, I was finally ready to start investigating the unanswered questions about what really happened in the Kea Channel on the fateful morning of 21 November 1916.

4

SCIENCE AND THE MODERN SHIPWRECK

I was never in any doubt that I was following in the footsteps of luminaries. Jacques Cousteau, a man with an unrivalled reputation in the world of underwater exploration, had located the *Britannic* in 1975 and carried out the first manned exploration the following year, while Bob Ballard, the man who found the *Titanic*, had used his remote technology to great effect in 1995, so we already had a far greater understanding of the wreck. By comparison, I was just an amateur historian who had got lucky, and the thought of somehow matching their accomplishments seemed little more than a pipe dream.

My ambitions, though, were far less expansive. Cousteau and Ballard were not just fixated on a single wreck, and while their *Britannic* expeditions had undoubtedly showed the way forward, there were still so many unanswered questions. Even so, my own efforts only seemed to be going back over ground covered after my first trip to the wreck in 1995. On the other hand, due to the imagery resulting from the three manned expeditions between 1997 and 1999, I now at least had a clearer idea as to the routes that would need to be followed if we were going to venture further inside the wreck. Furthermore, with the increasing use of rebreathers in the world of technical diving – a magic all-in-one box that absorbs the carbon dioxide exhaled by a diver and recycles the unused oxygen – it not only extended the depth capabilities and range of the individual divers, but by eliminating the exhaled gas bubbles it also had far less impact on the anaerobic interior of the wreck.

Despite the passage of time, however, my starting point was still very much where Cousteau had left off 27 years earlier. While the failure of the 1976 expedition to locate any evidence of an illegal munitions cache in the *Britannic*'s cargo holds was undoubtedly a good thing, it had also created something of a problem for Cousteau's team, as they needed to find some explanation for the mysterious 150-foot (46m) hole reportedly observed on the wreck. If the visible damage had not been caused by a secondary explosion of munitions, then it had to have been caused by something else. By chance, even a cursory glance at a set of the ship's deck plans seemed to indicate a possible candidate. Conveniently, cargo hold 3, extending between frames 95F and 78F, provided them with exactly what they were looking for. This hold was the fourth compartment aft of the *Britannic*'s stem, and the fact that it also contained a space at the level of the tank top where the ship's reserve coal was stored provided the perfect starting point to explore the exploding coal dust theory. To a certain extent the notion was plausible, and if such an explosion had occurred then it could, in theory, explain the scale of the damage. At the same time the question inevitably arose as to whether or not the conditions conducive to a coal dust explosion would have existed in the *Britannic*'s case.

As a rule, coal stored in bunker spaces creates finely divided particles of dust, which over a period of time will settle on various frames or brackets within the bunker. If the bunker is right next to the boiler room, which in this case the *Britannic*'s reserve bunker was

Above: A single coal sample, retrieved for analysis in 1999.

not, then the heat could also help to create the warm, dry conditions required to result in a rapid fire or explosion of the coal dust, if the dust is sufficiently disturbed to form a cloud in the presence of an ignition source. A small sample of coal was even retrieved from the seabed for analysis by the 1999 expedition, and to date it remains the only piece of *Britannic* coal to have been studied, although the subsequent investigation proved inconclusive. In the end, the retrieved sample was classed as 'bituminous' and with the volatile matter content ranging from 12 to 17.5 per cent, but after more than 80 years lying on the seabed there was nothing to be gained in analysing the methane content of the sample, as the methane would have evaporated through the pores in the coal long ago. Nevertheless, the indications seemed to suggest that the necessary conditions conducive to a coal dust explosion were not present in the *Britannic*'s case, essentially supporting the findings of the 1995 Ballard survey.

From a historical point of view, however, the most important question of all remained unresolved. Was it a mine or a torpedo that had sealed the *Britannic*'s fate?

Proponents of the torpedo theory have always had one great advantage in this debate, in that it is practically impossible to locate any physical evidence whatsoever of an exploded torpedo. While fragments of a detonated torpedo will certainly fall to the seabed after exploding against a ship's hull, the *Britannic* remained afloat for almost an hour after the explosion, during which time none of her movements can be ascertained with any great degree of certainty. The chances, therefore, of finding any traces of a German torpedo in relation to the sinking were always non-existent, effectively making it impossible to wholly prove the torpedo theory. With several witnesses claiming to have seen what they may have genuinely believed to be a torpedo, even though these sightings were relatively commonplace, their evidence could not simply be dismissed out of hand.

As for the mine theory, for decades there was ample documentation in the German U-boat archives to confirm that a minefield had indeed been laid in the Kea Channel, but as any good conspiracy theorist will argue,

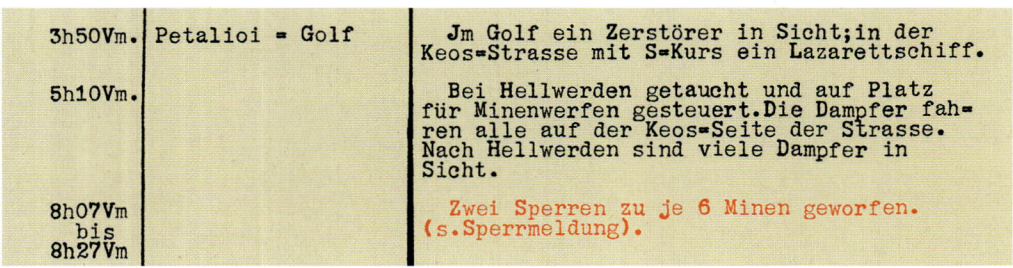

Above: The *U73* war diary entry, detailing the laying of the two mine barriers in the Kea Channel on 28 October 1916. (Titanic Historical Society)

SCIENCE AND THE MODERN SHIPWRECK

Above: The German EMA mines in the Kea Channel were laid deeper than usual, in order to bag a larger naval or transport vessel. (William Barney)

people can lie and documents can be faked, especially if those concerned had an interest in covering up what would effectively have been a war crime. Even so, after an interval of 87 years the chances of locating any physical evidence of a minefield on the seabed were always going to be considerably greater than finding any fragments of a detonated torpedo, and as long as you knew where to look there was always going to be at least an outside chance of success. Fortunately, we did know exactly where to look. Not only did the war diary of the *U73* provide reasonably precise details of the location of what the German Navy would refer to as 'Barrage 32', but there was also a considerable amount of information available on the German weapon of choice.

The type of mine laid by the *U73* was the first German mine with a chemical-horn firing system, designated Elektrische Mine type A (EMA). The EMA consisted of two steel hemispheres, joined by a 12-inch (30cm) cylindrical mid-section, resulting in an overall height of 46 inches (1.17m) and a diameter of 34 inches (86cm). Equally spaced around the top hemisphere of the mine were four soft lead horns, known as Hertz horns, each containing a glass phial filled with an electrolyte – in this case, potassium bichromate solution. Upon contact with a passing vessel, the glass tube inside the deformed lead horn would be shattered and the solution would leak into a

Above: The sonar team from the 2003 expedition.

small chamber containing one carbon and one zinc plate, connecting the two plates to form a simple battery able to generate sufficient electrical current to activate an electric detonator located in the bottom hemisphere of the mine.

Once the 150-kilo (330lb) hexanite explosive charge had been detonated, naturally you might not expect to find very much remaining of the mine itself, but unlike a torpedo, a considerable amount of undamaged evidence would remain on the seabed. Two lugs mounted on the mine's lower hemisphere connected it to a mooring bracket, which in turn would be released from the sinker as the apparatus came to rest on the seabed. The mine would then rise to a predetermined depth, controlled by a depth-taking hydrostat, in the process withdrawing a safety pin from the arming switch to complete the circuit between the horn battery and the detonator;

the mooring tension also extended the spindle of the white metal mooring switch, arming the internal circuit of the horn. In the *Britannic*'s case the water was deep, meaning that the anchor apparatus would have been at least 350 feet (107m) beneath the point of the explosion, so the answer seemed to be relatively simple. By locating either the mine fragments or the mine anchors, we would have the empirical evidence needed to confirm, once and for all, that the *Britannic* had indeed steamed into a minefield.

In itself, the practical technique used to locate what remained of the minefield was more or less the same as those used by Dr Harold Edgerton in locating the *Britannic* and Bob Ballard when looking for the *Titanic*. In 1975 Dr Edgerton, of the Massachusetts Institute of Technology, had been using his side-scan sonar to search the Kea Channel, whereas in 1985 Ballard, who likened the technique to 'mowing the lawn', used a 2-ton sled called *Argo*, equipped with video cameras, to explore a much larger swathe of the seabed. In each case, the search had been conducted by patiently towing a submerged imaging system back and forth across a designated search area, and in each case the technique had worked. As a result, in November 1975 the *Calypso* located the *Britannic*, just as almost ten years later, on 1 September 1985, the RV *Knorr* found the *Titanic*.

Of course, I wasn't looking for anything as grand as a shipwreck, but my chance would eventually come in September 2003, when *National Geographic* and Channel 5 co-funded the expedition I hoped would finally change the course of *Britannic* investigation. Our sonar vessel of choice, the Kea-based fishing boat *Stella*, was tiny by comparison to the 360-ton *Calypso*, or the even more impressive 2,685-ton RV *Knorr*, and *Stella* certainly had none of the technological wizardry necessary for a credible search of the seabed. That problem, however, was easily resolved when we called upon the expertise of Bill Smith, a sonar expert from Newcastle, to plug the gap. Bill was confident that his 410kHz GeoAcoustics towfish was up to the task, and with the necessary permission from the Hellenic Navy to carry out sonar operations in the Kea Channel, the *Stella* finally headed out of Port St Nikolo to commence the search for what I hoped would be the missing piece of this particular puzzle.

It may seem strange to think that one of the first items on my list was to explore an area of the Kea Channel approximately one mile from the location of my wreck, but finding the minefield had been a key item in my personal *Britannic* bucket list as early as the 1995 expedition. Even though we had the technology to do the job, however, doubts were never far from my mind as to whether the mine anchors would be too small for the sonar to detect, to say nothing of the more likely possibility of the mine fragments having been dragged God knows where by countless fishing nets or dredges over the 87 years they had lain on the seabed. The search process itself was also slow, not helped by the fact that on each trip Andonis, the skipper of the *Stella*, also needed to set aside enough time for his daily catch. Regardless of the interruptions and occasionally bumpy conditions in the channel, Bill and his team were always cheerful and optimistic. The data would still need to be

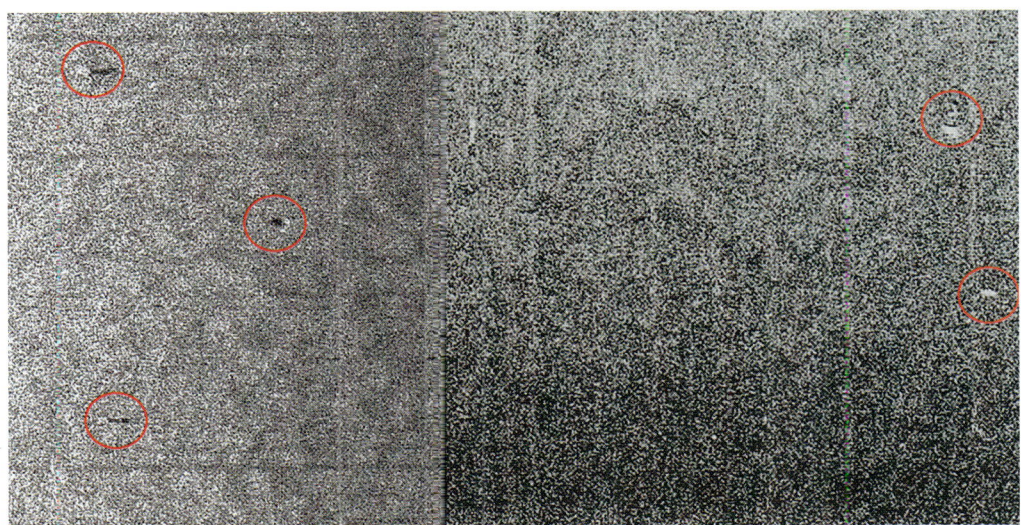

Above: The first sonar images of the mine fragments in 2003. (Bill Smith)

processed once back home in Newcastle, but while I seemed to be incapable of interpreting the obscure markings on the printouts, to Bill's more seasoned eye the evidence was inescapable. A series of tiny dots extending along a reasonably straight line could leave no further room for doubt – we had located the *U73*'s minefield!

Despite what at the time felt like an immense personal triumph, without a photographic image of a mine on the seabed I knew we would still have our detractors. However at that time it did not seem important. Our sonar towfish may not have incorporated an acoustic positioning system that would have enabled us to fix a definite position on each object, but with easily identifiable landmarks in the Kea Channel we could at least be confident that the minefield was well within the ballpark of the location recorded by the *U73*'s navigating officer, Oberleutnant zur See Martin Niemöller. True, it extended slightly further out into the channel than Niemöller's dead reckoning position on the war diary chart suggested, but the line was good and there could no longer be any doubt that the German records had been correct all along. Five years later I was finally able to return to the minefield and, courtesy of Bill's 2003 data, we used an ROV operated by the Hellenic Centre for Marine Research (HCMR), better known in Greece as ΕΛΚΕΘΕ (ELKETHE), to obtain that all-important photographic image of an exploded mine casing. QED!

Although the minefield survey had been crucial in correcting the historical record, other equally important scientific work needed to be carried out on the seabed in order to better understand not only the marine environment at the bottom of the Kea Channel, but also the effect that it was having on the wreck itself. Unlike the minefield, however, these results would take much longer to determine. For this reason, in September 2003 we also began the first investigation of the marine environment at the microbiological level.

Droycon Bioconcepts had been working on an analysis of the deterioration on the wreck of the *Titanic* since 1991, when biological activity reaction tests (BARTs) were deployed on the wreck in order to obtain as much scientific information as possible on the microflora, as well as the deterioration of the wreck itself. These BART platforms are used to determine the types and aggressiveness of the bacteria found on the wreck, which would then allow for a much more accurate determination of the flora. In the *Britannic*'s case, three different test vials were incorporated into a single platform, each being used to detect a different group of bacteria (sulphate reducers, slime-forming and iron related), but as an added feature, a strip of Kodak slide film was also used to gain as much information as possible. The test platform was then taken down to the wreck and placed in one of the forward windows (port side, B deck), where it would remain for 72 hours. During this time, the testers were exposed to the ambient

Right: An intact EMA mine captured in 1917, compared with images of one of the Kea Channel mine fragments photographed in August 2008.

nutrient flow, gases, currents and light present on that part of the wreck, before being returned to the surface, where analysis indicated a highly aggressive bacterial environment. The bacterial environment was actually so aggressive that, when the slide film test was examined, the etchings indicated that over 90 per cent of the gelatine emulsion had been removed by the bacteria present in the water.

The data from the BART platform reactions would prove to be very similar to those seen in the *Britannic* rusticle samples, which would also be taken that year. The *Titanic*'s hull has suffered badly as a result of the large number of what have now become more commonly known as 'rusticles', a growing mass of iron-rich bio-concretions on the steel surfaces, the word 'rusticle' being a derivation of the two words 'rust' and 'icicle'. The level of rusticle infestation on the *Britannic*, however, is significantly different, most likely resulting from the warmer water and natural light that exists at the bottom of the Kea Channel, as opposed to the *Titanic*'s eternally black and much colder resting place at the bottom of the Atlantic. As a result, there is a far greater variety of marine life on the *Britannic* than exists on the *Titanic*, with the constant competition for the available food sources keeping these micro-organisms at bay. On the other hand, the marine life on the *Britannic* differs considerably depending on where you go. At its shallowest point (about 86 metres/282ft) there is an abundance of colourful flora and fauna, but as you get progressively deeper the look of the wreck changes considerably. By the time you reach

HMHS *Britannic* BART platform results

HMHS *Britannic* Platform One	IRB	SRB	SLYM
PAC/ml	500,000	100,000	5,000,000
RPS	CL, FO, BR, BL	BA	CL, DS, TH, BL

the seabed at 114 metres (374ft), there is much less light and consequently much less sea life. As a result, it is here that the *Britannic*'s rusticles become more dominant.

In their simplest form, rusticles can be described as elongated structures incorporating organic filaments within a shell of iron oxide and/or calcite, their orange-brown colour entirely due to the highly oxidised ferric content, which could account for as much as 90 per cent of their dried weight. Microscopic examination of the *Britannic*'s rusticles shows a structure with an extremely tight matrix of growth. Due to the more temperate environment found in the Kea Channel, their characteristics were somewhat different from those on the *Titanic*, the complex structure of channels, reservoirs and crystalline formations having a more compact and tightly woven matrix. This variation of growth is most likely due to the conditions found on site, with the increased nutrient loading and the low levels of ambient light penetration at a depth of almost 400 feet (122m) allowing for a much wider group of organisms to be able to compete for nutrients, gases and habitat. As a result, the rusticles are not the dominant organisms on the wreck – at least, not on the upper reaches of the exterior

– and in adapting to their surroundings they have become more defensive in structure.

The final experiment to be conducted in 2003 would not yield quick results. A steel test platform, incorporating 12 metal coupons from a variety of steel types found in maritime vessels, was also used to analyse the deterioration of the hull steel. The platform was placed on the wreck – aft of the fourth window on the port-side bulkhead of the forward first-class main entrance on the boat deck – where it would remain undisturbed for at least five years. In the end, the platform would remain on the wreck for a total of 69 months, after which it was returned to the Droycon laboratory in Canada, where the individual coupons could then be weighed and measured to determine how much of the iron had been extracted from the steel.

Upon recovery, an intense growth of biomass was observed on the underside of the metal coupons, along with rusticles extending down the internal sides of the platform itself. This biomass was extremely irregular in form, incorporating so much dead animal life and marine shell fragments that it was not even possible to estimate an average thickness of the metal coupons until it could be removed. Once the individual coupons had been cleaned down to the steel surface, a gravimetric determination could then be made to determine how much steel had been lost after almost six years at the bottom of the Kea Channel. The cleaning revealed clear evidence that the steel was being attacked by several corrosive forces, and in some places the pitting corrosion had even turned into a total perforation of two of the

Chemical analysis of an *HMHS Britannic* rusticle

Metals Total (Fusion)	Units	Results
Aluminium (Al_2O_3)	%	0.3
Barium (BaO)	%	0.00515
Calcium (CaO)	%	0.516
Iron (Fe_2O_3)	%	76.9
Magnesium (MgO)	%	0.875
Manganese (MnO)	%	0.0613
Phosphorous (P_2O_5)	%	0.34
Potassium (K_2O)	%	0.37
Silicon (SiO_2)	%	1.8
Sodium (Na_2O)	%	2.19
Strontium (SrO)	%	0.01
Titanium (TiO_2)	%	0.02
Zirconium (ZrO_2)	%	<0.0007
Total oxides	ug/g	100
Beryllium	ug/g	3.6
Chromium	ug/g	15
Cobalt	ug/g	4
Molybdenum	ug/g	99
Valadium	ug/g	101
Zinc	ug/g	276
Loss on ignition	%	16.6

9mm steel coupons, equating to an average penetration rate of 0.13mm per month. Some of the steel coupons had lost significant steel through lateral corrosion (dishing), while

Above: The Droycon steel platform after recovery in May 2009, after 69 months undisturbed on the wreck.

several coupons also showed evidence of unusual lateral pitting occurring within the central 2mm of the coupon's steel. All these events combined clearly indicated that the environment in which the platform had been placed on the *Britannic* was undoubtedly conducive to microbiologically induced corrosion (MIC).

The individual gravimetric measurements were even more revealing, indicating that after 69 months of exposure on the wreck the coupons collectively had lost 662 grams of iron, equating to 6.9 grams per month, or 29 per cent of the total steel contained within the platform compared to when it was first deployed on the wreck.

The data resulting from the steel platform placed on the *Britannic* in September 2003 has since been incorporated into similar studies on other notable wrecks, including the USS *Arizona* and the KMS *Bismarck*, in the process materially expanding the knowledge of biological threats causing deterioration in these steel shipwrecks. In the case of the *Britannic*, though, one thing seems worryingly clear from the science. The analysis of the steel platform displayed an annual corrosion rate for the unprotected steel coupons nearly three times faster in the *Britannic* (5 per cent per year) than for the three platforms recovered from the *Titanic* (1.6 to 1.7 per cent per year). This faster corrosion rate may be a reflection of the greater and more diverse forms of life that would be attaching to the steels at the much shallower depths at which the ship rests on the seabed, suggesting that while the *Britannic* continues to look reasonably intact for the time being, this increased rate of corrosion could indicate that the wreck will be subjected to a more sudden collapse, as the steel eventually weakens to the point that the structure can no longer support its own weight.

While the initial data suggests that from a structural pint of view the *Britannic* is living on borrowed time, something is also happening at the bottom of the Kea Channel that may help to delay the process. Working in collaboration with the HCMR, in September 2008 we set out to survey and study the organisms settled on the shipwreck, utilising their submersible, *Thetis*, and *Max*, their underwater ROV.

Any artificial surface exposed to the marine environment typically develops a layer of attached organisms over a period of time, in a process that is generally referred to as 'biofouling'. The progression starts with the adsorption of inorganic material on hard surfaces, followed by the settlement of bacteria and diatoms, after which a complex and diverse fauna and flora community develops. To an untrained eye, the marine biomass may appear to be undermining the structural integrity of the wreck, whereas it may actually

> **Location of steel platforms:**
> *Titanic* A: Forward of the stern section keel, where the reciprocating engines were positioned
> *Titanic* B: Port-side boat deck, just aft of the port door to the bridge
> *Titanic* C: Immediately in front of the stem on the port side (close to a field of spent rusticles)
> *Britannic*: Forward port-side main entrance at boat deck level

	Months at site	Biomass/coupon (g dry weight)	Steel total loss (g)	Steel loss (g/month)	Annual steel loss (percentage)
Titanic A	72	106.5	18.87	0.26	1.7%
Titanic B	72	97.8	18.84	0.26	1.7%
Titanic C	84	15.2	21.81	0.26	1.6%
Britannic	69	64.1	55.21	0.80	5.0%

Coupon	Coupon weight	Metal weight	Biomass weight	% Metal loss
1	198.1	132.5	65.6	30.4%
2	199.3	142.7	56.6	25.0%
3	213.4	136.2	77.2	28.4%
4	209.6	135.8	73.8	28.6%
5	204.6	130.0	74.6	31.7%
6	210.8	133.0	77.8	30.1%
7	195.0	137.8	57.2	27.6%
8	163.2	136.8	26.4	28.1%
9	213.4	133.4	80.0	29.9%
10	195.2	131.0	64.2	31.2%
11	200.9	134.0	66.9	29.6%
12	187.0	137.9	49.1	27.5%

be helping to slow deterioration. The corrosive effect of seawater on a steel shipwreck begins the moment the hull touches the seabed, but there comes the point where a wreck eventually reaches a state of equilibrium with its marine environment. As the precipitates from the seawater settle on the steel surface, the process of colonisation by shells and barnacles results in concretions, mainly made of calcium carbonate, which are essentially the remains of dead sea creatures and which ultimately develop into a protective crust. These crusts can be as hard as rock, but, more importantly, they also create an anoxic environment, whereby the lack of oxygen getting through to the metal helps to preserve the structure. So, despite an understandable wish in some quarters to clean off the wreck, the *Britannic* will actually last much longer if these concretions remain undisturbed.

Through the combined use of the *Thetis* submersible and Max Rover, all told we spent a total of 17.7 hours over a five-day period studying only the marine environment. Based on the Elkethe data, the depth of the seabed varies from 105 to 114 metres (344–374ft). The predominant sediments in the Kea Channel are much as Cousteau described them – flat with gravel and muddy sand, with patches of rock further to the south to relieve the monotony of a relatively featureless seabed – but the presence of the maerl, a coralline red algae that is also harvested for use as a soil conditioner, confirmed that my old fears of dredging activities in the channel having possibly destroyed the evidence of the minefield were well founded. The large number of parallel trawling scrape marks on the seabed, not to mention the remains of a very large trawl net snagged on the bow of the wreck, provide ample evidence that the area had been quite extensively disturbed in the past; fortunately, most of the fishing nets that have attached to the *Britannic*'s hull are of the smaller type carried by the local traditional Greek caïques, so the human pollution of the wreck itself was still relatively limited.

Closer inspection of the wreck indicates that more than a century at the bottom of the Aegean has seen the *Britannic* transformed into a complex marine habitat and ecosystem. From the highest point of the structure to the seabed, a range of 86 to 114 metres (282–374ft), the hull is completely covered by settled fauna and flora, but with important variations in three distinct fouling zones. These variations could be due to a combination of any number of environmental factors, such as available light, depth, temperature, surface orientation of the individual habitats and even exposure to the prevailing currents, but the end result is an interestingly structured ecosystem. The fish life is particularly rich in terms of numbers and species, predominantly *Anthias anthias* – a marine goldfish, commonly referred to as the swallowtail seaperch – while a not insignificant number of lobsters (*Palinurus elephas*) can often be observed on the upper port side and forecastle. Divers also need to keep a wary eye out for more solitary Mediterranean moray eels, lurking menacingly in any of the numerous cavities and openings along the higher port side.

At the uppermost part of the wreck are

colonies of the serpulid polychaete worm *Filograna*, the upper edges of the wreck dominated by a variety of sponges, for the most part *Agelas oroides* and *Aplysina sp.* with some *Haliclona mediterranea* and *Ircinia sp.* around the deck railings and boat deck level. Below this area to the seabed is a flatter level of fouling, consisting of smaller sponges, hard and soft red coralline algae (*Lithothamnion*, *Lithophyllum* and *Peyssonnelia* types), some green algae and heavy deposits of saddle oysters (*Anomia ephippium*), while adjacent to the hull is a low berm, consisting mostly of saddle oysters resulting from fall-off from the wreck. On what would formerly have been the underside of the ship, where the angle is more acute and where the light level is generally lower, the surface is more prone to saddle oysters, while at the level of the seabed the marine fouling consists almost entirely of flat red coralline algae (*Lithothamnion*, *Lithophyllum* and *Peyssonnelia* types) with a clear sediment space where the wreck meets the seabed.

As a result of the marine biological surveys, one thing remains abundantly clear. It has taken more than a century to transform the wreck into an artificial reef. There is more life on the *Britannic* now than there ever was when she was in service and, despite my ambitious plans, I have never lost sight of the fact that I need to make sure it stays that way.

Below: One of the many Mediterranean lobsters that now inhabit the wreck.

5

CSI *BRITANNIC*

'Gradually the waters licked up and up the decks – the furnaces belching forth fierce volumes of smoke, as if the great engines were in their last death agony; one by one the monster funnels melted away as wax before a flame, and crashed upon the decks, till the waters rushed down; then report after report rang over the sea, telling of the explosion of the boilers. The waters moved over the deck still, the bows of the ship dipping deeper and deeper into the sea, until the rudders stood straight up from the surface of the water, and, poised thus for a few moments, dived perpendicularly into the depths, leaving hardly a ripple behind.'

In February 1917, Reverend John Fleming, the *Britannic*'s Presbyterian chaplain, published the first instalment of his story of the sinking of the *Britannic* in a two-part article in *The Record of the Home & Foreign Mission Work of the United Free Church of Scotland*. Several months later, the text would be republished in a single volume by Marshall Brothers in Edinburgh. This book is not what you might call truly definitive, the entire text coming in at marginally over 7,500 words and even then only about half of its length told the story of the actual sinking and its immediate aftermath, but for decades it has remained the only widely available contemporary publication of what happened aboard the *Britannic* on the day that she sank.

Fleming's descriptions of the *Britannic*'s last minutes afloat are all very dramatic, no doubt intended to appeal to his readership in both the religious press and the wider public, and to be fair much of what the book contains is reasonably accurate. Fleming notes that numbers of the crew agreed that they saw what they took to be a torpedo miss the rudder, while another would hit the ship in the bow, although the fact that most of the ship's personnel would have been at breakfast at the time of the alleged attack inevitably leaves

Left: Diver Rich Stevenson examining the stern of the Britannic, which on the day of the sinking was described as standing straight up from the surface of the water before diving perpendicularly into the depths. (Leigh Bishop)

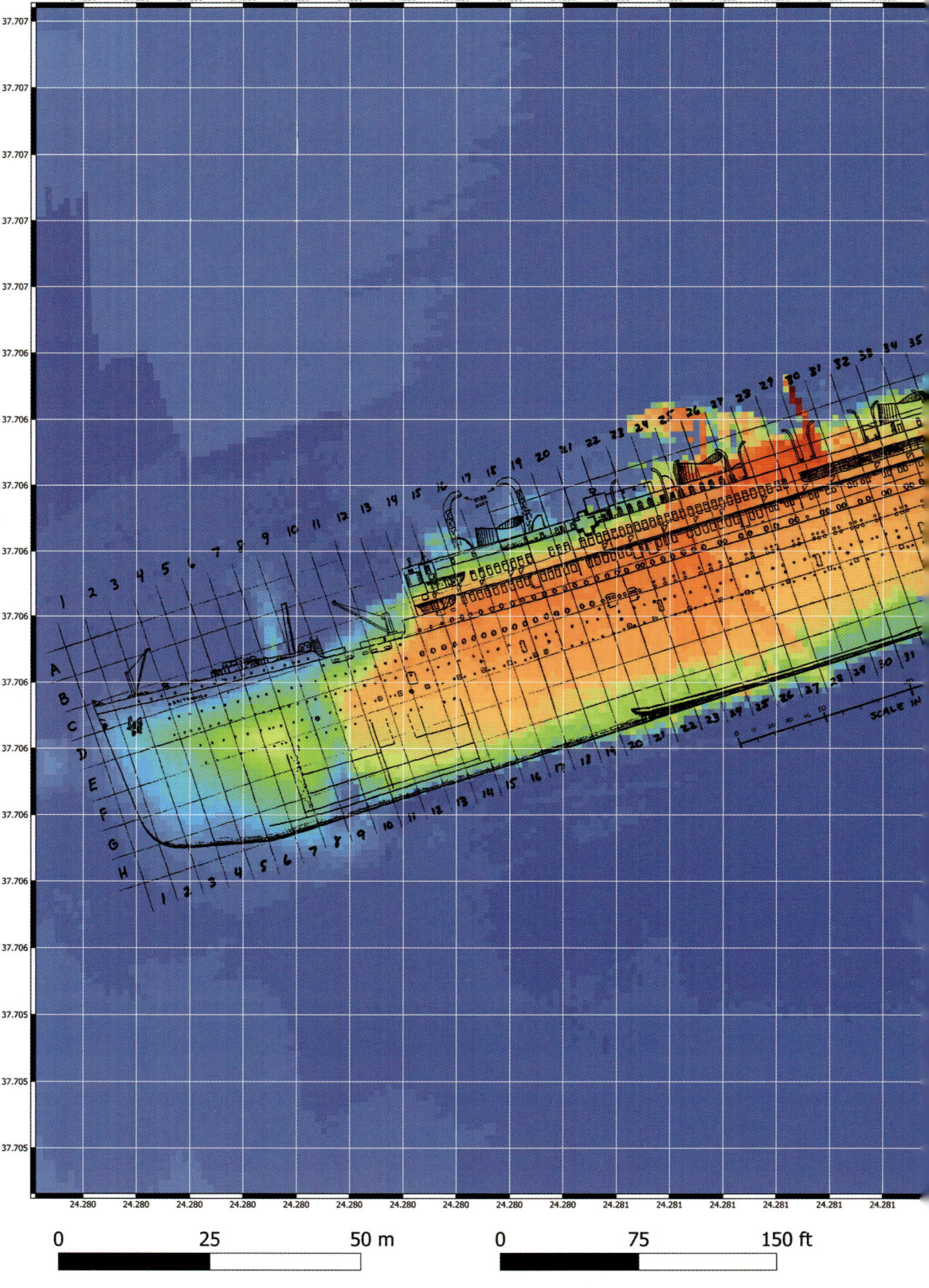

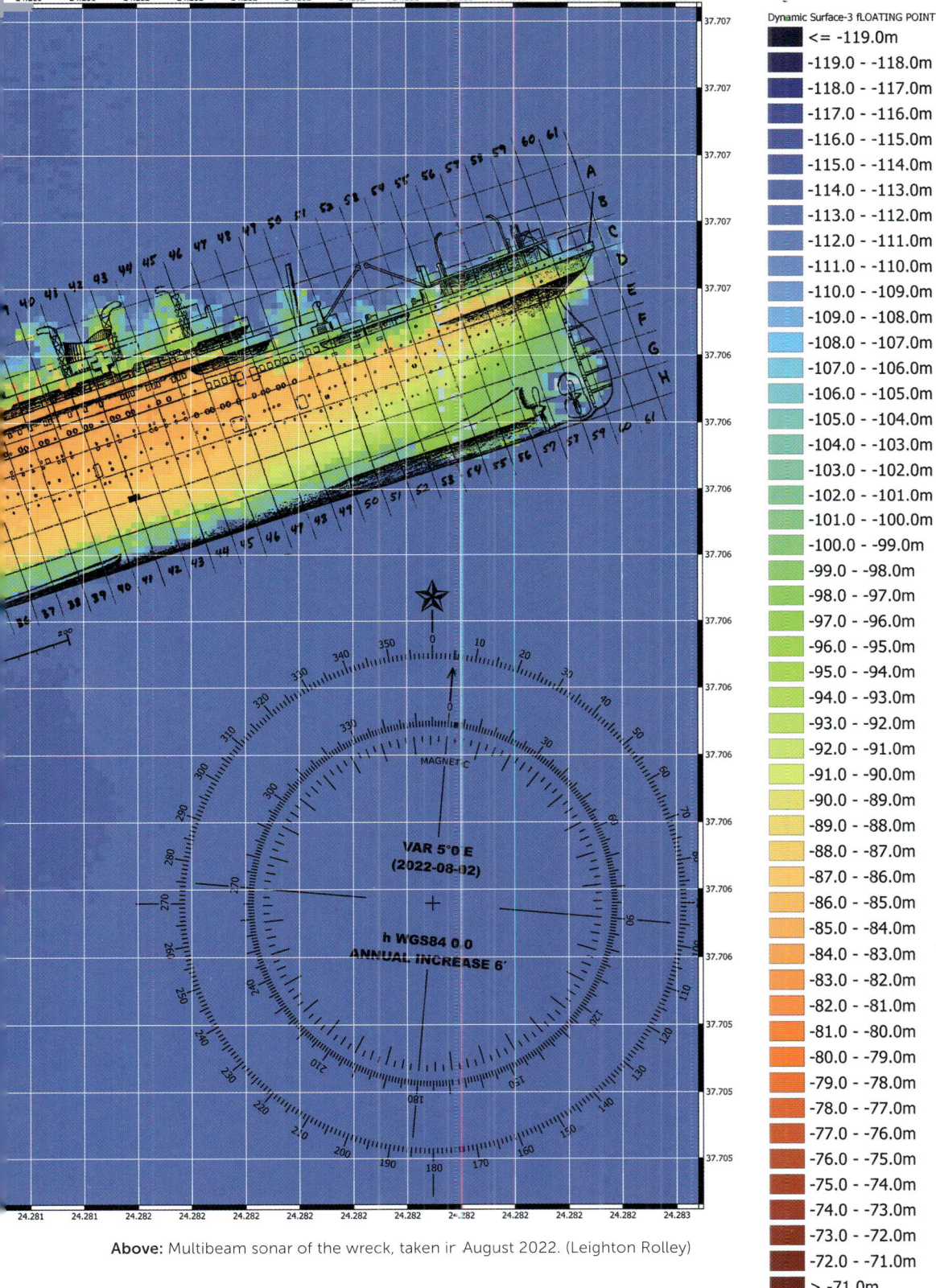

Above: Multibeam sonar of the wreck, taken in August 2022. (Leighton Rolley)

much of the witness testimony open to question. Fleming himself was in his cabin below deck, staring out of the porthole and absorbed by the sight of a Greek village nestling high up on the steep side of the island of Kea (almost certainly the island capital, Ioulis), when the breakfast gong snapped him back to reality. He was just leaving his cabin when there was a great crash, which he later recalled as '…if a score of plate-glass windows had been smashed together', before feeling the violent shudder throughout the ship. Less reliable, perhaps, was Fleming's assertion that the inhabitants of Port St Nikolo claimed to have seen a submarine in the Kea Channel earlier that morning, which inevitably raises the question as to how reliable any eyewitness statement can actually be.

Despite the passage of time, the physical evidence of the nature of the sinking can still be observed on the seabed, both in and around the wreck, but straight away we have a problem with Fleming's dramatic observation that the *Britannic* stood up on end before diving 'perpendicularly into the depths.' During the 2008 marine biological survey, the Hellenic Centre for Marine Research recorded various depths on the *Britannic* wreck site, ranging from 105 to 114 metres (345–375ft), which suggests that Fleming's description of the *Britannic*'s last moments afloat was either in error, or, more likely, embellished with a hint of artistic licence for his readership. After all, how could an 883-foot (269m) ship dive perpendicularly into water that is marginally less than 400 feet (122m) deep?

The solution to this particular mystery has always lain 114 metres (374ft) below the surface of the Kea Channel, but before proceeding inside the wreck, the exterior needed to be thoroughly mapped and recorded. The *Britannic*, almost completely intact, lies on her starboard side on an approximate bearing of 253 degrees, although the wreck is not quite parallel to the seabed. Recent internal measurements have now refined the angle of the hull to the seabed as being approximately 77 degrees, and as a result much of the superstructure is hanging unsupported over the seabed, rather than resting directly on top of it. Even at 114 metres (374ft) the ambient light and visibility provides ample opportunity to examine large areas of the wreck with the naked eye, although at that depth the colours with the longer wavelengths have been completely absorbed by the water molecules. The first colours to go in the water column fade in the same order as they appear in the colour spectrum: red will disappear first, usually at depths of about 5 metres (16ft), quickly followed by orange and then yellow, so that by the time you are at 20 metres (66ft) practically all of the green has also been absorbed. Blue light, having the shorter wavelength, is the colour least absorbed by the water molecules and, as a result, to the naked eye the light surrounding the *Britannic* is a deep blue, taking on a more grey appearance as the light level gradually drops later in the day. Despite the colour balance, however, it is not difficult to observe and photograph large expanses of the wreck, particularly when the midday sun is at its height, but for closer imagery the colour revealed by the incandescent camera

Above: Using a riveted seam and rusticle to estimate the wreck's orientation to the seabed. (Ken Marschall)

lights indicates a seemingly infinite number of visible colours.

Commencing at the *Britannic*'s forecastle, at the south-west end of the wreck, the survey would always move in a north-easterly direction towards the stern, so the individual frame numbers referenced in the following text will always be from forward to aft:

Forecastle (frames 153F to 101F)

The centre anchor of the Olympic class vessels came about with the realisation that in building ships of such a huge size, the traditional two-anchor arrangement in the bow was no longer sufficient to secure the vessel when at anchor. As a result, the *Britannic* was designed, like her two sisters, with a complement of five anchors – two anchors of the Dreadnought stockless type secured in hawse pipes at the bow, and a 16-ton Hall's patent stockless anchor, housed in a well immediately abaft the stem. A crane mounted on the bow would hoist this auxiliary anchor over the ship's side, while a 10-inch (25cm) steel hawser cable was passed through an additional hawse pipe in the ship's stem; once attached to the cable, the

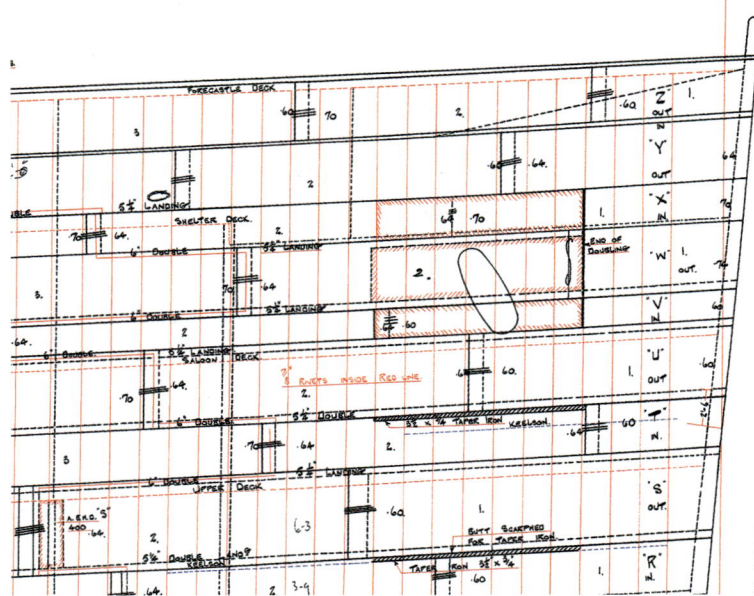

Left: Bow section of the Harland & Wolff hull plating drawing. (Harland & Wolff)

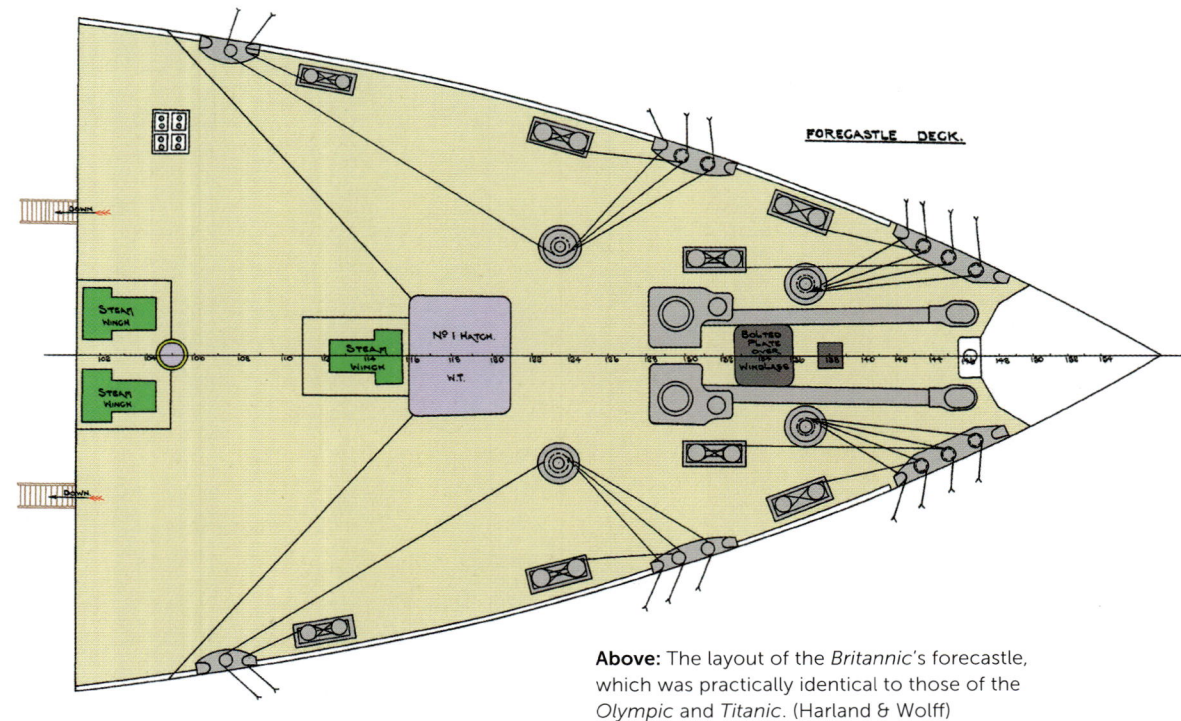

Above: The layout of the *Britannic*'s forecastle, which was practically identical to those of the *Olympic* and *Titanic*. (Harland & Wolff)

Above: A heavier trawl net, snagged on the ship's bow and partially obscuring the auxiliary anchor.

Above: The *Britannic*'s port anchor, still in the fractured hawse pipe.

anchor could then be lowered over the side, up to a depth of 175 fathoms (320m). To complete the arrangement, there was also a stream anchor of 20cwt and a kedge anchor of 10cwt.

Broadly speaking, the anchor arrangement in the *Britannic* was identical to that in the *Olympic* and *Titanic*, with each of the bow anchors connected to 330 fathoms (604m) of 3⅜ inch (8.6cm) stud-link chain cable. However, while the anchors in the two previous ships each weighed in at 7¾ tons, those in the *Britannic* were somewhat larger,

Above: Taking a closer look at the forecastle telephones.

the starboard anchor weighing some 11 tons, while at 9 tons the port anchor was slightly smaller. Similarly, at 16 tons the *Britannic*'s auxiliary bower anchor was also slightly heavier than those in the earlier ships; other than that, the arrangement and methods of deployment were identical.

The anchor gears, consisting of two cable holders mounted on the forecastle head, were both driven by engines from the shelter deck below, as was the steel wire windlass for working the auxiliary 16-ton anchor, but other customary fittings on the forecastle include the standard warping equipment that would be found on most vessels of that era. The forward warping gear, manufactured by Napier Brothers Ltd. of Glasgow, consisted of four capstans on the forecastle head; for the most part they were made from cast steel, while the various worm wheels linking the capstans to the engines below were made from gun metal. Beneath the foremast, electric winches manufactured by the Sunderland Forge and Engineering Company were designed to be particularly quiet, so as not to disturb the first-class passengers in the cabins at the forward end of the ship.

Although the *Britannic* has been lying on her side for over a century, all the heavy deck machinery remains firmly attached to the deck. The starboard side of the forecastle is now hidden from view by the seabed, but there is still considerable visible evidence to indicate the huge stresses that occurred in this area as the ship's bow ploughed into the seabed, with extensive deformation of the forward hull plating clearly visible, and some of the hull plating around the port side hawsepipe badly cracked. Once the ship's stem had come into contact with the seabed, the hull seems to have pivoted slightly, possibly contributing to the corrugated effect that can be observed at the bow, while at the same time further aggravating the scale of the damage inflicted by the mine explosion beneath the forward well deck. Even so, the two visible anchors are still exactly where they should be, and the detachable steel cargo hatch cover above the forward hold is also still in situ. Perhaps the most poignant sight on this part of the wreck is the foremast, complete with lookout's cage, still firmly attached to the forecastle but now crumpled at the base, its own weight causing it to sag down towards the seabed.

The investigation of the visible evidence at the bow does not provide any immediate answers as to what may have happened at the surface, but from a visual perspective it had been an absolute delight. The next section of the wreck, however, would be a more sobering experience.

Above: The collapsed and crumpled base of the foremast, bent towards the seabed, but still the mast itself remains attached to the forecastle.

Above: The lookouts' bell, located in May 2019, half buried in thousands of dead saddle oysters.

Forward well deck (frames 101F to 82F)

Perhaps the greatest surprise in this area of the wreck is that, despite the apparent devastation, both the Stothert & Pitt cargo cranes remain resolutely fixed in position. None of the deck structure immediately beneath them appears to display any significant visible damage, and although the higher port-side scantlings show signs of considerable structural damage – certainly the most extensively damaged area of the wreck – among the seemingly chaotic pile of twisted steel the evidence seems to suggest that the bow is still just about connected to the main hull, courtesy of a number of deck plates on the lower starboard side.

Even so, the structural collapse in this area of the wreck is considerable. Until the summer of 1976 the scale of the initial damage caused by the mine or torpedo (depending on your opinion at the time) could be based only on speculation, although it seems clear from Captain Bartlett's report following the sinking that whatever caused it, the damage was pretty extreme:

> 'The damage was most extensive, probably the whole of the fore part of the ship's bottom being destroyed and in my opinion penetrating to No. 6 boiler room. Water was seen to be thrown up to "E" or "D" deck forward at the time of the explosion, and a cloud of black smoke was seen, the fumes for some time being suffocating.'

Captain Bartlett's description of the damage is

particularly intriguing, as the depth of the actual explosion would also be critical insofar as the scale of the damage is concerned. When explosive shock waves travel through water they are generally dissipated in equal directions, either into the hull, away from the ship, or into the column of water, but for the captain of any ship the worst possible scenario is an under-bottom explosion, when over half of a mine's explosive force can be channelled directly into the hull. The fact that Siess had also set his mines deeper than usual was no accident, the wily U-boat skipper preferring to play a waiting game in the hope that sooner or later a larger battleship or transport vessel would pass over the mine, while countless smaller vessels might have passed over the two barriers in the 17 days before the *Burdigala* came to grief, oblivious to how close they had actually come to their own destruction. But for the reports of the phantom submarine observed by the *Burdigala*'s survivors, it is quite possible that the Kea Channel would have been swept for mines and the barrage located within days, but in the end a golden opportunity was lost; one week later, the *Britannic* steamed into the exact same waters, with exactly the same outcome.

There is no doubt that both the scale and location of the explosion was crucial to the survivability of the *Britannic*, but it is also clear that the scale of the observable damage beneath the forward well deck – at least, what remains of it – is much greater than a single mine of that era would have been capable of inflicting. Cousteau was certainly correct when he made that observation, but based on the limited diving technology and bottom time available in the 1970s, perhaps he can be forgiven for giving so much emphasis to the imaginary 150-foot (46-metre) hole, which in reality is simply not there. There is certainly a gap of approximately 50 feet (15m) between the aft port side of the forecastle and the main body of the hull itself, but just by studying the orientation of the two hull sections it is clear this was not caused by an explosion, either internal or external. A more focused visual analysis of the affected area indicates that the extensive gap in the hull was caused by the partially detached forecastle settling forward onto the seabed, which by default would have had the effect of further prising open the hull, not unlike cracking open an egg, causing additional areas of the structure to collapse in a random and unidentifiable manner. Admittedly, some deposits of coal can still be found scattered on the seabed in this area, which possibly served as the justification for the exploding coal dust theory, but in reality these are most likely only scattered deposits from the reserve coal bunker at the bottom of hold 3, which all but collapsed during the final stages of the sinking process.

The mechanism of the structural collapse in this area now looks to be relatively unremarkable. Once the bow had touched the seabed, it would have been impossible for it to pivot with the bulk of the main hull, which remained above water; with practically the entire weight of the vessel concentrated in the forward section of the ship's bow, which had already been weakened by the effect of the explosion, the stresses exerted in this area

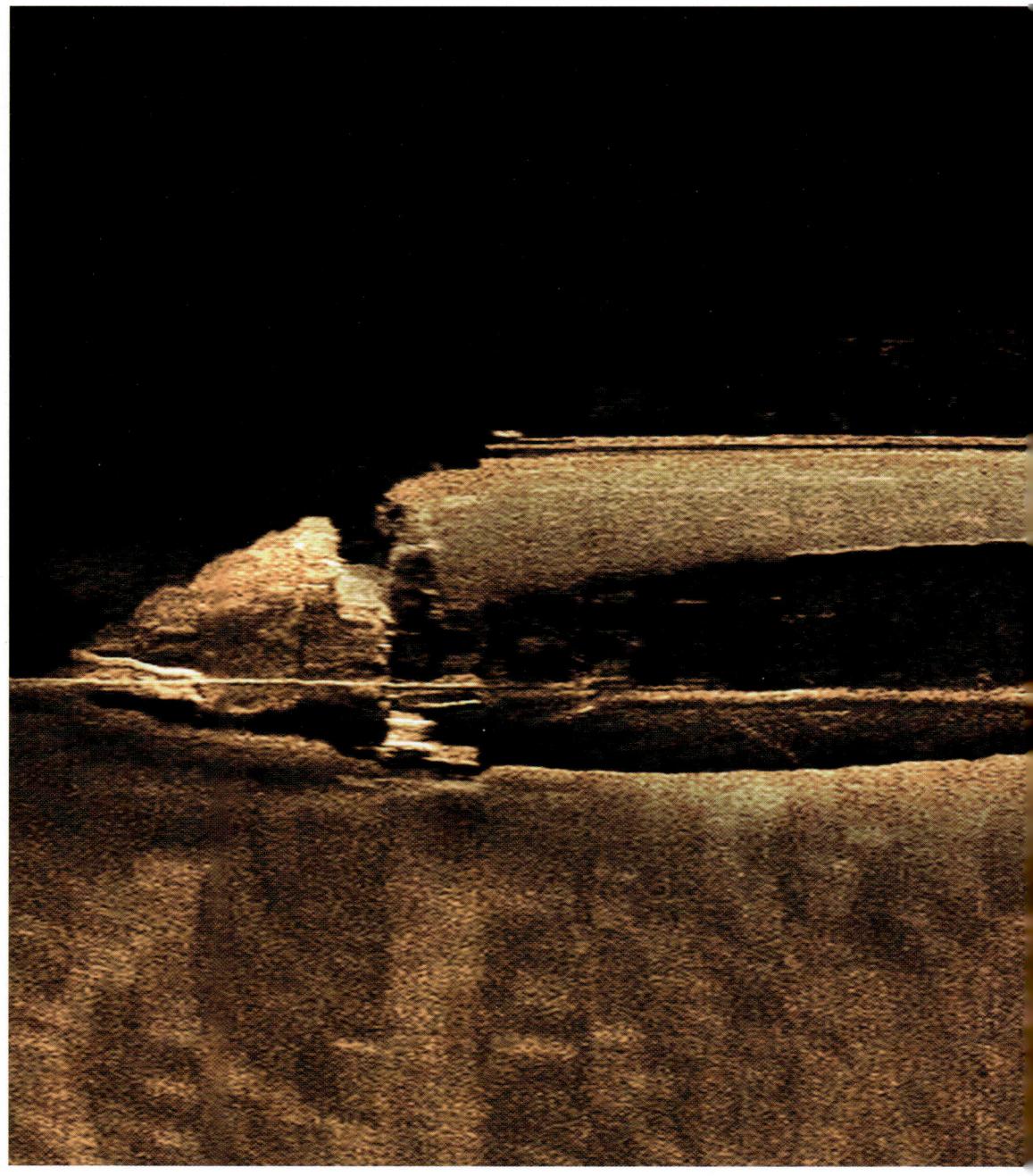

Above: Side-scan sonar of the wreck, with useful data on the nature of the underside hull break. (Dr. George Papatheodorou, University of Patras)

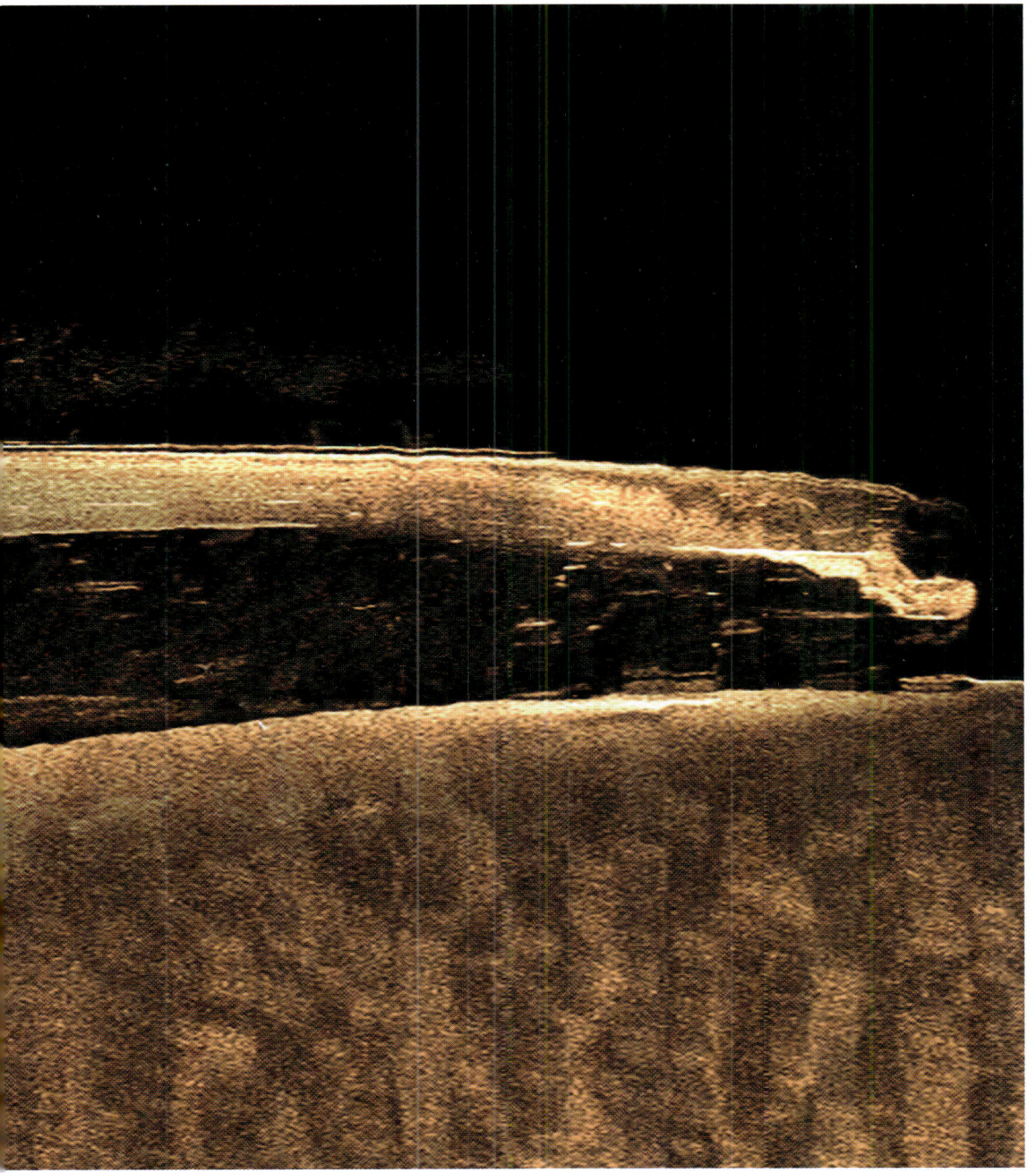

would have been massive. Consequently, the individual steel plates have fractured and buckled in a completely random manner, a phenomenon commonly referred to in the world of marine forensics as 'chaotic fracture'. Whether or not the subsequent collapse of the hull structure beneath the well deck was immediate, or occurred over a longer period of time, we cannot be entirely certain, but either way the resulting chasm is nowhere near to the 150-foot (46-metre) hole quoted in the post-expedition publicity of the 1976 dives.

The combination of the ship lying to starboard and the extensive collapse of the port-side hull plating presents little realistic chance of ever being able to identify or properly analyse the scale of the initial damage caused by the explosion. On the plus side, however, the location of the break, which seems to have occurred in the vicinity of frame 95F, would later provide a relatively straightforward entry point to the forward pipe tunnel, leading in turn to boiler rooms 6 and 5, and, crucially, the three forward watertight doors that would become vital factors in the ultimate loss of the ship.

Ship's superstructure (frames 82F to 87A)

With only the quickest of glances at the *Britannic*'s superstructure, it is perhaps understandable that so many people believe that the hull could be raised, cleaned up and restored for commercial service. Of course, this is just a pipe dream, but the fact that the *Britannic*'s superstructure appears to have stood up so well to the marine environment for more than a hundred years is still little short of miraculous.

The long-term prognosis, however, is not so encouraging. With the wreck lying at an angle of 77 degrees, much of the superstructure between frames 77F and 87A – the entire length of the boat deck – is almost completely unsupported. The situation is not too dissimilar to that of the wreck of the *Andrea Doria*, but whereas the *Andrea Doria*'s superstructure has now collapsed onto the seabed, for the time being the *Britannic*'s upper works remain largely intact. No doubt this is partly down to the skill of the Harland & Wolff shipyard, although modifications to the *Britannic*'s superstructure, based on previous experience with the *Olympic*, may also have played a role. Even so, the thicker external plating in this area has not stood up well to the marine environment, with practically all evidence of the former bulwarks now gone.

Another significant design modification was the arrangement of the expansion joints. The *Britannic*'s superstructure incorporated three such joints. The position of the forward joint at frame 49F was identical to those in the *Olympic* and *Titanic*, but in the *Britannic* the arrangement of the midship and aft expansion joints, located at frames 6F and 48A respectively, is significantly different from the single joint incorporated into the two earlier vessels at frame 28A. The joints were there in part to permit the hull to flex and respond to the bending forces of the sea conditions, but

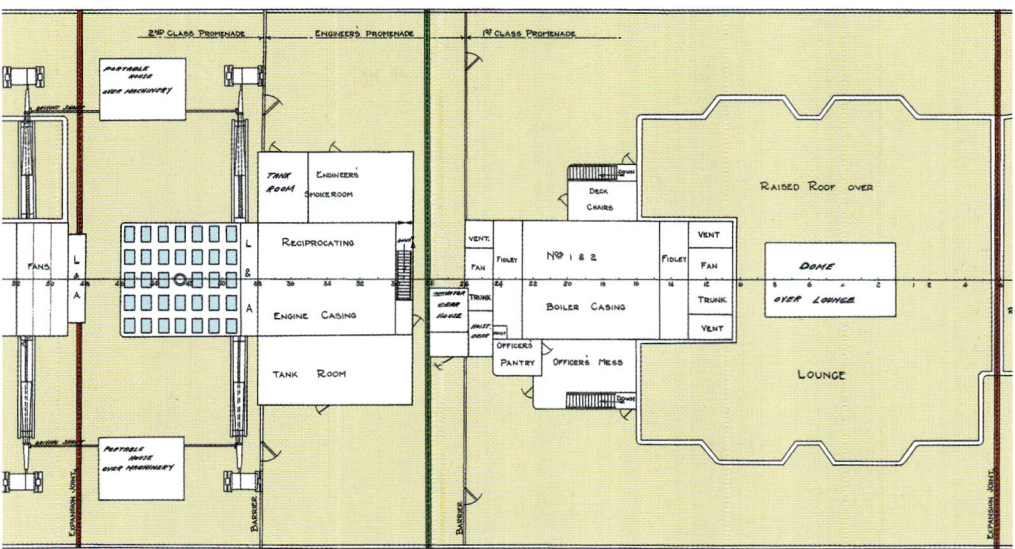

Above: The modified arrangement of the aft expansion joints in the *Britannic* (red), as opposed to the single joint in the original design in *Olympic* and *Titanic* (green).

they also served to isolate the superstructure from the hull stresses, enabling the top hamper to be of a lighter construction, with any loss of strength and stiffness of the ship compensated for by making the deck below of slightly heavier plate. Even so, structural issues in the *Olympic* during her later years of service would still be attributed to the stiffness of the superstructure, causing the flexure in the upper works to concentrate in the strength deck below, particularly in the area directly beneath the expansion joints. The Board of Trade's proposed solution for future reference would be to increase the number of expansion joints in order to distribute the flexing over a larger area, which, coincidentally, is exactly what Harland & Wolff had already done in the *Britannic*'s modified designs.

The *Britannic*'s superstructure, however, also needed to be radically different from the earlier design. On the one hand the design of the Armstrong davits had resolved the issue of the *Olympic*'s now overcrowded boat decks, but the enormous size and weight of the davits, not to mention the tiers of lifeboats concentrated at strategic points of the boat deck itself, still needed to be properly supported on the promenade deck below. Of the six sets of davits originally planned for the boat deck, only five had been installed by the time the *Britannic* was requisitioned, so the shortfall was partially offset by the installation of six sets of conventional Welin davits, running along each side of the central span of the boat deck between frames 40F and 35A. Each set of davits served one rigid and one collapsible lifeboat, and despite their relatively late installation practically all the davit arms remain firmly attached. The forward Armstrong davits on the lower starboard side

Above: The upper superstructure, although heavily encrusted with saddle oysters, remains largely intact.

(frames 69F to 54F) are still turned out, although badly damaged and twisted as a result of the impact with the seabed, while at the aft end of the boat deck nearly all the davits (between frames 38A and 76A) are in the outboard position, the exception being the forward set of Armstrong davits on the higher port side between frames 38A and 53A, which are stuck inboard, the forward davit having now dropped down practically to the level of the boat deck. The orientation of these davits seems to confirm the report of Fifth Officer Gordon Fielding that they went out of commission at a very early stage of the evacuation process, but one thing the port side Armstrong davits now have in common is that in all cases their lattice frame is almost completely obscured by the marine biomass, in this case mostly saddle oysters, in effect making them appear to be solid girders.

Once you see past the revised boat deck arrangements, in terms of layout the *Britannic*'s superstructure is on the whole similar to the earlier ships. The casings for the boiler uptakes are practically identical, with the forward casing serving boiler rooms 6 and 5 between frames 65F and 56F, the second funnel casing for boiler rooms 4 and 3 between frames 26F and 17F, and the third serving boiler rooms 2 and 1 between frames 15A and 23A. The funnels themselves have all gone, but not far. When interviewed in April 1999, George

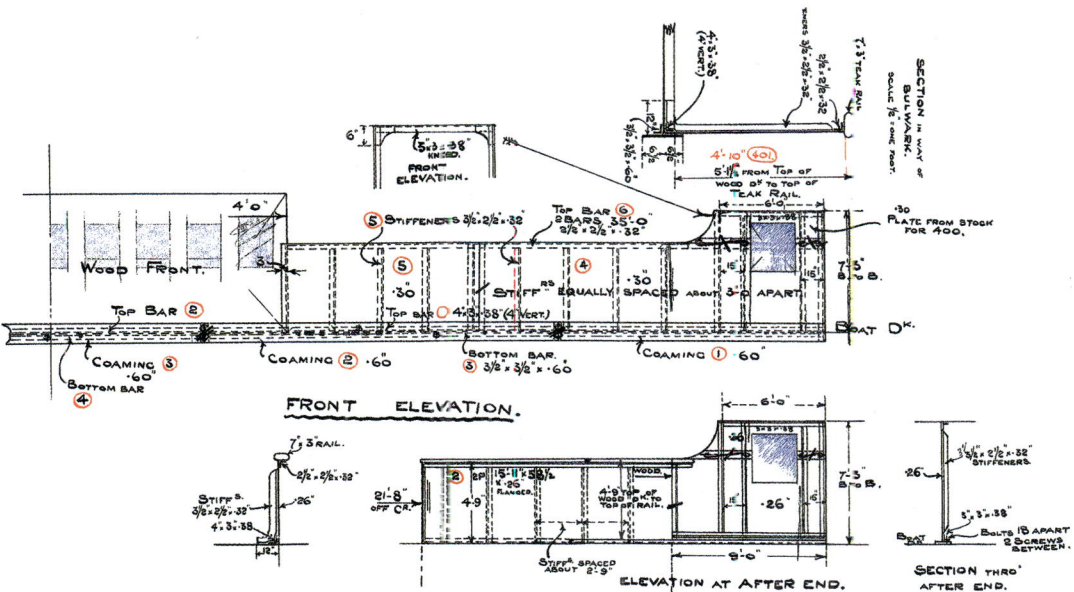

Above: Detail of forward boat deck bulkheads. (Harland & Wolff)

Perman recalled that he saw the funnels fall away in the order that the water reached them, and sure enough they all lie close by, just to the north of the wreck. Funnel 1 lies close to the bridge, while funnel 2 is a little further to the north-east; funnels 3 and 4 lie practically side by side and are a little further away. While it is interesting that the thinner metal of each funnel appears to have stood up well to its environment, none of them retain much of their original oval shape, having slowly compressed under their own weight over the years to the point where they now have an appearance of being almost completely flat.

Moving from forward to aft, the external survey of the superstructure begins at the navigating bridge, wheelhouse and chart room, located between frames 80F and 68F. The forward wooden bulwark and roof of the captain's bridge is long gone, possibly having broken free during the sinking process as nurse Sheila Macbeth, while onboard the HMS *Scourge*, recalled many familiar objects floating by, including the captain's bridge. Even if the bridge had remained intact, however, it is likely that the wood would have been eaten away within a few years. The steel bulwarks of the bridge wings are still completely intact, with much of the teak handrail still surviving, although the sea life attached to it does become increasingly sparse as you get closer to the seabed, revealing the teak to be moderately well-preserved.

While some of the smaller instruments, such as the helm indicator and the loud-speaking telephones, have yet to be located, nearly all the heavier bridge machinery is still in position, save for one bridge engine telegraph on the higher port side, which has fallen from its mounting. Three telegraphs ran direct from the bridge to the reciprocating engine room, two being connected to two 24-inch (61cm) engine room indicators, while the third was connected separately to two additional engine room indicators through an alternative route. The latter three instruments also formed an entirely separate emergency control in the event of the ordinary telegraphs being damaged. For the handling of the ship, fitted between the bridge and the after docking bridge were four 20-inch (51cm) double-dial brass telegraphs and one flange-back helm indicator. Two of these instruments enabled any possible order to be given to the engine room via the bridge, while the others enabled a complete set of docking and steering orders to be sent and received between the fore and aft bridges. The telegraphs were connected by a heavy chain of delta metal – a marine brass alloy – which seems to have been more than adequate as even today it is only these chains that have kept the remaining four telegraphs from falling to the seabed, each instrument having fallen from its original vertical mounting as the pine decking was gradually eaten away.

Also on the bridge was a standard ship's wheel, which was mechanically connected to the steering telemotor transmitter in the wheelhouse when steering from the bridge in piloted waters. The wooden wheel itself has long since rotted away; in fact, the wheel's original Brown Bros. brass band is one of a handful of items retrieved by Jacques Cousteau in 1976, with only the pedestal remaining on the bridge. That too has fallen from its deck mounting, whereas the wheelhouse telemotor pedestal seemingly remains as solid as the day the ship was built. The compass binnacle, forward of the bridge steering pedestal, has also detached from the deck and lies about 30 feet (9m) down towards the seabed, resting beneath a mass of saddle oysters right beside the forward starboard steel bulkhead.

The forward officers' deckhouse structure (frames 68F to 48F) seems to be reasonably intact, although some areas of the thinner metal are unquestionably showing signs of succumbing to the saltwater environment. On the higher port side, the steel bulkhead at the forward end of the deckhouse has rusted away completely, revealing one of the wreck's curious inconsistencies. Within this space is the much photographed 'captain's bath', yet none of the original plans show any provision for a bath of any description in this area. The original Harland & Wolff arrangements indicate that this cabin was originally intended to be occupied by the assistant captain, suggesting that because the *Britannic* was so far from being complete by the time she was requisitioned, we cannot simply continue to assume that certain areas of the ship would have been arranged on the same lines as those in the *Olympic* and *Titanic*.

Passing over the forward expansion joint at frame 49F, the joint itself shows no sign whatsoever of having opened up to even the

Opposite top: One of the bridge engine telegraphs on the lower starboard side, covered in red algae but with the markings still clearly visible in places.
Opposite bottom: The encrusted pedestal of the wheelhouse telemotor and compass binnacle. (Antonello Paone)

Above: The deteriorated forward bulkhead of the officers' deckhouse, revealing the unexpected location of the bath.

slightest degree, providing a sharp contrast to the forward joint on the wreck of the *Titanic*. Almost immediately after passing over the skylight to the wireless room (frames 48F to 45F), the elevator gear house provides the first substantial physical structure on top of the deckhouse, where the steel winch cables of the elevator machinery house (frames 42F to 40F) can still be clearly seen through the few remaining fragments of the roof itself. Almost immediately, the level of the roof then drops slightly, revealing the intact weather cover for the ornate glass dome of the forward first-class entrance between frames 40F and 31F. The entire roof structure of the forward deckhouse looks to be largely intact, but, worryingly, some of the side bulkheads of the structure, particularly on the higher port side, are exhibiting serious signs of long-term degradation. Save for only a couple of broken panes of glass, however, the weather cover remains completely intact.

Passing over the raised roof of the reading and writing room (frames 14F to 6F), followed by the first-class lounge (frames 6F to 16A), the second expansion joint at frame 6F also shows no external indication of any damage, the most noticeable anomaly in this area being the midship compass platform, located on the raised roof of the lounge between frames 6F and 1A. The four legs remain firmly attached to the steel deck, barely recognisable beneath the heavy covering of saddle oysters, but there is no visible evidence of either the protective

Top: The undamaged forward expansion joint, just forward of the ship's Marconi room.
Above: The winch cable for the forward starboard lift.

bulwark or the compass binnacle itself, which almost certainly lie below on the seabed. Another noticeable sign of deterioration in this area is a large hole that has appeared at the forward starboard end of the weather cover above the first-class lounge recess (frames 1A to 9A), where the electric chandelier would have been positioned.

Aft of the raised roof above the lounge is the funnel casing to boiler rooms 1 and 2, with the officers' mess on the lower starboard side between frames 16A and 22A. Immediately beyond that, just to starboard of the centreline, is the machinery house for the midship first-class elevator (frames 26A to 28A), an added feature incorporated into the *Britannic* but never installed in the *Olympic*. On the one hand the aft section of the boat deck looks to be remarkably intact, yet here we start to observe a number of external signs, suggesting that what happened in this area of the ship during the *Britannic*'s last moments afloat was of a far more dramatic nature when compared with the slower and more progressive flooding of the forward compartments. The skylight above the reciprocating engine casing (frames 30A to 38A) is now little more than an open void, while a closer look at the weather cover above the aft first-class entrance (frames 39A to 46A), in contrast to the cover above the forward staircase, indicates the first tangible evidence to suggest that the final moments afloat in the aft compartments may have been even more destructive. For years this evidence

Above: The legs of the midship compass platform, still firmly in situ, although the compass platform itself has now detached.

Above: Two of the ship's fallen Armstrong davits, now lying on the seabed.

had been partially obscured, not only by the biomass, but also by the forward set of damaged Armstrong davits, which had jammed and fallen inboard directly over the area where the weather cover is located.

The two remaining areas of interest on the boat deck are the open casing of the turbine engine room (frames 54A to 59A) and the second-class entrance and lift (frames 72A to 80A). Once again, the turbine engine casing held few surprises, being largely intact save for the missing funnel, which had detached during the final moments of the sinking, but the interior of the casing was an enticing indication of what seemed likely to be a relatively unobstructed route into the turbine engine spaces. The final structure on the boat deck, the second-class entrance, also remained largely intact, suggesting that the aft second-class staircase and elevator could also be in a far better condition than we might have hoped.

With the entrance points largely mapped out, even the external survey of the wreck had raised more questions than we had already answered, but the only place we were going to find those answers would be inside the *Britannic*.

6

WHAT LIES WITHIN

Planning a meaningful survey of the *Britannic*'s interior was never going to be as straightforward as most people might think. In this day and age, it is easy enough for technical divers to equip themselves with the latest in rebreather and imaging technology and then visit a shipwreck, but serious exploration is rarely that straightforward. Inside the *Britannic* it was not going to be a simple case of pointing a camera in a certain place and expecting to see something interesting; it would require a particularly detailed and well-considered dive plan, to make sure the divers knew where to go and, more importantly, exactly what to look for.

Although Cousteau had first explored the *Britannic* in the summer of 1976, it would be another 20 years before the world of technical diving was anywhere close to being able to follow in his footsteps. Curiously enough, I found myself entering the field of exploration at just about the right time, with Kevin Gurr's 1997 IANTD expedition, followed in quick succession by the *Starfish Enterprise* team in 1998, and Global Underwater Explorers the following year.

Bob Ballard's sonar survey of the wreck, combined with the video images obtained by the ROVs *Voyager* and *Phantom*, had provided an ideal starting point, while the manned diving team in 1997 had been the first step in being able to get closer in to some of the more specific areas of the wreck, using a manned diver in areas where the vulnerable tether of a very expensive ROV might easily have become snagged. As a result, a detailed survey inside the area of the hull break had not only revealed no sign of any munitions, but it had also confirmed that there was no evidence of any cargo whatsoever in the area of the ship where the explosion had occurred. Bit by bit, I was ticking off the list of external targets that needed to be investigated before moving to a more detailed examination of the hull's interior, but having now gained a lot more experience in the field of wreck exploration,

Right: Divers entering the water to commence the first internal survey of the wreck in September 2003.

not to mention a bit more confidence, I was starting to focus on the more challenging steps to come, and considering how to adopt a more forensic approach to the task in hand.

In September 1998, 'The Saga of HMHS *Britannic*' was included as one of the papers in the proceedings of the *From Research to Reality in Ship Systems Engineering* symposium. This conference was the first time that a paper specifically focused on the wreck of the *Britannic* had been thrown out for discussion at a more professional level, although, as a preliminary marine forensic analysis, by its very nature I had to acknowledge that much of what it contained was still reasonably speculative. Even so, in one important respect I was starting from a position of advantage, with a number of the more tenuous lines of investigation already debunked, along with the fact that at long last the evidence of what we were starting to see on the *Britannic* was undoubtedly taking the investigation in a more realistic direction.

Then again, if sections of the 1998 paper were speculative, it was at least based on relatively informed evidence. In 1996 two Harland & Wolff naval architects, Chris Hackett and John Bedford, had carried out an analysis to investigate the sinking of the *Titanic*, using modern computerised techniques. Aside from calculating the various rates of flooding in the *Titanic*, their paper also looked into the stability issues that may have resulted in the loss of the *Britannic*. Hackett and Bedford had estimated that it would have taken approximately 38,000 tons of water to enter the hull before resulting in the capsize of the *Titanic*, based on the rather

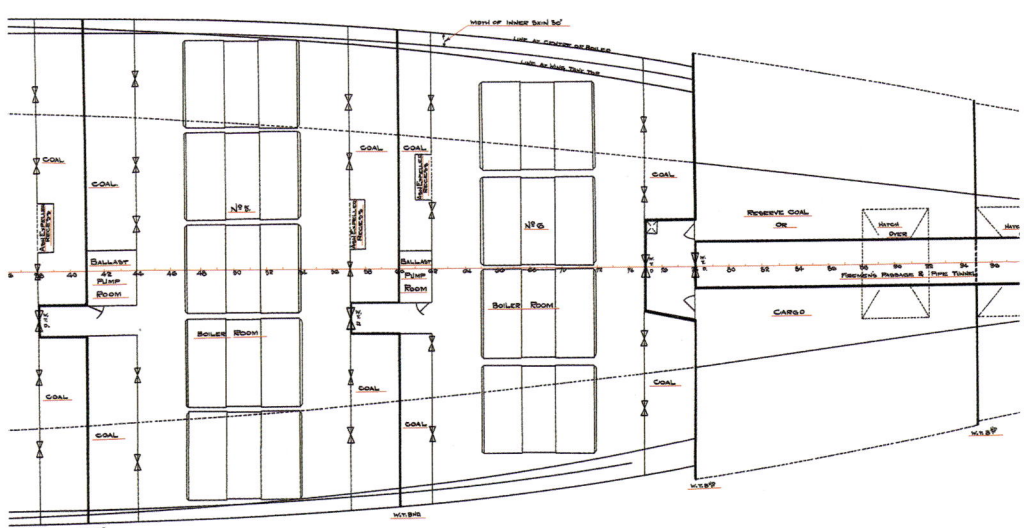

Above: The critical flooding of the two forward boiler rooms that ultimately led to the *Britannic*'s capsize. (Harland & Wolff)

Above and below: Several of the open portholes on the ship's higher starboard side.

unlikely stratagem of whether or not the sinking of the *Titanic* might have been delayed by leaving the watertight doors open in order to allow the ship to sink on an even keel. Interestingly, it revealed that had the *Titanic*'s crew taken this course of action then the ship would have capsized after about 90 minutes – some 70 minutes less than the time it actually took her to sink. The fact that the *Britannic* capsized 55 minutes after the explosion therefore also offered an approximate guide as to the scale of the damage resulting from the mine explosion, based on the assumption that it would also require something in the region of 38,000 tons of water – possibly slightly more if you take into account the increased beam – to cause the ship to capsize.

In the case of the *Britannic*, Hackett and Bedford concluded that despite the vessel's increased watertight integrity, the time difference between the *Titanic* and *Britannic* sinking was almost certainly due to the larger scale of damage and unsymmetrical flooding in the *Britannic*, with the scale of the initial damage to the *Britannic* probably being in the order of twice that of the *Titanic*. Based on observations in the official report into the sinking, they also calculated that some 15,000 tons of water would have needed to enter the hull for the water level to rise as high as the E deck portholes, after which it would take another 23,000 tons entering the hull over the next 35 minutes to equal the 38,000 tons that would have resulted in the ship capsizing. All told, this allowed for an estimated area of damage in the order of 40 square feet (3.7 sq m), but considering that a heel of 6 degrees, combined with the loss of forward trim, would have been enough to submerge most of the forward E deck portholes, with each porthole accounting for approximately 0.7 square feet (0.07 sq m) it would not have taken many of these potential openings to provide a significant additional source of flooding.

As to the factors contributing to the initial loss of stability, the paper considered that the *Britannic*'s metacentric height – GM – might have been reduced by the Armstrong davits and higher bulkheads incorporated into the design following the loss of the *Titanic*. In the world of naval architecture, a great many factors have to be taken into account when addressing issues of stability, but the GM is the distance between a vessel's centre of gravity (a force acting downwards) and her metacentre, the latter being a theoretical point formed at the intersection of a vertical line taken upwards through the waterline from the ship's centre of buoyancy (a force acting upwards) when the ship is in an upright position, and a similar line from the 'displaced' centre of buoyancy caused when the ship is inclined through a small angle of heel. In practice, this means that a ship with a larger GM will tend to recover from a list very quickly, in the process creating great discomfort to those on board, while a small GM results in a slower recovery from a roll; a negative GM will cause a ship to remain at a permanent angle of heel, or even capsize altogether. The *Britannic*'s sea-keeping characteristics might therefore have been somewhat different from those of the *Olympic* and *Titanic*, with the modified superstructure, additional lifeboats and Armstrong davits adding considerably to the top weight of the ship, but on the other hand this would have been offset to some extent by the increased beam and the additional weight of the lower hull, theoretically making her more stable.

All this scientific speculation, however, left us no closer to discovering what had been happening inside the wreck during the sinking process. All the survivors interviewed agreed that the *Britannic* shook for some time after the explosion, indicative of what is known as a hull whipping response, and while we can only speculate on the extent of the subsequent additional damage, it is not inconceivable that this shaking would have caused further damage to the hull, bulkheads, inner skin, or even the riveted seams. Once the water had penetrated the hull, it is also possible that the non-watertight bulkheads, such as the cabin walls of the lower decks on the starboard side, would have effectively helped to contain the initial flooding on this side of the ship, further contributing to the heel to starboard.

The focus on the interior, however, was not just a forensic analysis of what happened to the *Britannic* as she sank. Beneath the surface, the combination of the *Britannic*'s increased beam, additional expansion joints, stronger superstructure, higher and stronger watertight bulkheads and the double skin running the full 500-foot (152-metre) length of the boiler and engine room spaces had resulted in a markedly stronger and stiffer hull. The paying passengers, however, would have been far more aware of the magnificent first-class fixtures and fittings, which promised to outshine even the *Titanic*, than all the technical know-how that had gone into the ship's design. So what had happened to them?

As originally designed, the third and largest of the Olympic class liners was intended to retain, if not exceed, all the decorative magnificence of her sisters, although according to popular legend much of the panelling originally destined for the *Britannic* would later be removed by the Harland & Wolff workforce in November 1915, when the ship

Right: Press advertisement for the post-war auction of the *Britannic*'s unused panelling and fittings at Belfast.

was requisitioned for military service. Closer investigation of this story, however, indicates that this is by no means the case. The *Britannic*'s interiors were certainly somewhat basic. VAD nurse Daisy Spickett, who had joined the *Britannic* direct from the *Aquitania* on 19 January 1916, later recalled the White Star vessel as being very different compared to the *Aquitania,* which she described as 'palatial'. To be fair, the Cunarder had already been completed before the outbreak of war – if only just – so the fixtures and fittings were already on board, but while the *Britannic* was apparently very bare in comparison, Spickett still conceded that the furnishings and beds were comfortable enough. More importantly, the incomplete public spaces meant that many of the wards on the *Britannic* were far more expansive and a lot easier to run than they were on the *Aquitania*. In contrast, Vera Brittain, another VAD nurse being transported in the *Britannic* to her foreign posting on Malta in September 1916, would later write in her diary of having '...a most sumptuous first-class hotel meal in a beautifully finished dining room'. Brittain was evidently difficult to please, however, as she also wrote that while the first two or three meals on board were quite fascinating, she was getting extremely tired of them by the end of the voyage. The key point is that while the *Britannic*'s interiors appear to have been incomplete, some of the internal spaces may have been in a more advanced state of readiness by the time she was recalled to service in the autumn of 1916.

Inevitably, this would lead to speculation that despite the odds, it was still possible that we might find some of the rooms deeper inside the hull to be in a considerable state of preservation. Quite how realistic this hope really was in the warm and well-oxygenated waters of the Aegean was always going to be open to doubt, but we certainly had plenty of woodwork on which to base a useful comparison with the fittings in the *Olympic*, including the first-class lounge panelling at the White Swan Hotel in Alnwick, or even the à la carte restaurant panelling at one time preserved in the Celebrity Cruises' liner *Millennium*. Back in the real world, however, even a cursory glance at the advertisement for the extensive list of *Britannic* panelling auctioned off after the war included practically all the wood destined for the first- and second-class public rooms, including several hundred thousand square feet of pine, 70,000 square feet (6,503 sq m) of mahogany corridor panelling and 50,000 square feet (4,645 sq m) of oak. As a result, any hopes of finding very much wood inside the *Britannic* were, at best, extremely optimistic. Even if the anaerobic interiors of the *Britannic* were indeed conducive to preserving the wreck's internal environment, sadly most of the wood panelling, along with the estimated 4,000 wardrobes, dressing chests and bookcases, would probably not be there anyway.

The realisation that we would probably not find any surviving panelling to compare the interior of the *Britannic* with that of the *Titanic* was disappointing, until in May 2019 the *Britannic*'s first-class lounge and second-class library, long thought to be lost, were auctioned for a second time. Originally

Above: The Capitol Cinema in Princes Street, Dublin, home to the *Britannic*'s first-class lounge and second-class library panelling for fifty years.

bought from the Admiralty auction at Belfast in July 1919, the panelling would ultimately be used in the newly built La Scala Theatre and Opera House in Prince's Street, Dublin. The building would later become the Capitol Cinema, but prior to its eventual demolition in 1972, the panelling was once again recycled, this time for use in a private club in Baldonnell, a few miles south-west of Dublin. Although never utilised for its originally intended purpose, the panelling's rediscovery would provide an ideal opportunity to compare it with the original designs in the *Olympic*, now at the White Swan Hotel in Alnwick, on the one hand confirming the disappointment that the *Britannic* would never have had most of her sumptuous fittings installed, but on the other ensuring their survival. The subsequent discovery of the first-class lounge architrave at an office building in Shrewsbury is another sign that many of the *Britannic*'s other interiors will hopefully continue to emerge in the coming years.

Back in 1998, however, the forensic aspects

of the investigation were focused on the more pressing matter of the extent of the damage to the *Britannic*'s forward hull, and the thorny issue of why a second supposedly unsinkable ship had been sunk. Even the most fleeting examination of the hull plates beneath holds 2 and 3 could not fail to impress upon any diver the huge extent of the devastation in this area, not to mention the obvious hazards created by what remained of the overhanging hull structure, but the task of identifying the initial damage caused by the explosion would be almost impossible to determine. Captain Bartlett's official report already suggested that the whole of the fore part of the ship's bottom had probably been destroyed, but the crux of the issue was why, as referenced in Captain Heard's inquiry report, had the three forward watertight doors failed to close? Had any one of these openings closed properly, the *Britannic* would in all likelihood – on paper, at least – have survived the explosion.

Unfortunately, it was not that simple. In the late nineties, the option of just swimming into this part of the wreck simply did not exist, as while we had the capability to reach the depth of 114 metres (374ft), the available open circuit scuba technology of the time still had a number of shortcomings. True enough, the principles of using mixed gases in commercial diving at such depths were already well understood, but its application in recreational diving was less established. The mixed gases used on the 1997, '98 and '99 dives are known as trimix, which basically relied on helium being used to substitute some of the naturally occurring nitrogen in order to reduce the risks of nitrogen narcosis, but diving to 374ft (114m) requires several different mixes of gas, depending on depth and duration, with the percentage of oxygen used during the deepest phases of the dive also being reduced in order to reduce the risk of oxygen toxicity. With the additional risk of the exhaled gas bubbles stirring up the sediments inside the wreck, and the resulting effect on visibility, not to mention its effect on the anaerobic balance of the interior, the simple fact was that the divers themselves still had some way to go before they were ready to enter the wreck safely.

The solution to this problem lay partly in what is known as a closed circuit rebreather, now more commonly referred to in the world of technical diving as a CCR. To all intents and purposes the CCR is its own life support system, which not only absorbs a diver's exhaled carbon dioxide, but recirculates the exhaled gases in order to extend the endurance of what is essentially a limited gas supply. More importantly, it also eliminates the exhaled bubbles produced by open circuit scuba, not only reducing the risks to loss of diver visibility, but at the same time vastly reducing the negative effect on the anaerobic interior of the wreck. It was the perfect piece of kit and practically tailor-made for what I wanted to achieve inside the *Britannic*, and by the autumn of 2003 we finally had enough divers experienced with this technology to venture deeper inside for the first internal survey.

The answer to my initial questions lay at the end of the forward pipe tunnel, where the

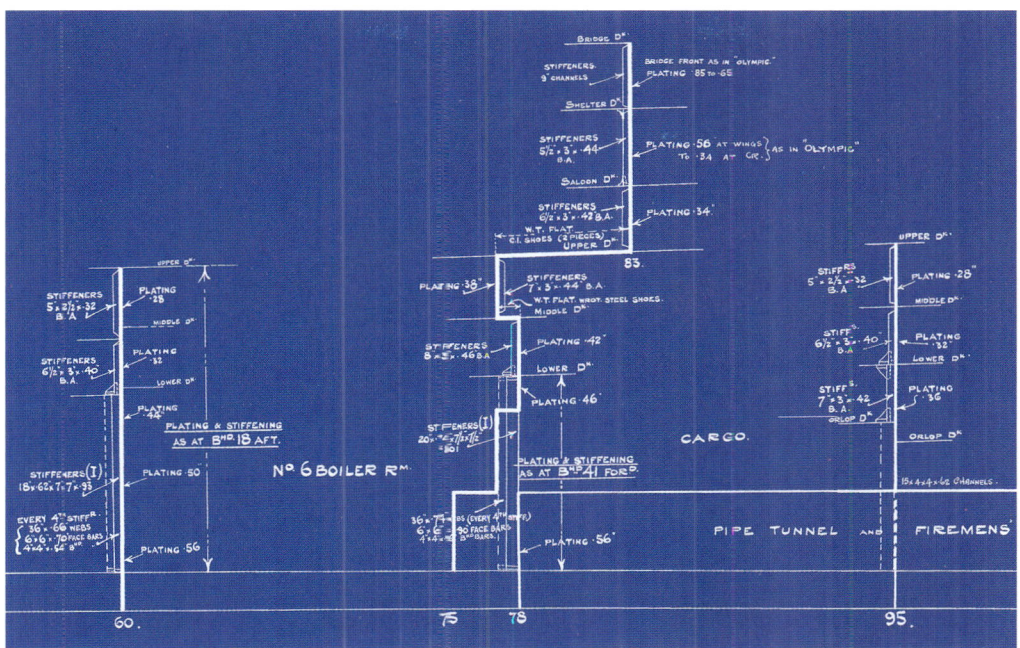

Above: Blueprint detailing the forward boiler room watertight bulkheads and stiffening. (Harland & Wolff)

three watertight doors, each measuring 5 feet 6 inches by 4 feet (1.7m x 1.2m), had failed to close following the explosion. Doors 1 and 2, located at either end of the forward vestibule, between frames 78F and 75F, were closest to the explosion, but door 3, located in frame 57F between boiler rooms 6 and 5, was more than 100 feet (30m) aft of the estimated blast location, and although it was thought to have been at least partially closed, it is clear that something had gone badly wrong with the system in the forward part of the ship.

To maintain optimum watertight integrity in a war zone, the standard practice in a military transport vessel was to keep all critical watertight doors closed. This was certainly the practice on board the *Olympic*, when in particularly hazardous waters the watertight doors would not only be kept in the closed position at the level of the tank top, but the lifeboats would also be kept in the swung-out position. On the morning of 21 November 1916, however, these critical doors inside the *Britannic* were open, but while it is easy to point the finger and say that this should not have been allowed to happen, it has to be remembered that the boiler room doors would have needed to be open at the time of the explosion – 8.12am – in order to facilitate the scheduled changing of the stokehold crews.

Questions have also arisen as to the potential for a faulty design of the *Britannic*'s watertight doors, although perhaps such accusations have missed one rather important point. As a merchant ship, the *Britannic*'s hull was never designed to take into account the scale of the shock loadings that result from a large explosion, and it has to be said that even warships, with reinforced hulls specifically designed to withstand such underwater damage, were no less vulnerable to German mines. The 25,000-ton British battleship HMS *Audacious*, barely a year old, ran foul of a German mine on 27 October 1914, while the older armoured cruiser HMS *Hampshire* also sank after hitting a mine on 5 June 1916. Both vessels succumbed to a single explosion, the latter with the loss of 737 lives, including Lord Kitchener and his entire staff on a diplomatic mission to Russia, proving that merchant vessels such as the *Burdigala*, and even the practically unsinkable *Britannic*, were no more or less vulnerable.

Intriguingly, however, there was crucial evidence in the archives as to why the watertight doors may not have closed. Launched a little over six years before the *Britannic*, the A-class Royal Mail Steam Packet Company liner *Asturias* was also a product of the Harland & Wolff shipyard. Shortly before midnight on 20 March 1917 the *Asturias*, while also serving as a hospital ship, was in the English Channel, eastbound for Southampton, when she was deliberately torpedoed off Start Point by the *UC66*, commanded by Oberleutnant zur See Herbert Pustkuchen. The torpedo struck the *Asturias* in the stern, beneath the aft peak tank on the starboard

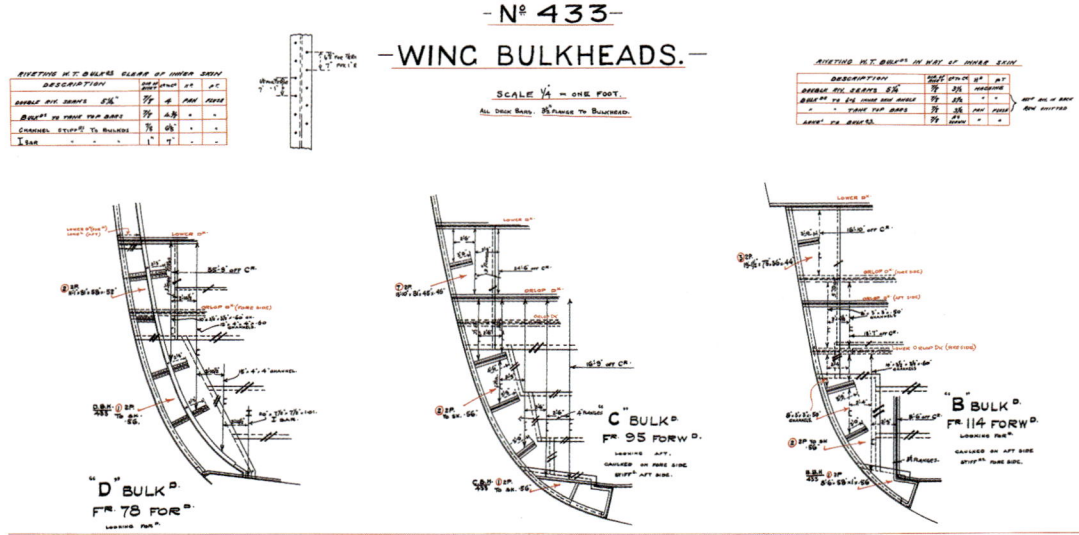

Above: Details of wing bulkheads in the forward pipe tunnel, in the location where the explosion occurred. (Harland & Wolff)

Above: HMHS *Asturias*, beached on the Great Eelstone, Starehole Bay, in May 1917.

side, resulting in a large hole beneath the ship's counter. The starboard propeller was totally destroyed in the explosion while the sternpost was blown away and the shell plating in the area completely shattered, but fortunately the port propeller remained operational and Captain Frederick Laws was able to beach the ship in Starehole Bay, just to the west of Salcombe, Devon. Several days later the salvage vessel *Ranger* arrived on the scene, the subsequent inspection of the damage indicating that the internal stepped bulkheads had proved to be a particular weakness, as was the problem of ventilating shafts and piping passing through the watertight bulkheads. But there was one other observation that also had a particular bearing on the loss of the *Britannic*:

> 'Although the WT doors to Shaft tunnel were closed as soon as possible after the explosion, the bulkheads and framework of the doors were distorted by the explosion to such an extent as to prevent the complete closing of them.'

Although the *Asturias* and *Britannic* were damaged at opposite ends, there were clear similarities as to the nature of the secondary damage suffered by both vessels, and it was with this in mind that the first expedition to explore the interior of the *Britannic* would start in the firemen's tunnel, before moving into the more vital areas of the forward stokeholds.

Curiously enough, it was here that the huge scale of the damage beneath the forward well

Above: A submersible illuminates the divers' route to the pipe tunnel opening.

deck would, for once, work to our advantage. The combination of the shattered hull plates and the effective prising open of the hull during the sinking had resulted in a virtual chasm opening up between the forward end of the superstructure and the aft end of the forecastle, in the process collapsing the area of the hull immediately forward of bulkhead C. The forward pipe tunnel ran directly through this bulkhead and the structural collapse had, by default, also opened up a relatively direct route to the watertight doors. Although this would still be a potentially hazardous penetration, fortunately the *Britannic*'s specification book provided the divers with the precise detail they needed on the layout and structure of the forward pipe tunnel:

> 'To be fitted between Frames 78 and 112 forward; plated horizontally, the edges and butts of the plating being lapped and double riveted; the seams to be joggled. Channel stiffeners fitted on the inside one frame space apart, channel being connected to the tank top by large double riveted single angle on the inside. A walking platform to be arranged about 2'6" above the Tank Top consisting of two widths of

chequered plate flanged on the outboard edges and resting on athwartship angle bearers; stanchions 6'0" apart with tube handrail to be fitted up the centre of the tunnel. The semi-circular top of the tunnel to be insulated to the depth of the stiffeners, the insulation plates attached by bolts to the channel stiffeners. An escape trunk to be arranged at the forward end of the tunnel, the plating being stiffened with bulb angles. The tunnel and trunk to be watertight throughout.'

Rich Stevenson was the lucky diver tasked with the first penetration of the forward pipe tunnel in September 2003, and on paper at least the route from the opening in bulkhead C to the first watertight door at frame 78F looked to be quite straightforward. It is only a relatively small matter of 51 feet (15.5m), although the passage was still filled with potential hazards. The raised walking platform served as the main thoroughfare for the firemen, as they moved to and from their quarters in the bow to the boiler rooms, but while it looked to be reasonably intact in places, the damage to the hull has nevertheless resulted in the extensive dislocation of numerous structural members in this area, to say nothing of unexpected obstacles, including a trimmer's wheelbarrow, which evidently slid into the tunnel from the forward stokehold as the ship's angle of trim gradually increased. Several fallen handrails and supporting beams

Above: The raised walkway, leading directly to the boiler rooms.

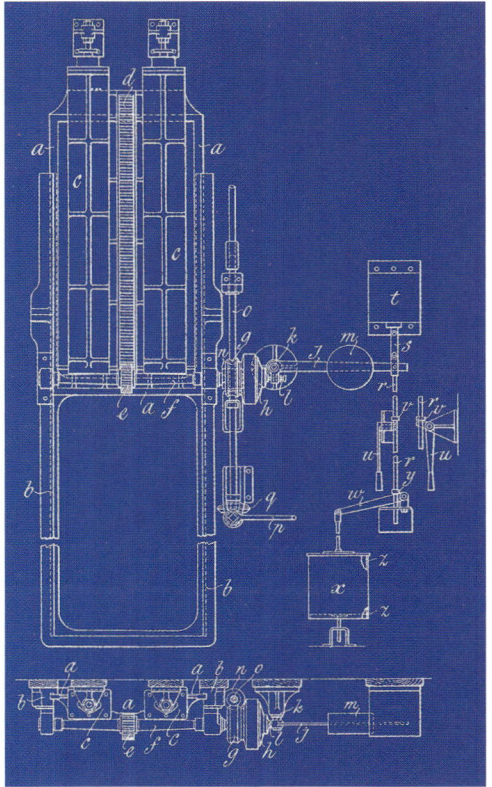

Above: A schematic of the dropping watertight doors. (Harland & Wolff)

had also combined to obstruct the way forward, but none of the obstacles were so great as to block the way completely. Before long, the outline of the first watertight door began to emerge from the gloom, providing an open void leading directly into the vestibule where, immediately overhead, the escape ladder that had provided stoker Albert Smith with emergency access to E deck could still be clearly seen. Immediately ahead lay the second watertight door. Both of the watertight doors at either end of the vestibule were wide open and showing no evidence whatsoever of being even partially closed. Had either of these two openings been sealed then the damage to the *Britannic*, although extensive, would not have proved fatal. Despite its proximity to the explosion, the vestibule reveals little in the way of any visible structural damage, while both watertight doors exhibit no visible sign of damage, suggesting that the *Ranger*'s assessment of the distorted bulkheads and framework of the watertight doors inside the *Asturias* may well be equally relevant to the forward damage sustained in the *Britannic*.

Perhaps the greatest and, it has to be said, most pleasant surprise during the 2003 pipe tunnel survey was the brief glimpse that it afforded of the forward stokehold, showing all four double-ended boilers, each weighing in excess of 100 tons, to be firmly mounted on their stools. The boilers showed no indication of having exploded when the cold seawater flooded into the compartment, and, more importantly, in the more than one hundred years that the ship has been lying on its starboard side, not one of the boilers gave any indication of having shifted to the slightest degree. At the start of the day the goal had simply been to confirm that the two forward watertight doors were open, and in that respect the box had undeniably been ticked, but even as I was watching the video that same evening, I was already pondering what, until hours before, I had previously thought would be impossible. Next time, I wanted to make it as far as the third watertight door in bulkhead E.

Based on the 2003 footage, this was not just an idle fancy on my part. There seemed to be just enough space between the boilers through which a diver could squeeze, and in September 2006 another opportunity finally arose on a project being sponsored by The History Channel, with US divers John Chatterton and Richie Kohler making the next attempt. They would ultimately come within spitting distance of making it to the crucial bulkhead between boiler rooms 6 and 5, only to find their way blocked by a trimmer's wheelbarrow, jammed in the lower starboard boiler passage. Unfortunately, no amount of gentle persuasion could shift the obstruction, and ultimately the attempt had to be abandoned; but if nothing else it had at least confirmed in my mind that the strategy was practicable, and that when we returned we would just need to take a different route. It never occurred to me that it would be another nine years before we would be in a position to make the next attempt, when, in June 2015, Richie Kohler and Evan Kovacs were finally able to return to where we had left off in 2006 to make one last attempt to pull off what I had originally thought would be the impossible.

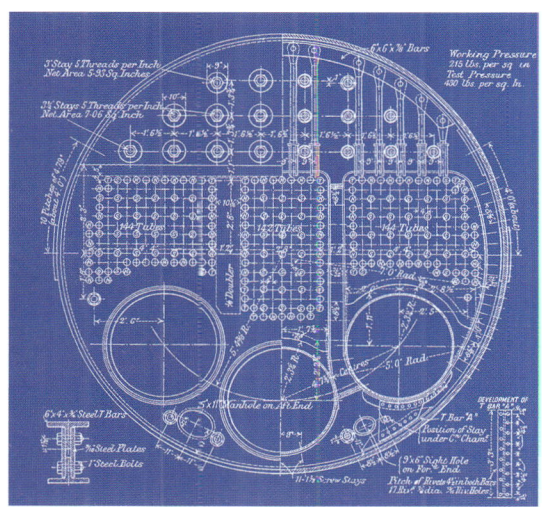

Above: Blueprint of the *Britannic*'s Scotch marine boilers. (Harland & Wolff)
Below: The confined space between the boilers leading to the next watertight door and boiler room 5.

7

THE SUPERSTRUCTURE

Glancing at the *Britannic*'s large-scale general arrangement plans, to all intents and purposes the planned layout of the deckhouses is so similar to that of the *Titanic* that any diver might be forgiven for thinking it would be a simple case of following a relatively well-known path. Unfortunately, the reality was never going to be quite that straightforward. Once the *Britannic* had been requisitioned for government service, military constraints meant there was no time for Harland & Wolff to remove what little wood panelling might already have been installed, and with their priority being to have the ship ready for sea as quickly as possible, they would naturally have worked around the existing layout, making the occasional modification as required in order to fine-tune the ward layouts.

In truth, the full extent of the work completed by December 1915, both internally and externally, remains unclear. The ship had lain incomplete for over 15 months, with little more than essential maintenance being carried out on the ship's machinery and other vital systems during this time, although it had still been possible to continue work on the fitting out during the occasional hiatus in Admiralty orders. By May 1915 enough work had apparently been completed on the ship's engines for them to undergo their mooring trials, while additional work would also have been possible on the electrical and plumbing installations, but even so, the *Britannic* was still a long way from being ready for commercial service on the North Atlantic. What we do know for sure, however, is that by November 1915 Harland & Wolff could at least say they were 'confident' that the *Britannic* could be made seaworthy in approximately four weeks, provided that the Admiralty gave the ship priority. Sure enough, on 13 November 1915 the *Britannic* was duly called up for service as a military hospital ship.

We can also be certain that when the

Left: The forward bulkhead of the Marconi room, with a solitary wall-mounted control panel remaining in situ.

Above: The 'captain's bath', actually in the location of the assistant commander's cabin.

Britannic eventually left the shipyard, huge quantities of wood panelling remained in storage in Belfast, where it would eventually be auctioned off in July 1919 before finding its way into other vessels, public buildings or even private houses. All of this therefore begged the question as to how much reliance could be placed on the available GA plans, on which any internal survey had to be based. There is certainly evidence to suggest that Harland & Wolff had at least created a tracing of the *Britannic*'s internal arrangement as a completed hospital ship, but sadly these plans appear to have gone astray sometime in the early 1980s, so in all respects the *Britannic*'s interiors were always going to be a mystery.

The boat deck

The first indication that something was different came the moment we entered the forward deckhouse on the boat deck, immediately aft of the wheelhouse. This structure extended for well over a third of the boat deck, between frames 72F and 13F, the forward section being used exclusively for the navigating officers' accommodation. Broadly speaking, the interior was arranged on similar lines to the comparable accommodations in the *Titanic*, but while the dive team always seemed to take pleasure in photographing what they refer to as 'the captain's bath', doubtless as a comparison to Captain Smith's bath on the

Titanic prior to the collapse of the overhead deckhouse roof, closer inspection of the GA plans actually shows this bath to be in an area where it simply shouldn't be. Aside from the fact that Captain Smith's bath is located in his quarters, on the starboard side of the deckhouse (between frames 60F and 57F), the *Britannic* bath is actually further forward and on the higher port side, in a cabin space located between frames 72F and 69F. Even a cursory inspection of the GA plans indicates that this space was originally intended for the assistant captain's cabin, the presence of the bath therefore suggesting that a good many makeshift alterations had been carried out while getting the ship ready for sea.

Nearly all the wooden dividing walls inside the forward end of this deckhouse are also gone, giving little idea as to the final layout of this area in the ship, or of any makeshift materials that might have been used in the *Britannic*'s incomplete state. The ghostly outline of where the red and white floor tiles once lay can still be seen, even if practically all the tiles in the area have since fallen away, while the forward external steel bulkhead in front of the bath has almost completely rotted away. The more substantial metal sides of the forward funnel casing and ventilator shafts remain, but to all intents and purposes much of this area has become an open void.

The Marconi wireless

Moving further aft, questions arise as to just how much the lack of wood partitioning

Above: Closer detail of the bath's four taps, with hot & cold running fresh and salt water.

might be explained by biological activity in the marine environment, as opposed to the more violent force of water flowing into this part of the ship during the final stages of the sinking process. Immediately aft of the officers' accommodation are the remains of what should be the Marconi wireless room, between frames 48F and 45F, but aside from a single control panel affixed to this compartment's forward metal bulkhead, there is practically no evidence that the Marconi room ever existed. A large pile of silt-covered debris against the starboard bulkhead of what would have been the third officer's cabin (frames 48F to 45F) bears silent testimony to some of the equipment and fittings that would have occupied this space only a few feet above, but an important clue as to how this part of the interior might have fared during the *Britannic*'s last remaining seconds afloat would come later with the discovery of the multiple tuner for the Marconi apparatus. I had expected to find this delicate piece of equipment either in the space occupied by the Marconi rooms or perhaps somewhere in the pile of debris immediately below, but when it was located in September 2003, it was nowhere near either of these two locations. In fact, it was found four decks beneath where it should have been, presumably swept away by the surging water halfway down the forward main entrance before, by some miracle, coming to rest on one of the D deck supporting beams in the staircase opening. The fact that this delicate piece of equipment lies at an approximate distance of 60 feet (18.2m) from where it should be is a strong indication that the final stages of the sinking in this part of the superstructure were especially violent.

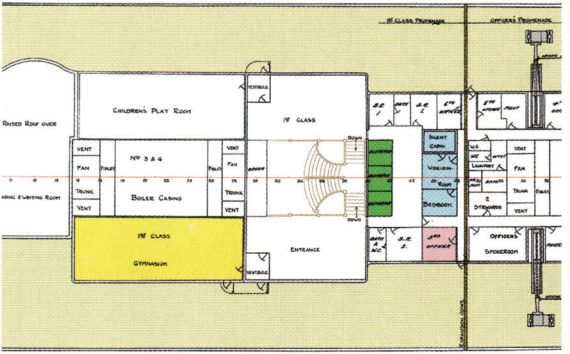

The first-class elevators

Immediately aft of the wireless rooms, the internal structure is of a more solid construction, with the metal bulkheads

Top right: General arrangement of the boat deck area, in the region of the forward first-class main entrance.
Above: The debris atop the third officer's cabin, likely containing much of the heavier Marconi machinery.

seemingly standing up well to the marine environment. In fact, the layout in this part of the ship is in such good condition that we have even been able to make a much closer examination of one of the major alterations incorporated into the *Britannic*'s design.

No one on the dive team was particularly surprised to come across the first-class forward elevator shafts, located between frames 42F and 40F, as these elevators were a well-advertised fixture in the Olympic class ships. The only difference we expected to find was an open space, where, in the two previous ships, the motor and winding gear room for the three forward elevators was housed, on account of the fact that the *Olympic* and *Titanic*'s lifts only extended as high as the promenade deck, whereas the lifts in the *Britannic* extended all the way up to the boat deck. The actual lift arrangements, however, turned out to be completely different.

Although the lift machinery was supplied by the Waygood-Otis company, the original cages would have been built and decorated by Aldam Heaton & Co., a company owned by Harland & Wolff that had carried out much of the interior design and furnishing in the *Olympic* and *Titanic*. The order for the *Britannic*'s lifts had originally been placed in January 1914, and from the Waygood-Otis records it appears that everything was pretty much ready for delivery by the end of July, so even though work on civilian contracts at Belfast was not being given priority, the lack of Admiralty work at the time meant that the lifts could still be installed by the end of October.

Above: The sliding Bostwick gates for the elevator on the lower starboard side of the boat deck main entrance.

At first there was no difference in the arrangement of the three forward lifts, each designed to handle loads of up to 15cwt, equating to about ten passengers. Even so, an intriguing alteration seems to have been under discussion since at least 26 October 1915 – almost three weeks before the *Britannic* was officially requisitioned – when Harland & Wolff changed the original specification in order to make the lifts 'suitable for hospital work'. The starboard lift remained largely unaltered, but a considerable modification was made to the centre and port-side lifts, with the runners for those two lifts being removed and replaced by a single runner to operate a single but larger lift in the space previously occupied by two, more suitable for handling larger surgical trolleys and medical equipment. In the meantime, the elaborate lift gates in the original Aldam Heaton designs would also be dispensed with for the duration, to be replaced instead by larger and more functional Bostwick gates at each of the deck landings. After more than a century, practically all of this machinery remains intact, the only visible sign of any damage on the boat deck level being the partially detached port-side Bostwick gate, which has fallen back and into the lift shaft. The smaller starboard gate, however, remains completely in situ, the gate itself still as firmly closed as it was on the morning of 21 November 1916.

The forward main entrance

'We leave the deck and pass through one of the doors which admit us to the interior of the vessel, and, as if by magic, we at once lose feeling that we are on board a ship, and seem instead to be entering the hall of some great house on shore. Dignified and simple oak panelling covers the walls, enriched in a few places by a bit of elaborate carved work, reminiscent of the days when Grinling Gibbons collaborated with his great contemporary, Wren.

Above: The modified runners of the port side elevator.

In the middle of the hall rises a gracefully curving staircase, its balustrade supported by light scrollwork of iron with occasional touches of bronze, in the form of flowers and foliage. Above all a great dome of iron and glass throws a flood of light down the stairway, and on the landing beneath it a great carved panel gives its note of richness to the otherwise plain and massive construction of the wall. The panel contains a clock, on either side of which is a female figure, the whole symbolizing Honour and Glory crowning Time. Looking over the balustrade, we see the stairs descending to many floors below, and on turning aside we find we may be spared the labour of mounting or descending by entering one of the smoothly-gliding elevators which bear us quickly to any other of the numerous floors of the ship we may wish to visit.

The staircase is one of the principal features of the ship, and will be greatly admired as being, without doubt, the finest piece of workmanship of its kind afloat.'

[*Olympic* and *Titanic* publicity booklet, May 1911]

The forward staircase was always designed to be the main focal point of the ship, through which the first-class passengers could access the boat deck and the public rooms of the promenade deck, as well as the reception room and dining saloon on D deck. The *Britannic*'s forward main entrance would have been very similar to those in the *Olympic* and *Titanic*, and it is known for a fact that the panelling in all three staircases would have been of oak, but inevitably there would also be a number of subtle design alterations to differentiate between the three ships, giving them each a certain character and 'feel' of their own. One minor difference in the *Britannic* would have been the curved tops of some of the wooden balustrades, or, perhaps more noticeable, the elaborately carved figures of Peace and Commerce on either side of the ornamental clock at the mid-landing of the staircase between the boat and promenade decks, as opposed to the well-known figures of Honour and Glory crowning Time in the *Olympic*. However, as a much younger ship, not to mention the significant additional competition from Cunard's *Aquitania*, or the Hamburg-Amerika Line's even larger trio *Imperator*, *Vaterland* and *Bismarck*, the commercial realities meant that the White Star Line once again needed to raise its game and create an even more sumptuous interior. This was partly achieved by extending the forward elevators up to the boat deck, although the upper levels of the main entrance would also differ in one key respect.

By the early 20th century, player organs had become an important status symbol of the wealthy. Orchestrions – a pneumatically operated organ without a keyboard, to which a number of orchestral effects, such as drums and a xylophone, might be added – were manufactured in both Europe and the USA, in particular by M. Welte & Söhne, of Freiburg im Breisgau, to the point where Philharmonies (Philharmonic in England and America) were developed through crossing orchestrions with console-played organs. As a result, they could be played either by an organist or through a built-in roll-playing apparatus, similar to a player piano. When the SS *Olympic* was launched on 20 October 1910, Philharmonies were still some way from being actively marketed by the Welte company, until in November 1911 – the same month that the *Britannic*'s keel was laid – they exhibited their first Philharmonie in Turin. It is quite evident from the original Olympic class design that neither the *Olympic* nor the *Titanic* were ever intended to be fitted with an organ of any description – certainly there is no existing White Star publicity to suggest that any such plans ever existed – whereas in the case of the *Britannic*, the evidence for a Philharmonie being fitted is irrefutable. By the time Harland & Wolff had completed their initial designs for the ship, Welte's Philharmonie was widely available in a range of specific models, and, crucially, adequate space for 'an Aeolian organ with two chests for music rolls' had been allocated in the *Britannic*; in this case, it would be located between frames 31F and 29F, at the aft end of the first-class main entrance on the boat and promenade decks. Interestingly, the 1914 Welte catalogue also carried an illustration identifying the organ of the 'Welte-Philharmonieorgel auf S.S. *Britannic* der White Star Line' ('Welte Philharmonie on the White Star Line's steamship *Britannic*'), the illustrated roll player hinting at a console and possibly the wind apparatus being located underneath, with wind chests and pipes on top. Although the Welte catalogue shows the roll playing mechanism, no keyboard is apparent, which might lead to a belief that this instrument was a large orchestrion, but the Welte publicity specifically referred to it as a 'Philharmonie', meaning that the *Britannic*'s instrument would therefore have had a keyboard.

Sadly, the organ would never be installed. In normal circumstances the schedule would have allowed for the organ to be built and installed in ample time, but the outbreak of war in August 1914 changed everything. The Philharmonie intended for the *Britannic* might have been completed in Freiburg by late 1913, ready to be shipped to Belfast, but it

Opposite right: A fish eye image of the main entrance, taken at the level of the boat deck. The green hue is caused by the colours with a longer wavelength being filtered out in the water column.
Below: The promenade deck arrangement, extending from the forward main entrance to the aft superstructure. (Harland & Wolff)

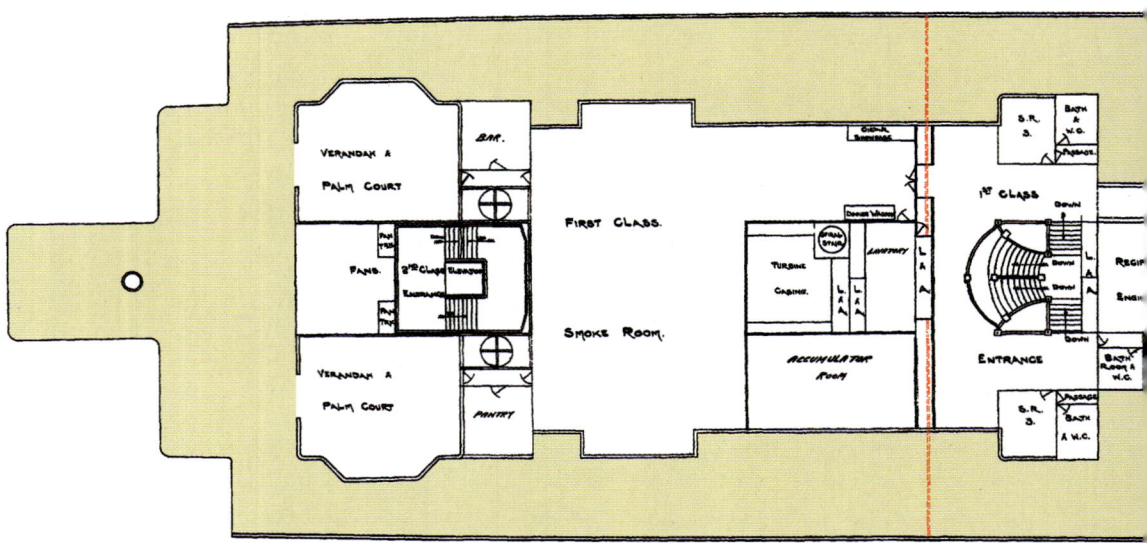

THE SUPERSTRUCTURE

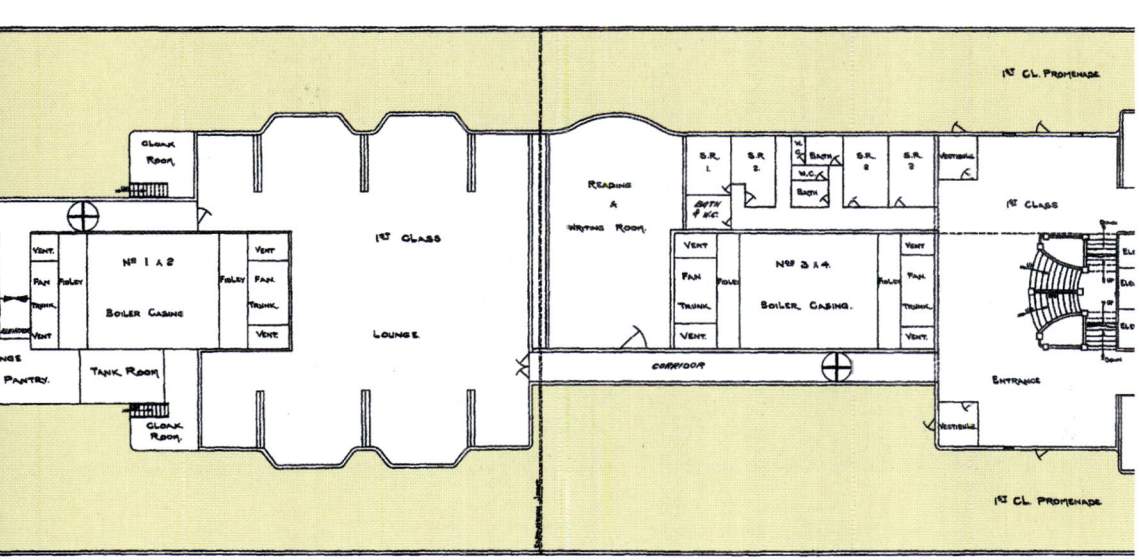

seems that by August 1914 it was still in Germany. We know this because when the organ was undergoing restoration in early 2007, the first '*Britanik*' inscriptions were observed around the original wind chests. Expert advice independently concluded that the beams and the organ were part of the original instrument, confirming that the organ was indeed the instrument originally intended for the *Britannic*, the only major modification to the instrument in its 91-year existence being the installation of a larger keyboard. As such, the organ is probably now the most typical, intact and best-preserved instrument of its size and kind, and, having narrowly missed being installed inside the *Britannic*'s main entrance, it can now be seen and, more importantly, still heard, at the *Museum für Musikautomaten* at Seewen, in Switzerland

Inside the wreck, the space where the organ was to have been installed is now an open void, with no visible evidence observed to date of any of the required Welte fittings, or of the organ pipes that some have alleged were observed by Jacques Cousteau in 1976. On the other hand, while the lack of wood panelling or the organ is a disappointment, the size of the open space remains an undeniable sign of the intended scale and planned magnificence of this part of the interior.

The forward first-class main entrance was always going to be one of the key areas of interest in the exploration of the *Britannic*. The staircase opening extended all the way

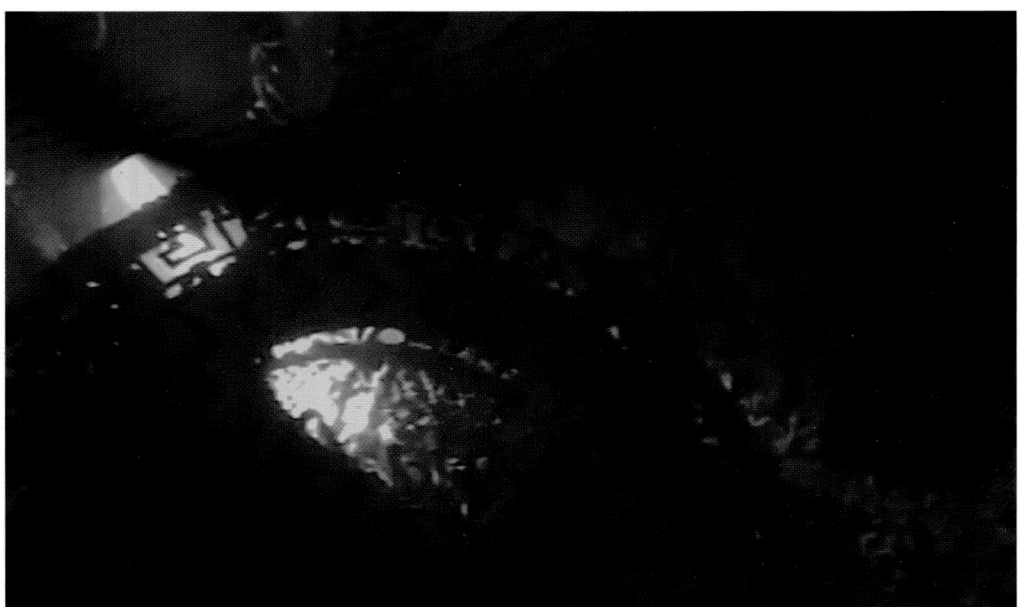

Above: The electric chandelier in the forward main entrance. This image was taken in 2003, but the chandelier appears to have fallen since then.

Above: A larger fragment of the glass dome above the forward first-class staircase.

down from the boat deck to the upper deck (E), although with the wreck lying on its side it is more akin to swimming along a tunnel, rather than down a shaft. Consequently, the dive team could move easily through all six decks without actually increasing depth, but sadly as we moved deeper into the hull it confirmed that there was little evidence of the oak panelling or the elaborately curving stairs described in the White Star publicity. Instead, there are only bare steel bulkheads, which, save for a few holes in the area where the ornamental clock would have been mounted, seem to be largely intact. While there is practically no evidence remaining of the wooden stairs, one thing that does remain completely intact is the heavy steel frame that supported the entire staircase. Just as the first-class passengers would have been able to look over the balustrade and see the stairs descending through many floors below, so the dive team could follow the steel framework all the way to the level of the E deck landing, without coming up against any physical obstruction whatsoever. The original oak balustrades are also all gone, although scattered in the debris we can still observe sections of the decorative iron and bronze scrollwork used to help support the balustrade.

One key difference between the wreck of the *Titanic* and that of the *Britannic*, however, is the top of the staircase. On the *Titanic* the external weather cover has collapsed completely, and as a result the glass dome and electric chandelier at the top of the staircase lie broken and scattered across the wreck site. In the *Britannic*'s case, however, the weather cover remains almost completely intact, and as a result it is not so difficult to find evidence of the elaborate glass dome that once adorned this part of the ship. There is no doubt that the glass dome had been installed by the time the *Britannic* was requisitioned, as we can still observe numerous broken sections of the iron framework, complete with intact white glass panes, scattered throughout the entrance, but perhaps the greatest surprise of all was not only locating the electric chandelier, but finding it to be substantially intact, in stark contrast with what we would later find in the aft first-class entrance.

The gymnasium and children's playroom

In terms of location, the *Britannic*'s first-class gymnasium was located in the exact same area as in the earlier ships, at the top of the forward main entrance, on the starboard side of the boat deck. VAD nurse Marjorie Barber, when travelling on the *Britannic* in September 1916 to her posting on the island of Malta, noted that there was a gymnasium on the boat deck reserved for the *Britannic*'s medical staff, indicating that this room was at least partially

Above: A fallen cast iron balustrade is the first substantial evidence of the forward main entrance being at least partially complete.

Above: The Marconi multiple tuner lies halfway down the forward staircase opening, some four decks lower than where it was originally located.
Below: One of the more utilitarian hospital ship light fittings found throughout the ship.

Top: Only a few fragments of wood now remain attached to the steel frame of the forward staircase.
Above: Returning safely to the top of the forward entrance.

THE SUPERSTRUCTURE

completed in line with its originally intended purpose. The actual deckhouse structure, measuring 44 feet x 18 feet (13.4m x 5.5m), remains almost completely intact, but little evidence remains of the gym equipment that would have filled this room. A few fallen metallic objects now lie against the inner starboard bulkhead of the room, but only one piece of equipment still seems to be attached to the featureless deck, in this case the support for one of the rowing machine's oars.

On the higher port side of the main entrance, the children's playroom was a feature unique to the *Britannic*, having never been included in the approved design of the first two ships. The layout of this room exactly mirrored that of the gymnasium, the only difference being that while the gymnasium was panelled in oak, the playroom panelling was apparently intended to have been finished in walnut. Unfortunately, the open expanse of deck space in this area gives little clue as to how this space might have been utilised, but based on the description of the layout on the promenade deck below, the likelihood is that it would also have been used as an additional officers' ward.

The promenade deck (A)

With the interior layout of the *Britannic* still such a mystery, once again the diary of nurse Marjorie Barber helped to give some idea as to what would be found in certain parts of the ship. Because Barber was a passenger rather than a part of the *Britannic*'s permanent

Above: A piece of unidentified fallen gym equipment resting against the starboard bulkhead of the gymnasium.

medical staff, she was assigned a bed in one of the wards, her description of the swinging iron beds riveted to the floor, being next to a big window and lots of bathrooms nearby indicating that she was placed in one of the enclosed promenades for the outward journey. Her description of A deck, however, has helped to fill in many of these gaps, noting that there were large officers' wards located in this area, a lounge, writing room and two libraries.

The enclosed promenade

The enclosed promenade, an unmistakeable feature in the *Titanic* and *Britannic*, extended along the forward end of the first-class promenade deck, between frames 70F and 6F on either side of the ship. In its original configuration, the enclosed promenade was intended to offer the first-class passengers protection from the weather in stormy conditions, but with windows that could be raised or lowered as required so that they would still be able to enjoy the conditions as they preferred. Interestingly, when the *Britannic* was requisitioned, Harland & Wolff realised that simply by installing an additional bulkhead at the aft end of each promenade, in the approximate location of frame 6F, two additional enclosed ward spaces could be created out of thin air.

It comes as little surprise that the attractive views of the sea and the fresh air, both made possible by the sliding windows, meant that these wards would be allocated to the officers, but sadly the higher port side enclosed promenade has not fared well over the years. Only broken fragments of glass in the window openings bear testimony to the sliding panes that once enclosed this space, while the temporary aft bulkhead has also disappeared completely, either swept away by the force of the water surging along the enclosed promenade during the ship's last moments afloat or decaying in the marine environment over the following years. Large deposits of marine biomass have built up on the port side of the deckhouse, and the medical cots, made from iron, appear to have fared particularly badly in this more exposed area of the ship, with parts of their structure even crumbling to dust as the divers move past. It was an ominous sign, and we could only hope that the medical equipment inside the darker and less oxygenated compartments of the wreck would be coping better than the cots in the more open marine environment.

The aft superstructure

Moving aft of frame 13F into the area of the *Britannic*'s first-class reading and writing room, everyone on the team was conscious of the fact that we were effectively entering into dark territory. Although the moderately intact bow section of the *Titanic* has been partially explored and studied for decades, the weakened structure aft of the second funnel casing has for a long time been in the process of gradually collapsing in on itself. The *Titanic* actually broke in half in the area of the third funnel, and practically all of the structure previously located between frames 12A and 36A now lies broken and scattered across the seabed to the east of the stern section. As for the aft section of the wreck, although it remains recognisable in places, from frame 12A to the end of the stern it is essentially a devastated pile of compacted and twisted steel. This means that practically every space explored inside the *Britannic* aft of frame 13F – representing well over half the ship's length – is completely new. The equivalent spaces in the *Titanic* will likely never be fully explored to the same extent because they simply no longer exist as a structural entity, whereas in the *Britannic* everything remains largely intact.

The reading and writing room

'The pure white walls and the light and elegant furniture show us that this is essentially a ladies' room.

Through the great bow window, which almost fills one side of the room, we look out past the deck on which our companions in travel are taking the air, over the vast expanse of sea and sky.

An atmosphere of refined retirement pervades the apartment; a homely fire burns in the cheerful grate: our feet move noiselessly over the thick, velvety carpet, and an arched opening leads to an inner recess – a sanctuary so very peaceful that here it would seem as if any conversation above a whisper would be sacrilege.'

[*Olympic* and *Titanic* publicity booklet, May 1911]

Although broadly speaking similar in decor and furnishings, this room in the *Britannic* was somewhat smaller than the equivalent spaces in the *Olympic* and *Titanic*, with part of the original layout given over to one of the four additional port-side cabins extending between frames 29F and 14F. These cabins would have provided accommodation for an additional nine first-class passengers, and the assumption can only be that part of the original reading and writing room layout was dispensed with because the space was considered to be excessive. There is no indication as to why this might have been the

Above: Looking down the corridor between the lounge and forward main entrance. The internal bulkhead to the reading and writing room seems to have disappeared completely.

case, although there is evidence to suggest that in the *Olympic* and *Titanic* this room may also have served in part as an area for the first-class children to play, in which case the addition of the children's playroom in the *Britannic* would have precluded the need for so much space in this room. Certainly, today there is no indication of the room's final configuration, a brief glance along the corridor running between frames 29F and 5F indicating that the inner wall for this room has now completely disappeared.

The first-class lounge

'The lounge, being a room dedicated to reading, conversation, cards, tea-drinking and other social usages, is decorated in the style which was in vogue in France when Louis XV was on the throne, when social intercourse was the finest of fine arts, and when the Salon was the arena in which the keenest intellects of the age "crossed swords" and exchanged the most delicate conversational thrust and parry.

Now, as then, the British workman is supreme in the production of the finely-carved 'boiseries' with which the walls are covered, and in which, without interfering with the symmetry of the whole, the fancy of the carver has everywhere shown itself in ever-varying details.

When talk becomes monotonous, we may here indulge in bridge and whist, or retire with our book or our letters to one of the many quiet retreats which reveal themselves to the thoughtful explorer. The chairs and sofas are so soft and cosy, however, that on them inducements to slumber may easily prevail, to the detriment of our literary efforts.'

[*Olympic* and *Titanic* publicity booklet, May 1911]

Above: Publicity drawing of the *Britannic*'s planned first-class lounge. (Harland & Wolff)

The conditions inside the *Britannic*'s first-class lounge are little different from those of the reading and writing room, with bare steel walls and little visible evidence of the room's furnishings. However, in one key respect we now know so much more about this room than would have been thought possible, with the recent discovery of considerable amounts of the panelling originally intended for this space.

Much of this Louis XV-style oak lounge panelling was originally purchased at the auction in July 1919 to be incorporated into the new La Scala Theatre and Opera House, in Prince's Street, Dublin, along with the sycamore panelling intended for the ship's second-class library. The La Scala also served as a cinema, and in 1927 the building was leased by Paramount Pictures, in the process becoming the Capitol Cinema, although live acts would remain a regular feature until 1953. The Capitol would continue as a cinema until the building was demolished in 1972 to make way for a department store, but far from being the end of the line for the panelling, it was once again reused.

John 'Bosco' O'Brien, the owner of Demolition Ireland, the company contracted to pull down the Capitol, was also one of the directors of the motor race circuit at Mondello Park, in County Kildare. Bosco, however, had a problem, as Mondello Park was an hour's drive from Dublin, so his plan was to establish the Mondello Club House at Baldonnell, which was much closer to the city. The old panelling from the Capitol Cinema was ideal for the new club house, which opened in May 1974, the opening ceremony being performed

Above: A section of the auctioned lounge panelling. (John Hynes)

by Formula 1 drivers José Carlos Pace and Jean-Pierre 'Jumper' Jarier. Sadly, the venture didn't last long, allegedly on account of the Gardaí raising concerns over the growing number of traffic accidents involving inebriated members on the Baldonnell to Dublin road, but Bosco managed to cut a deal whereby the house and panelling could be saved.

Perhaps it could only happen in Ireland. In July 1977 Bosco was in his car, stopped at traffic lights, when he spied his friend, John Hynes, headed in the opposite direction. Rather than drive on, as the lights turned green they both stopped their cars in the middle of the road, rolled down the driver's window and started to chat. Knowing of John's liking for the house, the conversation went something like this:

'Will you give me £45K for that auld club house?'

'I will.'

Above: One of the piles of unidentified debris in the lounge.

'Will you give me £5k for the panelling?'
'I will.'
'Have you got anything on you?'
'Two grand!'
'Pull in over there!'

And so the deal was done. For the next 40 years, Aqua House would be the home of the Hynes family, before John – who believed that the panelling originated in the RMS *Celtic*, which had gone aground off Cobh (formerly Queenstown) in December 1928 – decided the time had finally come to part with it. It was only when the unmistakeable Harland & Wolff 433 markings were identified that the true provenance of the panelling came to light, before once again being sold at auction.

Less extensive, but undoubtedly more elaborate, were the oak architrave and swinging double doors intended for the forward end of the starboard corridor (frame 5F), which led to the starboard-side corridor linking the lounge to the forward main entrance. The doors and architrave were originally sold to another shipbuilder in Birkenhead, before being purchased in 1922 by Morris & Co. for the main entrance of the company's office in Shrewsbury. The discovery of this piece also highlighted a number of subtle variations when compared to the design of the same architraves in the *Olympic* and *Titanic*, but as a result of finding this door and the panelling in quick succession, it is finally possible to envisage more accurately how the *Britannic*'s first-class lounge would have looked, had it ever been completed.

As for what remains in the *Britannic*'s lounge inside the wreck, no apparent evidence survives of the more elaborate White Star furnishings or sconces intended for this room, although large deposits of unidentified material remain, much of it piled against the lower starboard-side bulkhead. Considerably more intact, however, is the lounge pantry, slightly aft of the casing for boiler rooms 1 and 2 between frames 23A and 31A, where a small cooking range remains intact and still firmly attached to the steel deck Even some of the shelving at the forward end of the compartment remains recognisable, providing the first indication that as we moved further inside, we might still find better-preserved areas of interest.

Above: The opening where the decorative lounge architrave would have stood.
Above right: The first-class lounge and doorway architrave, now located at the entrance of *Morris & Co.* in Shrewsbury.

Above: Two views of the interior of the promenade deck pantry, used for the first-class public rooms on that deck.

Above: The imploded weather cover above the aft first-class staircase.

The aft first-class entrance

Like the forward main entrance, when completed this space would have been panelled in polished oak and finished in the Georgian style. While the weather cover of the forward main entrance remains largely intact, the cover above the aft staircase shows every sign of having imploded as the differential in water pressure outside the hull overwhelmed the cover above the ornamental glass dome and electric chandelier at the top of this staircase. Assuming they were fitted, which the completed dome in the forward entrance suggests they could have been, then the violent implosion of the weather cover, and the resulting torrent of water into this still unflooded section of the hull, has swept away any evidence of the glass dome that might once have existed in this space.

So far, not a single fragment has been observed of the dome near the base of the staircase at the level of the shelter deck, although the elegant curved steel frame of the staircase itself seems to be largely intact. The clearly visible footprint of the wooden oak balustrade certainly suggests that the staircase itself was at least partially complete, but perhaps more tellingly, the partially buckled C deck support stanchions serve as a clear indication that the damage inflicted to this part of the interior during the sinking would have been considerable.

The first-class smoking room

Back at the level of A deck, as we move further aft into the first-class smoking room, we pass a small compartment enclosing the aft expansion

Above: The base of the aft first-class staircase, the slightly bent support stanchions giving the first indication that the aft structure may have suffered additional damage as it impacted on the seabed.

joint inside the superstructure, which exhibits not even the slightest sign of having opened up either during the sinking process or as a result of the hull's subsequent impact on the seabed. Interestingly, the *Britannic*'s smoking room appears to have been the one public room in this part of the ship that would have differed significantly from those in the *Olympic* and *Titanic*. While the mahogany panelling of the two earlier ships was in the early Georgian style, described by *The Shipbuilder* as 'the finest apartment of its kind on the ocean', according to the 1919 auction publicity the panelling of choice for the *Britannic*'s smoking room would have been cedar of Lebanon with lime tree carvings, supposedly in the lighter style of one of the apartments at Hampton Court. Nor was the *Britannic*'s smoking room as large as those in the two earlier vessels, on account of the additional accumulator (battery) room located on the starboard side between frames 49A and 59A.

A number of bed frames resting in the debris against the port-side bulkhead of the turbine engine room casing also suggest that this space was almost certainly being utilised as a ward. This ward space was so close to the living accommodations of the medical staff, it once again seems likely that this area would also have been prioritised for officers. As with the other public rooms surveyed in this part of the superstructure, there is little evidence of any fabric or wood having survived in this area, although large deposits of unidentified debris have also piled up against the lower starboard bulkhead, which in time may reveal equally substantial finds.

The veranda cafés

'Passing through the silently-revolving doors, we emerge upon a gay little veran-dah, over whose green trellis grow climbing plants, which foster the illusion that we are still on the fair, firm earth; but one glance through the windows, with their beautifully-chased bronze framing, adds to the charm, and we realize that we are still surrounded by the restless sea, once so dreaded a barrier to national intercourse. Set in this flowery arbour are numerous inviting little tables, at which we can take our coffee or absinthe in the open air, much as we do in our own summery gardens on land.'

[***Olympic*** and ***Titanic*** publicity booklet, May 1911]

There is little surviving evidence of the veranda trellis, or even of the large windows with their 'beautifully-chased bronze framing'. An educated guess suggests that these spaces may have served as the two libraries to which Marjorie Barber referred in her journal, and which were run by the ship's chaplain. All that remains now is a largely open space, with the opening for the aft sliding doors leading to the broken stump at frame 59A, indicating the location where the fallen mainmast was once attached to the promenade deck. Unlike the foremast, the mainmast has completely detached from where it was mounted, and now lies on the seabed, directly beneath where it would have originally been fitted.

The stump of the fallen mainmast also marked the conclusion of the promenade deckhouse survey, meaning that we could turn our attention to other enticing targets deeper within the hull.

Above: Piles of debris, including cot frames, lying against the port-side bulkhead of the turbine engine room casing in the first-class smoking room.

8

THE BRIDGE DECK

While it is evident that the staterooms for the *Britannic*'s medical staff lacked the finished elegance of the more complete accommodations in the *Aquitania*, there is enough photographic evidence to suggest that the arrangements were at least moderately comfortable. Compared to a dugout on the western front, if anything the doctors and nurses would have been positively spoiled for choice, but even though the interiors were incomplete, Harland & Wolff had at least done what they could to make them as comfortable as possible.

The original B deck arrangements in the *Britannic* resulted from a mixture of the features in the earlier two vessels. When the *Olympic* first entered service in June 1911, the ship featured an enclosed promenade extending along the entire length of the bridge deck. While this seemed to offer adequate promenading space for the first-class passengers, Joseph Bruce Ismay, the chairman of the White Star Line, still considered the available open space to be excessive, and it was at this point that the notion of utilising the B deck promenade for additional cabins in the *Titanic* first took hold. As a result of Ismay's observations, the *Titanic*'s B deck layout would be substantially different, with practically all the previously open space being utilised to increase the revenue-earning aspects of the ship. The first-class à la carte restaurant, between frames 59A and 74A, was extended out to the ship's port side, while an entirely new feature, a Café Parisien, took up the previously open space along the aft starboard promenade located between frames 46A and 74A. The most noticeable difference, however, is that the *Titanic*'s first-class B deck cabins were also extended out to each side of the vessel aft of frame 13F, while between frames 29F and 13F the two first-class parlour suites were given their own private promenade, affording an additional touch of luxury for the particularly well-heeled passengers. Forward

Right: The doorway between the private promenade of the port-side parlour suite, leading into the first-class enclosed public promenade on B deck.

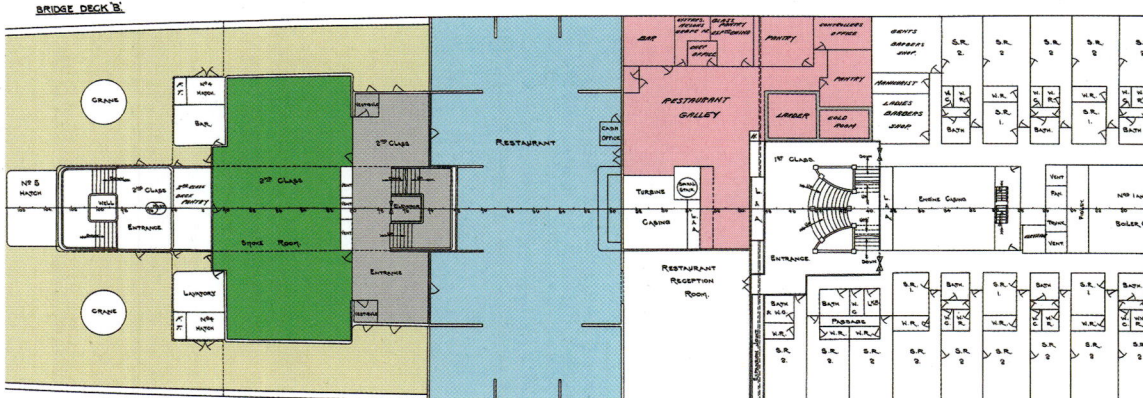

Above: General arrangement of the *Britannic*'s bridge deck. (Harland & Wolff)

of frame 40F, once again additional cabins extending to frame 66F took up what remained of the originally open space in the *Olympic*, ensuring that the available deck space was utilised to maximum effect.

Following the loss of the *Titanic*, during the winter of 1912/13 the *Olympic* was also modified to include an enlarged first-class restaurant and a Café Parisien, both of which had proved popular with the first-class passengers. Even so, much of the enclosed promenade remained untouched, presumably because the additional lifeboats installed on the boat deck occupied so much space that the previously unappreciated B deck promenade had now become that much more appealing. In the *Britannic*, however, the novel design of the Armstrong davits effectively meant that some of Ismay's original recommendations could still be incorporated into the B deck arrangements. As a result, the forward promenade between frames 74F and 40F would be reinstated, as per the original layout in the *Olympic*, while aft of frame 40F the arrangements would be more akin to those in the *Titanic*. Both parlour suites would continue to feature in the layout, with the port-side arrangement reminiscent of that in the *Titanic*, while the starboard suite would instead incorporate a smaller private veranda between frames 24F and 17F, rather than a private promenade.

In terms of the B deck staterooms, aft of frame 13F it was very much à la *Titanic*, with the cabins extending as far back as the aft first-class entrance, the cabins on the starboard side extending slightly further to the aft expansion joint at frame 49A. It is at this point, however, that the arrangements inside the *Britannic* become noticeably different from those in the *Olympic* and *Titanic*, with the à la carte restaurant reception room, galley and restaurant occupying the remaining space as far aft as frame 74A. Crucially, in the *Britannic* the restaurant extended the full width of the promenade deck, with no provision at all

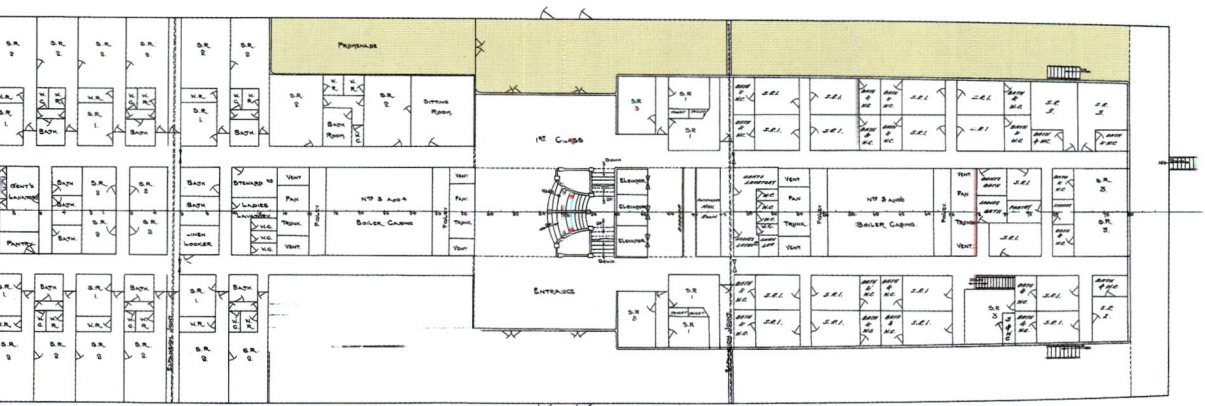

being made for a Café Parisien. The reasons for this feature not being included in the *Britannic*'s final configuration are unclear, the likelihood being that the two veranda cafés on the promenade deck, combined with the additional seating created by a much larger restaurant reception room, were instead considered to be sufficient.

Once again, the 1911 White Star publicity booklet for the *Olympic* and *Titanic* gives the first-class traveller a taste of the intended ambience of the restaurant:

'The Restaurant is of the Louis XVI period in design, and is panelled from floor to ceiling in beautifully marked French walnut of a delicate light fawn brown colour, the mouldings and ornaments being richly carved and gilded. In the centre of the large panels hang electric light brackets, cast and finely chased in brass and gilt and holding candle lamps. On the right of the entrance is a counter with a marble top of fleur de pêche, supported by panelling and pilasters recalling the design of the wall panels.

The room is well lighted by large bay windows, which are a distinctive and novel feature, and give a feeling of spaciousness. These are draped with plain fawn silk curtains with flowered borders and pelmets richly embroidered. The windows themselves are divided into squares by ornamented metal bars. Every small detail, down to the fastenings and hinges, has been carried out with regard to purity of style.

The ceiling is of plaster, with delicately modelled flowers in bas relief, forming a simple design of trellis in the centre and garlands in the bays. At various well-selected points hang clusters of lights ornamented with chased metal gilt and crystals.

The floor is covered with a rich pile carpet of Axminster make, and a non-obtrusive design of the period in a delicate vieux rose, which forms an admirable background, and

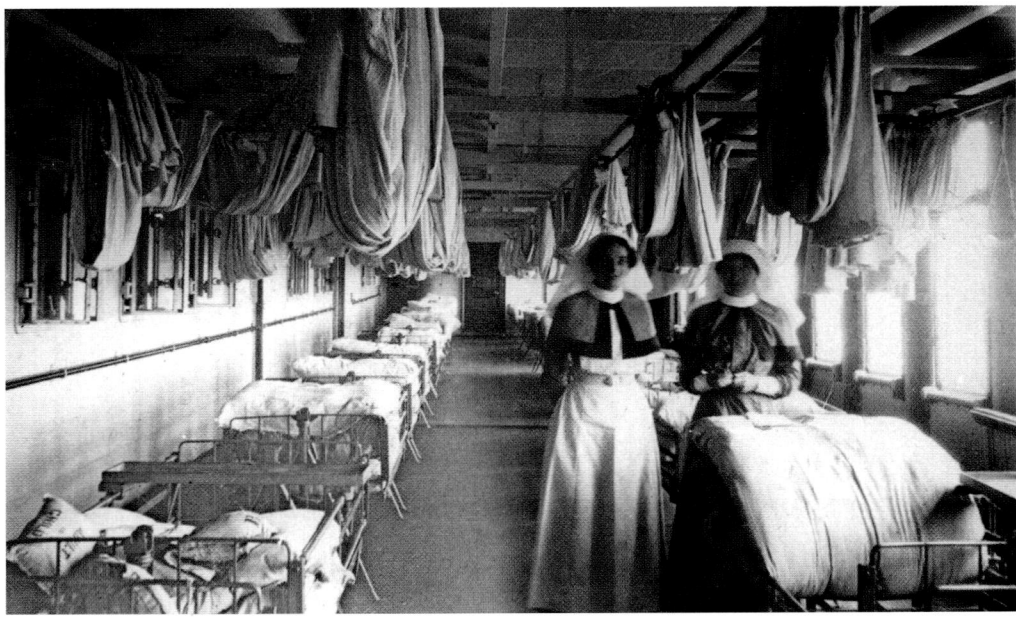

Above: One of the officers' wards, beside the port-side promenade deck sliding windows, providing relatively easy access for the divers.

completes the harmonious ensemble.

Comfort has been well considered in the arrangement of the room. It is furnished with small tables, to accommodate from two to eight persons, with crystal standard lamps and rose-coloured shades to illuminate each table.

The chairs have been particularly well studied, and are made in similar light French walnut to the walls, carved and finished with a waxed surface and upholstered with an interesting tapestry representing a treillage of roses in quiet tones assisting the general harmony of colour.

For convenience of service there are several dumb-waiters encircling the columns and forming part of the decorative scheme.

On one side is ample accommodation for an orchestra, partly recessed and raised on a platform, flanked on either side with a carved buffet, the top part being a vitrine to hold the silver service, and the lower part for cutlery, thus completing the necessities for a well-appointed restaurant to satisfy every requirement.'

The 1919 auction advertisement suggests that the *Britannic*'s intended restaurant style would have been of a broadly similar specification, the only real difference being that the builders would instead be using Italian walnut panelling, rather than French, suggesting that the *Britannic*'s panelling would have been slightly darker. The question, however, was how much of this panelling, if any, would remain?

B deck enclosed promenade

Although for many years divers have been able to access the more open A deck promenade with little difficulty, access to the B deck promenade has been more problematic. Permissions for suitably qualified recreational divers to visit the wreck can now be obtained more easily, but it can never be forgotten that 30 British crew and servicemen lost their lives on the day the *Britannic* sank, which by default raises issues in terms of respect for war graves. The *Britannic* is also a listed monument according to Greek law, so any permits issued by the Greek Ephorate of Marine Antiquities are only granted on the absolute condition that all diving activities remain restricted to the exterior of the wreck, and that nothing is disturbed. Even so, while the large sliding windows, which extend along the entire length of the promenade, have always provided a relatively easy opportunity to image the equipment strewn along this area of the interior, the 2021 internal survey enabled us to physically move into this previously excluded area, and to take a closer look at the key areas of interest.

The B deck enclosed promenades extend between frames 72F and 29F, with the private promenade of the port-side parlour suite extending back an additional 45 feet (13.7m) to frame 13F. Practically every one of the 33 brass-framed sliding windows, each measuring

Below: A sink now occupies the forward corner of the parlour suite promenade.

37 inches x 31 inches (94cm x 79cm), are either open or smashed, while nearly all the smaller upper panes, which did not open, remain intact. The smaller private promenade shows no evidence of any medical equipment, the only noticeable modification in this area to the original design being a utilitarian sink installed against the deckhouse at the forward inboard corner of the promenade itself.

Passing through the bulkhead opening at frame 29F, the promenade widens slightly, leading into the forward main entrance where it is still relatively clear of debris; but forward of frame 40F it is another matter, with practically all the swinging medical cots having fallen from where they were riveted to the pine decking, which slowly rotted away after the sinking until the surface was so deteriorated that the wooden planks were no longer strong enough to bear the weight. Fragments of these medical cots can still be seen all along the promenade, resting against the lower deckhouse walls, although their condition does not seem to be quite as fragile as the medical cots on the more open promenade deck above. Interestingly, one of the cots has come to rest directly over the forward expansion joint at frame 49F, which, unlike the forward joint on the *Titanic*, shows not even the slightest indication of having been affected in any way during the sinking process.

Nearly all the deckhouse windows along the promenade are closed, and, for the most

Above: The doorway into what would have been the sitting room of the port-side parlour suite.

THE BRIDGE DECK

Above: A fallen medical cot above the forward expansion joint, which shows no sign of any damage.

part, remain largely intact, suggesting the possibility that when venturing into these areas forward of frame 49F, we might find the interior to be better preserved. On the other hand, subsequent examination of the B deck cabins further aft indicated that this might be something of a forlorn hope. In any event, the level of preservation along the promenade seems to be consistent with other parts of the wreck observed up to that point, with little or no evidence of any surviving wood or fabric being observed along this space.

Intriguingly, as we arrived at the forward end of the promenade, passing through the doorway in the forward bulkhead at frame 70F is the first indication in this part of the wreck that some of the harder teak wood seems to have survived. Fragments of the

Top: Closed windows along the promenade, possibly suggesting a better-preserved interior.
Above: Another enclosed promenade deck window, but wide open.

stairway leading up to the boat deck can still be clearly seen, although like the rest of the wood in this area, the steps have not fared well after more than a hundred years on the seabed. Nonetheless, the teak steps have stood up better to the marine bacteria and biomass when compared to the pine decking, of which practically no trace remains, although it is only the sight of the elongated stumps, reminiscent of dragon's teeth, protruding through the thick covering of saddle oysters that provide any clue as to the purpose of the original structure.

The first-class restaurant galley

The decay of the medical cots and the wooden stairwells would turn out to be a worrying indication of what we would later find further aft. Access to the first-class restaurant galley had always been one of the main targets of the 2021 survey, the original plan being to enter the first-class smoking room in the aft deckhouse, move into the aft first-class staircase and descend to the level of B deck, before entering the restaurant itself via the

Above: The jagged remains of the forward teak staircase leading up to the promenade deck.

restaurant reception room. The initial penetration on 22 September confirmed that this route was certainly practicable, but two days later Irish divers Stewie Andrews and Barry McGill found themselves exploring the aft port promenade deck where, between frames 40A and 44A, a large hole has formed in the area of the deck immediately above the restaurant's pantry, larder and cold room. On the one hand it was an unexpectedly useful entry point – just about large enough for a diver equipped with a rebreather and bailout tanks to penetrate – but it was also a worrying indication that this part of the ship's structure had deteriorated to a more alarming extent, begging the inevitable question as to how many other areas would be equally decayed.

The hole in the deck would provide us with the first glimpses of the collapsed internal dividing walls and numerous pieces of twisted and broken refrigeration piping, but with the way to the galley itself seemingly wide open, it was an opportunity that simply had to be taken. No sooner had the divers passed through the opening than we had our first glimpses of scattered White Star Line plates and cutlery that we always knew would be somewhere inside the wreck. There was never a realistic chance of finding any of the famous Royal Crown Derby chinaware used in any of the Olympic class vessels – in fact, I was expecting to come across far more significant deposits of the less attractive but far more durable Adams third-class crockery – so the

Above: Refrigeration piping for the first-class restaurant larder and cold room.

Top left: Broken plates in one of the sinks in the first-class restaurant pantry.
Top right: Large numbers of White Star Line plates lie scattered around the pantry of the first-class restaurant. The blue 'Bradford' pattern was used for second-class passengers, and was manufactured by the Copeland Spode pottery in Stoke-on-Trent.
Above: The manufacturer's details stamped on the back of each plate before firing.

sudden vision of dozens of blue plates scattered around the pantry and galley came as something of a surprise.

Closer investigation quickly revealed that the plates were a standard White Star second-class pattern; the design was known as 'Bradford' and was manufactured by the Copeland Spode pottery in Stoke-on-Trent, Staffordshire. According to the Spode records, the Bradford pattern was registered with the British Patent Office as early as 31 July 1905 (patent no. 461740), so it was by no means created for the exclusive use of the White Star Line, and the plates could be manufactured in

Top: One of the many earthenware pots lying scattered across the galley floor.
Above: An unexpected find in the first-class restaurant galley. A pair of binoculars, possibly used by one of the chefs to peer through portholes at a particularly interesting passing vessel.

Above: Part of a corroded but still easily recognisable silver-plated serving platter, in this case of the Reed and Star pattern normally used in first-class.

any number of colours, including red, green and brown. The White Star colour of choice was printed in blue, before being covered in a ceramic glaze and fired in a kiln. This 'underglaze' technique not only made the decoration more durable, but it also had the added benefit of requiring only a single firing, thus making it cheaper to manufacture than the more elaborate gilt-edged first-class chinaware, which would require a second firing.

Earthenware jars and kitchen utensils of every description lie scattered across these compartments, to all intents and purposes frozen in time since the morning of 21 November 1916, when the kitchen staff were busily preparing breakfast for the medical officers and nurses. Once again, the *Britannic*'s specification book provided a tantalising clue as to what we might find as the dive team moved further aft, but inevitably much depended on exactly how much of the interior had been installed by the time the *Britannic* was requisitioned for military service. The presence of so many plates and plate silver service items lying around the compartment confirmed that the galley was certainly being utilised for its original intended purpose, the only question being how much of the 12-foot by 6-foot (3.7m by 1.8m) island range would we find still in situ?

The cooking ranges for use in the Olympic class were manufactured at the Cornhill Street works of Henry Wilson & Co., in Liverpool. Until recently, only a glimpse of the occasional

Above: Publicity drawing of the *Britannic*'s enlarged first-class restaurant. (Harland & Wolff)

archival image has provided any indication as to how this compartment might have been laid out, especially as the wrecked stern of the *Titanic* is so badly damaged that it is practically impossible to access this area. However, with the *Britannic*'s aft structure still largely intact, the route into the main area of the galley quickly revealed that the island range, complete with overhead canopy and pan rack, was still firmly fixed in position.

Sadly, the elation at finding one section of the interior to be so well preserved was quickly dampened by the fact that as the divers returned to their entry point, additional deterioration in one of the internal non-structural bulkheads allowed them to

Above and opposite: The first-class restaurant cooking range, manufactured by Wilson & Co. of Liverpool, still intact and firmly attached to the steel deck.

Above: The bare interior of the first-class restaurant, as it looked in September 2023. Only a few of the iron table supports now remain in situ.

move almost effortlessly through the pantry wall and into an area that, in commercial service, would have been occupied by the first-class ladies' and gentlemen's barbers and manicurist (frames 37A to 40A). Beyond this point lay the aft port-side first-class staterooms, which are known to have served as accommodations in the ship for the medical staff, but in common with the rest of the wreck, practically all the wooden dividing walls in this area have now disappeared.

Even more concerning is the fact that exploration of this more open area has also shown that many of the supporting stanchions are badly deformed. Whether this distortion was caused by the racking forces transmitted through the hull as the ship rolled over to starboard and impacted with the seabed or has developed post-sinking and over a longer

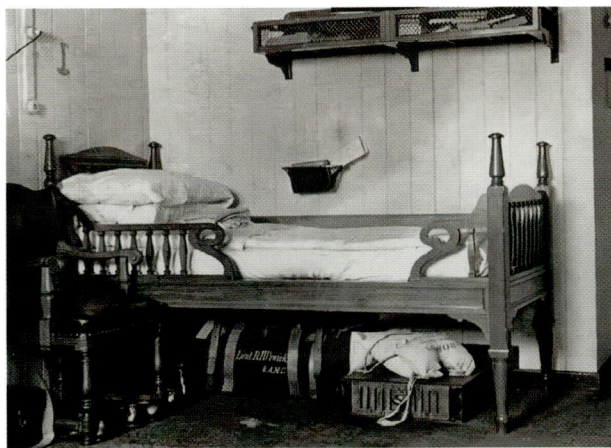

Right: One of the medical officer's cabins located on the *Britannic*'s bridge deck. (Ronald Goodman)

Above: A chamber pot rests against the frame of one of the doctor's bed frames.

period of time is unclear at this time. Perhaps it is a combination of both factors, but either way, this extensive deformation indicates a potential weakening of large areas of the aft structure, particularly in the higher and lighter parts of the structure. To date, the dive team has only penetrated about 60 feet (18m) into this area of the ship, but it is clear that a more representative number of these stanchions need to be earmarked for future examination within the various levels of the wreck.

The second-class entrance

Unlike the promenade deck above, which was reserved exclusively for the first-class passengers, save for the small enclosed area through which the second-class stairwell and elevator passed between frames 72A and 80A, the aft section of the bridge deck between frames 74A and 103A was intended for the use of the second-class passengers.

As with the other staircases, the second-class entrance was also panelled in polished oak, the entrance extending down through seven decks, although the original arrangement was such that there was no access to the promenade deck. The remaining six decks were also served by an elevator incorporated into the centre of the staircase, although as with the forward port first-class elevator, the size of this lift cage may have been modified when the *Britannic* was converted into a

Above: The now open area of the bridge deck where the medical staff were once accommodated. Further aft, the damage to the deck support stanchions becomes increasingly noticeable.

hospital ship, necessitating the repositioning of the original cage runners and modified Bostwick gates for each landing.

Between frames 74A and 80A the entrance is still relatively open, with no evidence of the vestibules originally intended for either side of the entrance space. Like the two first-class entrances, much of the wooden staircase is now gone, although like the first-class main entrance a few fragments of wood remain tenuously attached to the metal framework. The runners for the single central elevator,

extending all the way down to F deck, seem to be largely undamaged, and based on the imagery obtained at the upper levels of the lift shaft itself, it is not unreasonable to assume that the structural conditions further down in decks C to F, which have yet to be surveyed, would allow for relatively easy access to the internal spaces in this part of the hull. The lift cage itself has not yet been seen, suggesting that it is probably located somewhere in the lower part of the structure, although a large number of now exposed electrical distribution boxes are clearly visible in this area, all of which appear to be in an almost pristine state of preservation.

The second-class smoking room

Located on B deck, between frames 80A and 94A, as with the rest of the superstructure there is little or no evidence of any of the oak panelling originally intended for this space. Once again we need to address the question of how much of this panelling might have been installed before the *Britannic* was requisitioned, although this public room does seem to have been outfitted to a greater degree of readiness than some of the others, with traces of the original linoleum flooring still

Left, above and overleaf: Little remains of the aft second-class entrance, although some elements of the floor tiling and electrical boxes still look to be in an almost pristine condition.

Titanic, while the Veitchi flooring beneath the fallen tiles remains largely intact, with no significant sign of any damage being observed to date.

The initial survey of the boat, promenade and bridge decks have been both illuminating and concerning. On the one hand there is no doubt that, even after a century on the seabed, many parts of the structure still seem to be standing up well to the marine environment, but at the same time there is no denying the worrying evidence of our own eyes that, in other areas, parts of the structure are displaying considerable signs of decay. The boat deck's vanishing exterior bulwarks had not come as any great surprise to anyone, but the deterioration in the promenade deck above the restaurant pantry, along with the numerous twisted stanchions observed in the B deck cabin spaces, as well as the bottom of the aft first-class entrance, clearly indicate that all is not well inside the *Britannic*'s upper works. The question was, would it be any different deeper inside the main body of the hull itself?

evident. Many of the linoleum tiles have now fallen from the floor into the jumbled heap of debris on the lower starboard bulkhead of the smoking room space, but enough fragments remain attached to the floor for us to be able to reconstruct the original floor pattern with almost complete accuracy. Intriguingly, all the indications seem to suggest that the floor pattern in this area of the ship would have been identical to those in the *Olympic* and

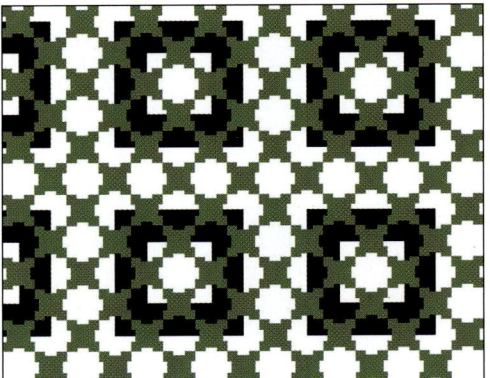

Above: A reconstruction of the linoleum pattern.

THE BRIDGE DECK

Above: Fragments of the linoleum flooring, still attached to the Veitchi base in the smoking room.

9

THE SHELTER AND SALOON DECKS

The *Britannic*'s shelter deck (C) was the highest deck to extend along the entire length of the ship from stem to stern; it was also the first deck to incorporate elements not only from all three classes of passenger, but also some of the crew accommodations.

Inside the ship's forecastle, the space extending between frames 122F and 101F was, for the most part, given over to the crew's working areas, with the crew's galley and seamen's mess on the port side, the firemen's and trimmers' WCs on the starboard side, along with the firemen's wash place and a smaller compartment for the greasers' mess. Forward of frame 122F, extending all the way to the ship's stem, two compartments housed not only the windlass and warping machinery, but also the steel wire windlass for working the auxiliary 16-ton anchor.

The windlass and warping gear was designed and manufactured by Napier Brothers Ltd. of Glasgow. The anchor gears consisted of two cable holders mounted on the forecastle head, and were driven from the deck below by two 18-inch x 14-inch double-cylinder engines through worm gearing, the engines being coupled in such a way that either or both could be connected to one or other of the cable holders. The forward warping gear comprised four capstans, two of which were also driven from the deck below by separate 18-inch x 14-inch double-cylinder engines through spur and bevel wheel gearing, while the other two were connected to the windlass engines by bevel gearing. There was also an additional capstan on the shelter deck, aft of the windlass engines and connected by bevel gearing. To ensure an ample margin of strength, the gears throughout were manufactured from cast steel wherever possible, while the worm wheel rims were made of gun metal.

Left: One of the visible windlass engines, still completely intact and undamaged. (Leigh Bishop)

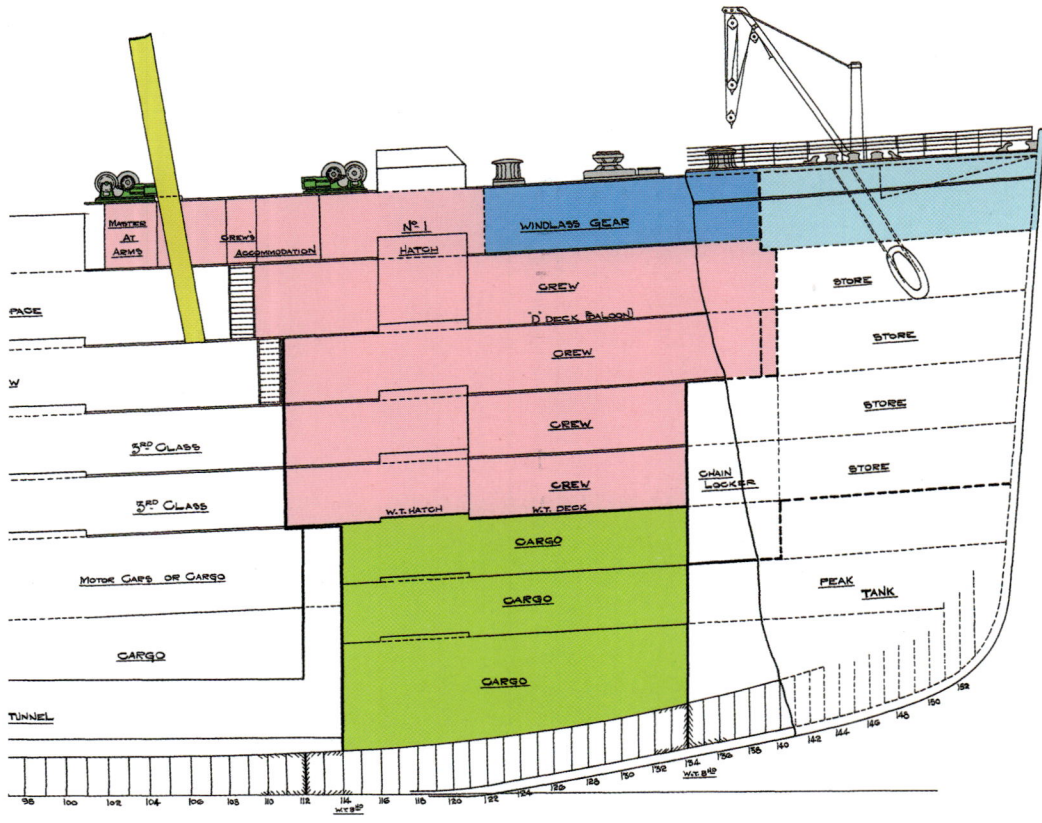

Forward of the collision bulkhead, at frame 139F, is the steel wire windlass for working the auxiliary 16-ton anchor, powered via a bevel and worm gearing linked to the windlass engines. This windlass has a grooved barrel some 7 feet 8 inches (2.3m) in diameter, and 8 feet 7 inches (2.6m) in length, and was capable of taking 175 fathoms (1,050 feet or 320 metres) of 10-inch steel wire. The brake gear of the cable holders and cable drum was also designed so that the load itself governed the grip, meaning that once the brake was put in gear it could be safely left alone, the theory being that the greater the strain on the cable, the tighter it was held.

For the dive team, entering the forecastle could be achieved with the minimum of effort. The steel cargo hatch on the forecastle deck above (frames 120F to 116F), although completely intact, was originally fitted with two hinged wooden flaps, one on each side, both of which had rotted away decades earlier. As a result, a diver could easily squeeze through the remaining 42-inch by 36-inch (107cm by 91cm) openings, even with a bulky rebreather on their back.

Once inside the forecastle, the resulting images would be a revelation. Inside the

THE SHELTER AND SALOON DECKS

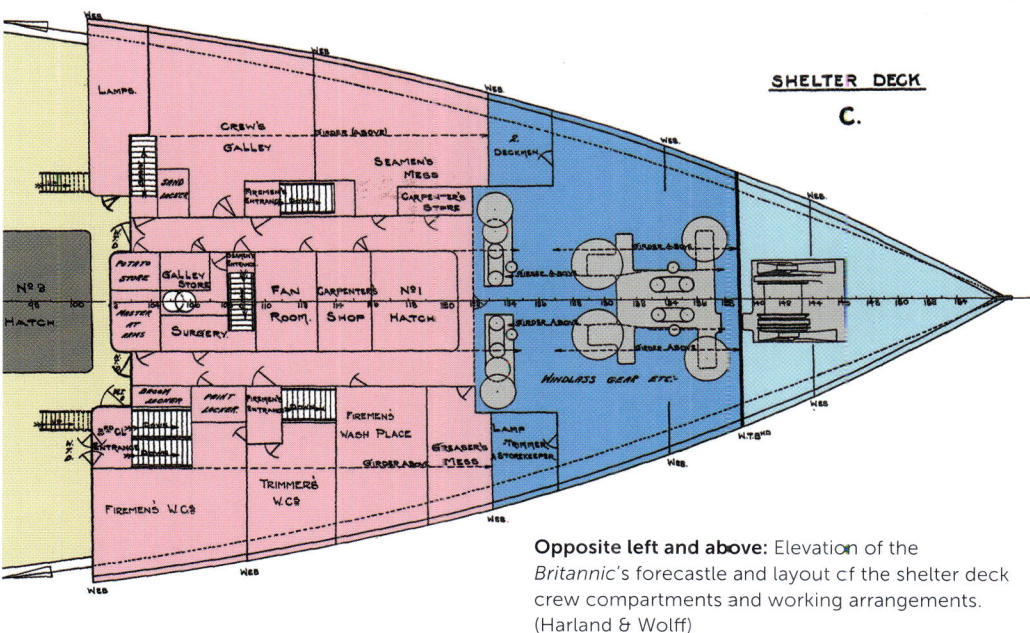

Opposite left and above: Elevation of the *Britannic*'s forecastle and layout of the shelter deck crew compartments and working arrangements. (Harland & Wolff)

Titanic there is generally very little visible evidence of the floor coverings, on account of the wreck being largely upright and the heavy deposits of silt that have built up after more than a century on the seabed, whereas inside the *Britannic* it is completely the opposite. With the *Britannic*'s hull lying at an approximate angle of 77 degrees to the seabed, the internal silt deposits nearly everywhere inside the wreck have largely collected lower down, on the internal starboard bulkheads, while the more acute angle, combined with the smoother working surface of the non-slip tiles, means that few marine organisms have been able to establish a foothold. Despite the general lack of wood throughout the interior, the anaerobic environment inside this part of the wreck, combined with the materials used, seems to indicate that there has been very little in the way of degradation inside the forecastle since the day the *Britannic* sank.

Passing through the weather cover flap openings, immediately forward on the right-hand side, at frame 122F, is a vertical metal grille. The surprisingly good level of preservation in this area is already clearly indicated by the condition of the teak decking utilised in the working areas of the ship, while a partially open gate in the grille points tantalisingly to the well-preserved windlass engines slightly further forward. All the visible elements of this apparatus are still completely in situ, indicating that the forward section of the ship's structure at least internally, seems to have stood up remarkably well to the forces exerted in this area during the stem's prolonged impact with the seabed.

It is here that the first indications as to the

Above: The spiral staircase at a lower level, with the beautifully preserved ceramic tiling.
Opposite left: The top level of the spiral staircase on D deck, extending all the way down to the tank top. (Leigh Bishop)

standard of the fittings inside the crew's quarters also become apparent, with colourful non-slip tiles taking the place of bare steel decks in order to ensure as safe a working environment as possible. This particular transit area would probably have been one of the busiest in the ship, with the stokehold crew accommodated in the forecastle regularly passing through this space while en route to their allotted duty station in the stokeholds. Indeed, the route to the boiler rooms was remarkably easy. Two spiral staircases, located at frame 113F, extended from the saloon deck (D) all the way down to the bottom of the ship, passing through the stokehold crew's accommodations on the upper, middle and lower decks, before entering an enclosed watertight escape trunk, which effectively enveloped the remaining descent to a raised walking platform, about 2 feet 6 inches (0.76m) above the tank top. At the bottom of the winding staircase, a watertight pipe tunnel, extending some 100 feet (30m) aft between frames 114F and 78F, provided direct access to the boiler rooms; in fact, this very tunnel would also be used by the divers for that exact

Above: The iron railings leading to the windlass gear. (Leigh Bishop)

same purpose, except that they would enter from the exterior, via the break in the forward hull at frame 95F.

Perhaps the most pleasant discovery in this area of the wreck was that despite the bow's initial contact with the seabed, and the huge stresses concentrated in the forward part of the ship during the latter stages of the sinking process, the cargo hold directly beneath the watertight lower deck (G) not only displays practically no evidence of any significant internal damage, but, crucially, remains completely empty. There is no evidence whatsoever of any cargo being carried in this area of the ship, and with the entire space seemingly clear of any debris all the way from the orlop deck to the top of the keel two decks below, the allegations that the *Britannic* was being used to transport illegal military cargo now look to be even more doubtful.

THE SHELTER AND SALOON DECKS

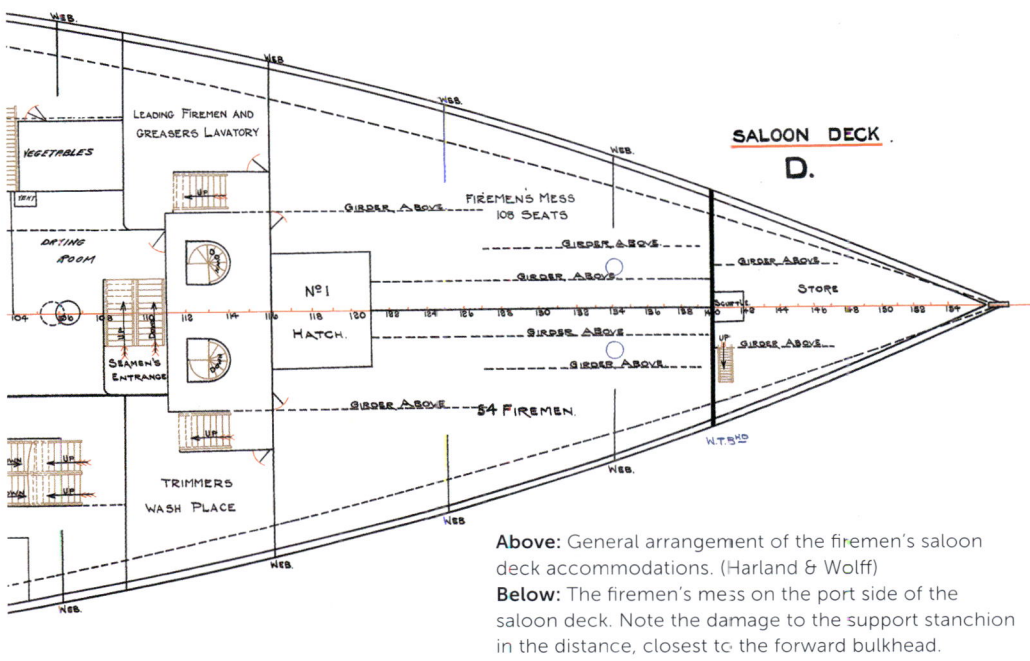

Above: General arrangement of the firemen's saloon deck accommodations. (Harland & Wolff)
Below: The firemen's mess on the port side of the saloon deck. Note the damage to the support stanchion in the distance, closest to the forward bulkhead.

Above: The bottom of cargo hold 1, all the way down to the tank top.

The forward well deck

The *Britannic*'s forward starboard well deck, extending between frames 102F and 85F, is the one part of the wreck where practical exploration by a manned diving team is all but impossible. The reason for this limitation is that the scale of the damage to this area is not only such that to all intents and purposes holds 2 and 3 no longer exist – at least, not to any practical extent – but also because the twisted and weakened steel structure in the collapsed area of the hull presents a clear and present danger to anyone venturing into this part of the wreck. A remote operated vehicle is probably the safer option here, although even the ROV operator would need to display maximum caution when working in this area, the jagged and twisted hull plating capable of snagging and even inflicting considerable damage to the trailing fibre-optic cable of any submersible craft. Once again, you can almost understand why Cousteau might have speculated on his internal explosion theory, but while the exploding munitions hypothesis undoubtedly had its attractions for a television audience, the lack of any explosive ordnance on the seabed is enough to undermine it. It cannot truly be said that the forecastle is now completely detached from the main body of the hull; however the scale of the damage is such that any thoughts of attempting to lift the wreck intact would only result in the total collapse of what little remains of the structure in this area. This may be a bitter pill to swallow for those who believe the wreck could still be raised; nevertheless, it is the reality.

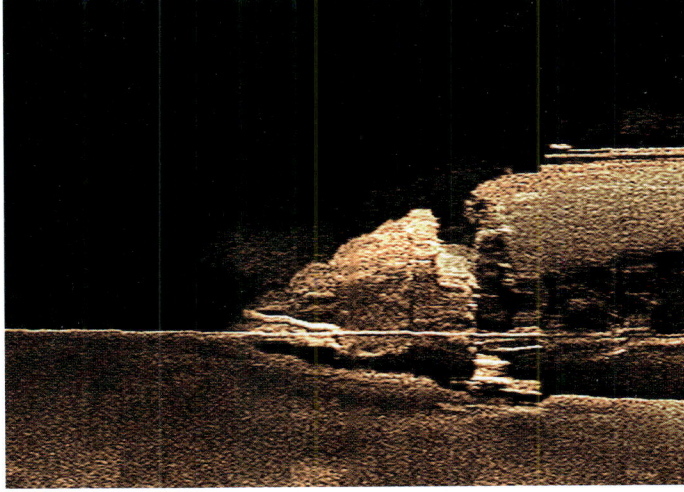

Above: Closer side-scan sonar image of the break in the hull beneath the *Britannic*'s forward well deck. (Dr George Papatheodorou, University of Patras)

The scale of the damage to the well deck itself also prevents us from examining more closely another significant design alteration incorporated into the *Britannic*, although it is rarely commented upon. In the *Olympic* and *Titanic*, this area of open deck was given over entirely to the steerage passengers, but while the same could also be said of the layout in the *Britannic*, two additional third-class entrance houses had been incorporated into the design, along the centreline forward and aft of the bunker hatch leading into hold 3. This entrance has now all but collapsed, although some of the original structure does still appear to be attached to what little remains of the shelter deck plating in this area, while other parts lie scattered in the twisted and broken hull plates that have fallen into the chasm between the forward superstructure and the aft end of the forecastle. In common with the *Olympic* and *Titanic*, the two Stothert & Pitt electric cargo cranes, each capable of handling loads of up to 50cwt, were fitted at the aft end of the well deck, each with an outreach of 29 feet 6 inches (9m) and a lifting speed of 160 feet (48.8m) per minute. Despite the huge scale of the damage in this area, the circular steel casings that house the cranes' machinery remain firmly attached to the deck itself, the jib arm of the higher port crane still lying in its support cradle, while the jib arm of the lower starboard crane is turned down towards the seabed.

In the *Britannic*'s intended commercial configuration, the entire deck space extending between frames 83F and 70A on the shelter deck would have consisted almost entirely of first-class cabins. Many of these spaces are now taken up with forests of dangling electrical cables, but passing through the foyer at the bottom of the aft first-class staircase, the space once again opens up to reveal a relatively intact and more spacious interior.

Aft of frame 70A, we once again find ourselves entering the second-class areas, in this case the enclosed promenade enveloping the second-class entrance and library, which would also have functioned as the second-class lounge. As with the smoking room on the bridge deck immediately above, the interior of this room is now almost totally bare, and yet strangely it was also one of the easiest to picture in its completed form. The 1911 White Star publicity booklet for the *Olympic* and *Titanic* devoted only five lines to this

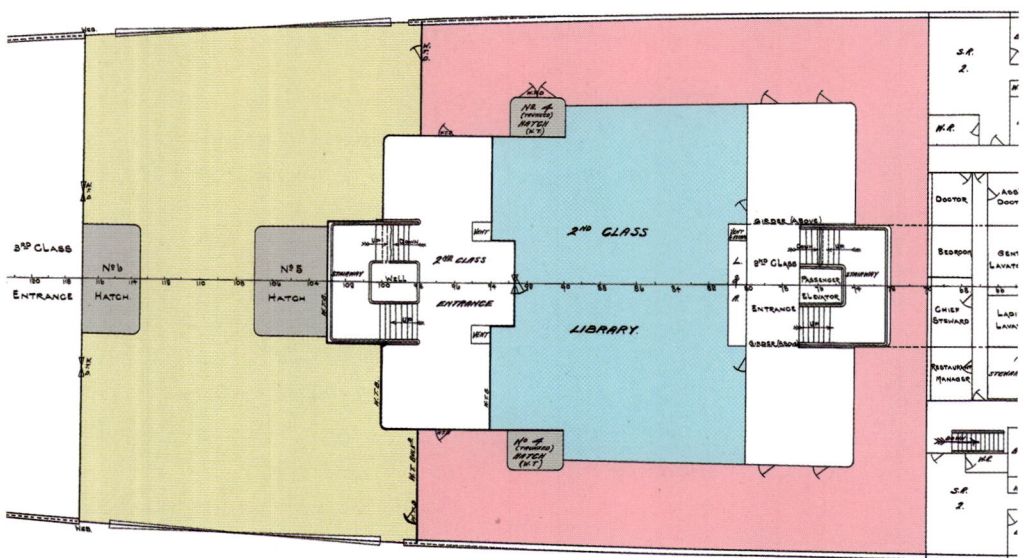

Above: General arrangement of the *Britannic*'s aft second-class public rooms on the saloon deck. (Harland & Wolff)

Above: A lonely anthia, attracted by the camera lights, in the second-class enclosed promenade.

room, extolling the handsome sycamore panelling, carvings, mahogany dado, specially designed furniture and handsome Wilton carpet, but while no evidence remains to suggest that any of this room's intended fittings were installed, some of the 4,000 square feet (372 sq m) of surviving second-class library panelling, sold at the July 1919 auction for the interior of the La Scala Theatre and Opera House in Dublin, makes it easier to imagine just how this room would have looked had it ever been completed. For those with a particularly overactive imagination, it's not difficult to recollect the final scene in James Cameron's 1997 *Titanic* movie, as the camera match moves along the wrecked promenade deck into the forward main entrance, while the rust fades away as the interior is once again transformed into its original beauty. Working at depths in excess of 100 metres (328ft), divers do not have the luxury of being able to pause and daydream about what could have been, but when reviewing the footage obtained in this area of the ship, it is curious that this is one of the very few occasions where I allowed my imagination to get the better of me.

Back in the real world, the occasional glimpse of White Star cutlery scattered around the compartment indicated that this room had served an altogether different and more functional purpose in a hospital ship than that of a library. Private Percy D Tyler, formerly of the 1st Anglo Belgian Ambulance Corps before being transferred to the *Britannic* during her second period of service, provides the only truly detailed contemporary

Above and opposite: The panelling originally intended for the *Britannic*'s second-class library. It was later resold for use in the La Scala Theatre in Dublin, and subsequently the Mondello Club House. (John Hynes)

THE SHELTER AND SALOON DECKS

Above: The second-class library was utilised as the RAMC orderlies' mess, where White Star first-class cutlery, manufactured by Elkington & Co., now lies buried in the silt.

description that we have of this part of the ship, noting that the RAMC parade ground was located in the area of the enclosed well deck, next to the medical orderlies' mess aft on C deck. Until now there was no conclusive proof that Tyler's memory was completely accurate, but the sight of the White Star cutlery scattered in the debris inside this room seems to suggest that his recollections were spot on.

The saloon deck

According to the White Star Line publicity, the main characteristics of the Olympic class first-class reception rooms were 'dignity and simplicity', with beautifully proportioned and delicately carved white panelling in the Jacobean style, providing 'a fitting background to what will probably be the most brilliant mise-en-scene on the ship'. Images of the

THE SHELTER AND SALOON DECKS

Above: White Star Line publicity image of the *Olympic*'s first-class reception room, which would have been practically identical in the *Britannic*.

Titanic's handsome bronze ceiling lights, the magnificent Aubusson tapestry facing the staircase, capacious Chesterfield sofas and armchairs, upholstered grandfather chairs or comfortable cane furniture upon a dark, richly coloured carpet all serve to further emphasise the delicacy and refinement of the panelling, but it has to be said that my expectations were low even before we had entered this area. In this case, it had nothing to do with the catalogue listing the panelling to be auctioned off after the war, but rather more to do with the very precise recollections of nurse Daisy Spickett, whose audio recollections, recorded for posterity in 1974 by the Imperial War Museum provide probably the most detailed information available on this area of the ship. Spickett unquestionably found the 'perfectly lovely' *Aquitania* to be the more attractive vessel of the two, recalling that while the *Britannic* seemed to have 'a most peculiar roll', the Cunarder was much more steady. Nor, in her opinion, was the *Britannic* as well run as the *Aquitania*, as they didn't have daily inspections, but at least her recollection of the *Britannic*'s D deck ward, capable of accommodating up to 288 patients, was more appreciative:

> 'One huge deck, nothing down the middle, just one enormous part of the deck. Two rows of portholes, one on each side, it had been intended for first-class dining room and lounges, now known as Hickeys, after the designer of the ship as a hospital ship ... it was a lovely big ward...'

Based on Spickett's memory, it therefore seemed unlikely that we would find any elaborately furnished areas in this part of the ship, even if they had been installed; but despite this disappointment, these two first-class public rooms were still going to be full of surprises.

The first-class reception room and dining saloon

Although they are deep inside the *Britannic*'s hull, accessing the saloon deck public rooms would turn out to be a relatively straightforward penetration. The numerous boat deck access points to the forward main entrance provide no serious obstacle to a diver, and, once inside, the fact that the *Britannic* lies on her starboard side meant that rather than having to descend deeper into the wreck, accessing the first-class reception room involved little more than a horizontal swim of barely 40 feet (12m) from the entrance point.

Curiously enough, the most intriguing find of all in the reception room would in no way be linked to the general arrangement in this part of the ship. When the divers on the 2003 expedition first reached the level of the saloon deck, they had observed what they took to be a relatively unimportant electrical box of some description. For reasons unknown, they decided to pause for a few seconds to obtain some closer shots of the unidentified and harmless-looking piece of electrical machinery before moving on, little realising that what they were filming was the multiple tuner, a crucial part of the Marconi wireless apparatus, which would originally have been located in the wireless room four decks above. The fact that it had by some complete fluke come to

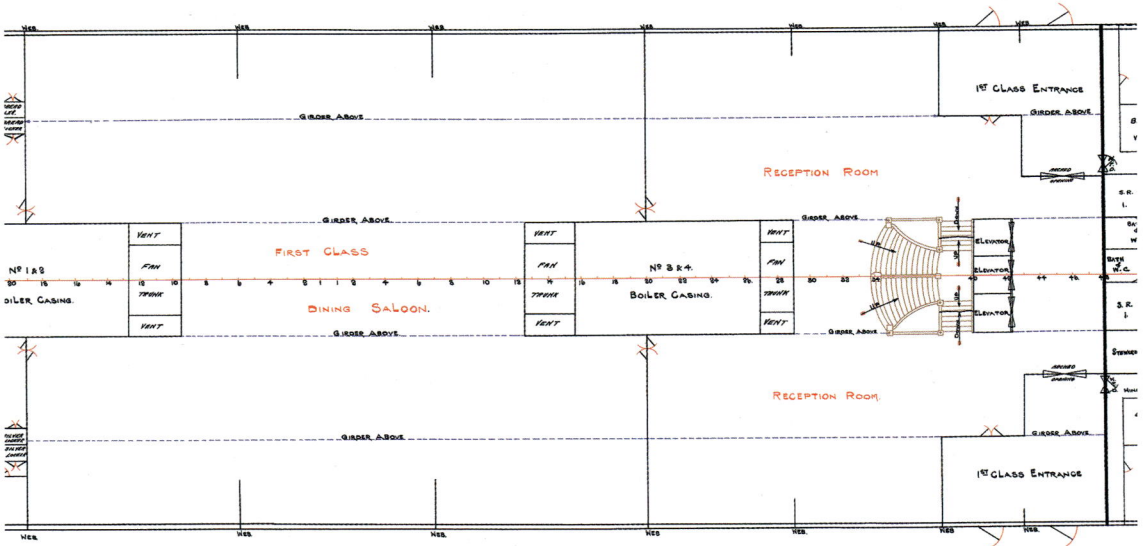

Above: General arrangement of the first-class reception and dining rooms on the saloon deck. (Harland & Wolff)

rest on the lower supporting deck beam around the stairway opening was even more miraculous, suggesting that a more detailed search of this area might reveal additional components of the Marconi apparatus, which may also have been torn from its original position and swept deeper into the ship's interior by the deluge of incoming seawater.

The main area of the reception room immediately confirmed that Spickett's recollections of one of the *Britannic*'s largest wards were pretty accurate. The area contained a large number of medical cots, most of which have over the years fallen towards the ship's lower starboard side, almost certainly because the pine decking to which they were attached has been eaten away by the legions of marine organisms. A few of the cot supports remain attached to the steel deck, and even though they had fallen from their mountings, it was noticeable that nearly all the observed cot frames in this area are in a far more robust state of preservation than those in the more exposed wards housed in the enclosed A and B promenades. Once again, ridges of caulking give the appearance of the decking being largely intact, indicating that even if the panelling had not been installed by November 1915, work on the internal outfitting in this area of the ship was at least underway.

With the recording of the reception room largely complete, the time had come to move further aft, entering the area previously occupied by the first-class dining saloon. At first glance, there was no indication of the wooden wall defining exactly where the reception room originally ended and the

Above: One of the lower wards in the *Britannic*, providing a useful indication of the standard of internal completion in some areas of the ship. (Angus & Jonathan Mitchell)

dining saloon began, which essentially would have been on a line with frame 20F, yet it seems evident that there was once a division of some description. Some traces of a dividing wall are still attached to the deck itself, beyond which, on the higher port side, a line of nine white porcelain WCs clearly indicate some of the makeshift sanitary arrangements installed by Harland & Wolff to suffice for some of the three thousand sick and wounded.

Beside the WCs there is still significant evidence of dozens of fallen bed frames,

Above: One of the sliding Bostwick gates for the lift lying on top of a fallen medical cot, which has come to rest on a seemingly undamaged deck support stanchion in the reception room. The ridges of caulking indicate that the flooring in this space was largely complete.
Above right: A closer view of the line of WCs, detailing the nature of the temporary arrangements carried out at Belfast to make the *Britannic* ready for war. What little remains of the base of the original oak partition is still attached to the steel deck.
Right: A revealing fish-eye image of a line of nine WCs, located in the approximate area where the wooden dividing wall between the first-class reception room and dining saloon would have been situated.

Top: Further aft in the area where the reception room and dining saloon meet. Note the several white ventilator covers lying in the debris.
Above: Closer detail of the ventilator covers, this one still attached to what little remains of the wooden ceiling.

interspersed with other assorted debris and lying on top of the casing that served boiler rooms 3 and 4. Included in this debris are a number of white, diamond-shaped metal grilles. There was nothing similar in the *Olympic* and *Titanic*'s dining saloon when the two ships entered service, which at first suggested that these ornate-looking objects may have been something to do with the medical fittings, until the sight of additional grilles fixed to the ceiling indicated a more meaningful improvement in the *Britannic*'s interiors.

When first entering service, there had been a number of issues with the ventilation in the *Olympic*'s dining saloon, so much so that additional fans were later fitted in a number of areas in the dining saloons in both the *Olympic* and *Titanic*. There was not enough time to improve the ventilation in the *Titanic* before the issue in the *Olympic* became apparent, but it seems evident from archival images that it was only by the late 1920s that a number of small grates, similar to those now scattered atop the *Britannic*'s funnel casings, had also been installed in the *Olympic*'s first-class dining saloon ceiling. Because work on the *Britannic* was less advanced, however, it would appear that Harland & Wolff had already improved on their original design during the earlier stages of the *Britannic*'s outfitting.

Beyond the aft edge of the funnel casing, in line with frame 13F, the room opens up to reveal the full width of the dining saloon. The area, which in happier times would have been occupied by the captain's table, is completely open, with absolutely nothing to see except for

Below: The first-class dining saloon, photographed at Belfast prior to the launch. (Harland & Wolff)

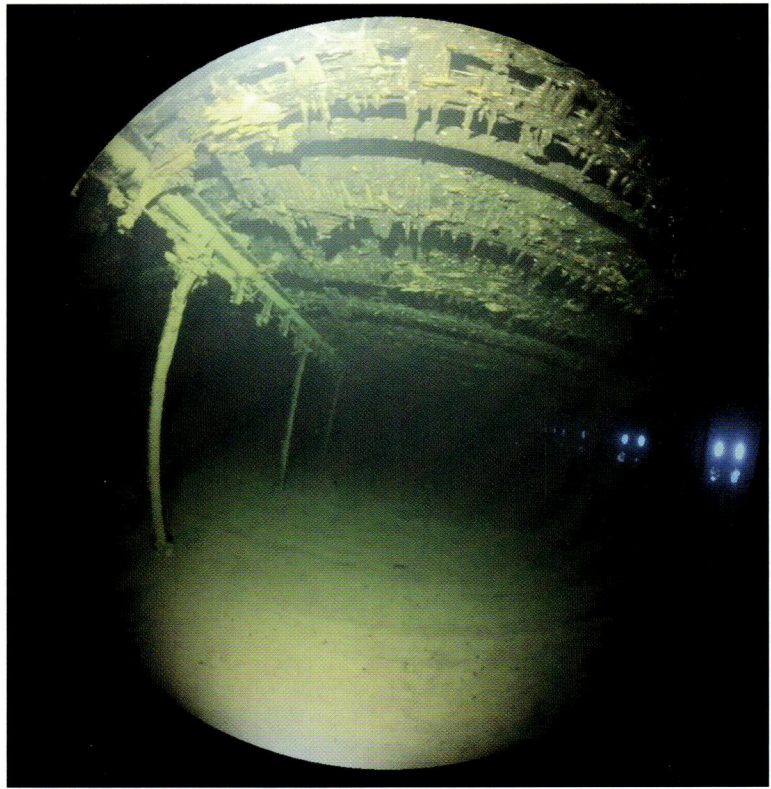

Above: The completely open void of what would have been the first-class dining saloon, taken in September 2023.

a single water fountain attached to the aft side of the boiler casing on the port side, as the available visibility gradually fades to black until it completely obscures any sight of the starboard bulkhead some 50 feet (15m) below. Looking forward, the limited illumination provided by the sun's blue-tinted light filtering through the distinctive line of double portholes overhead reveals only an empty space, beyond which lies the solid bulkhead at frame 19A, delineating what would have been the forward extent of the first-class pantry. It was barely 100 feet (30m) away, which would have been a walk in the park for an ROV, but for a manned diver, working at an approximate depth of 100 metres (328ft) and with a limited bottom time, it might just as well have been the far side of the moon. Even so, a huge amount of data on these important and, until now, previously unexplored internal spaces has already been pulled together from the imagery, and future exploration in this area, as we continue to survey the midship pantries, galley and second-class dining saloon, will only add to this knowledge of the *Britannic*'s military configuration.

Top: A fallen sink and other debris resting on the starboard side of the casing for boiler rooms 3 and 4.
Above: A drinking fountain, still attached to the aft side of the casing for boiler rooms 3 and 4.

10

THE UPPER AND MIDDLE DECKS

The working passage on the upper deck (E) was always going to be one of the potential goldmine areas in terms of accessing many of the *Britannic*'s internal spaces. This passage extended for the entire length of the superstructure, between frames 83F and 86A. While in the *Titanic* the passageway was completely open forward of the watertight door in bulkhead K, in the *Britannic* strategically placed watertight doors in frames 83F, 43F, 30A and 86A (bulkheads D, F, K and N, respectively) made the prospects of a successful penetration from one end of the passage to the other unlikely at best. The only way we were going to crack this particular nut was to adopt a more piecemeal approach.

The open port-side shell door, located between frames 78A and 81A, provided an ideal starting point, in theory making it possible to swim along this passageway to at least as far forward as the watertight door in bulkhead K, in the process taking us right into the areas originally inhabited by the ship's engineering officers. Although it looks straightforward enough on a deck plan, the dive team would effectively be entering another relatively unknown part of the ship, as this same area inside the hull of the *Titanic* is now little more than a devastated mass of steel, which collapsed and compacted as the stern section impacted with the sea floor and corkscrewed into the mud at the end of its 12,500-foot (3,800-metre) journey from the surface. With the *Britannic*'s aft hull still completely intact, however, it inevitably prompted the feeling that we were once again entering into dark territory, effectively making everything we were about to observe a completely new discovery.

Despite the shadowy gloom lurking just within the open shell door, as entrance points go this was by no means the most intimidating. More to the point, the Harland & Wolff deck plans indicated a reasonably open way forward, with little in the way of obstructions

Right: The open shell door, allowing the dive team to enter Scotland Road for the first time in 105 years.

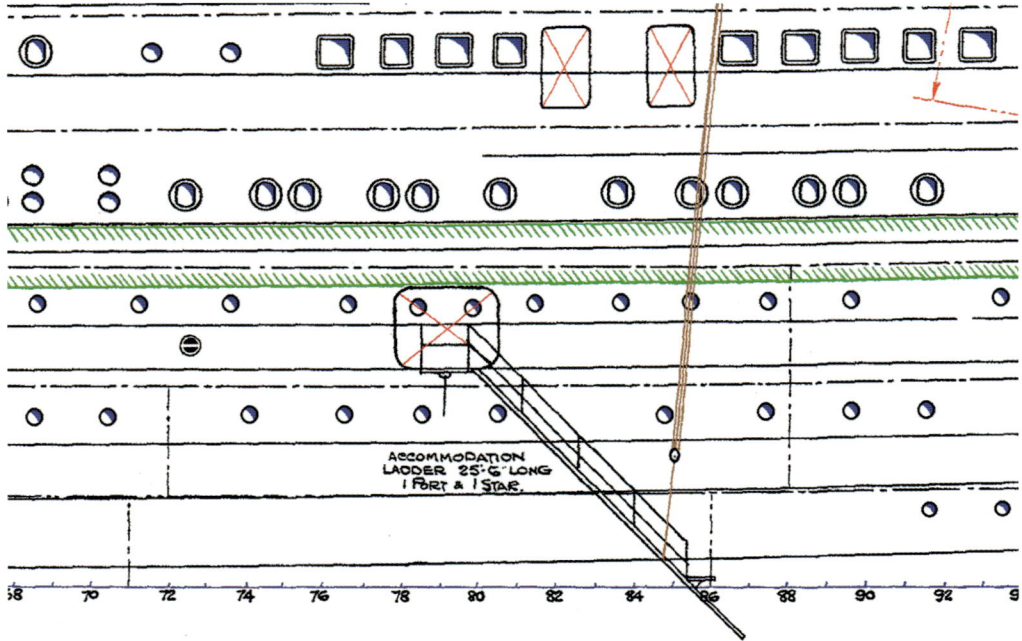

Above: A port elevation of the hull section incorporating the E deck shell door. (Harland & Wolff)

to impede the individual divers, although inconsistencies in the various drawings sometimes added to the element of expectation. One set of plans indicated that the first room immediately to the left of the shell door served as the potato wash room, which made sense as directly opposite was the potato storage room, whereas in another set of plans the room was clearly identified as the ship's printing room. The only way we would know for sure was to enter these spaces and, we hoped, find the desired physical evidence of the ship's printing press.

The way into the working passage was easy to locate, at the level of E deck and directly in line with the second-class entrance and elevator. Externally, the easiest reference point was the aft Armstrong davit on the boat deck, but the open door would prove to be as much a curse as a blessing. On the one hand it had simplified the point of entry into the hull, but on the other it also meant that the internal environment – at least in the area closest to the door itself – was more exposed to a combination of well-oxygenated water and light. As the divers moved through the opening, the sight of the two badly corroded metal bulkheads on either side of the door provided visual testimony that all may not be as well with the interiors in this part of the wreck as we had hoped. It was also an important telltale sign that this part of the interior would be in a far more advanced state of deterioration.

Almost immediately, to the right-hand side

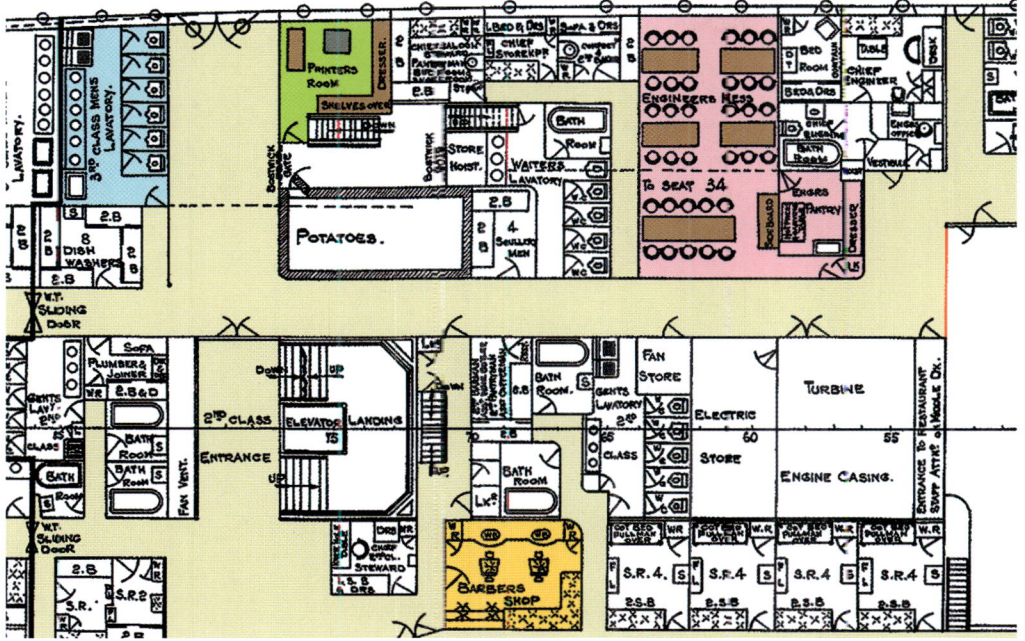

Above: General arrangement of the aft working passage leading to the reciprocating engine room casing. (Harland & Wolff)

of the entrance was the well-preserved tiled flooring of the third-class men's lavatory, the design identical to the non-slip tiles observed in the firemen's accommodation in the forecastle. The only noticeable difference was that while the tiles in the forecastle were of a lighter shade, Harland & Wolff had instead opted for a different colour combination of a red and darkish grey-blue colour scheme. Or so we thought. A quick wipe of a small surface area, however, indicated that what we were in fact seeing was a thin layer of marine growth, which, by darkening the floor, had only given the impression of a darker-coloured tile combination being used, the cleaned surface quickly revealing that they were in fact identical to the other tiles previously observed.

The six porcelain WCs remain firmly fixed to their mountings, although several are very badly cracked just above the base, suggesting that this damage may well have been caused by the shock of the impact as the stern section hit the seabed. After more than a century on the seabed, the wooden walls dividing the individual cubicles have long since disappeared, while the six stainless-steel wash basins, also minus their original wooden surround, remain firmly attached to the aft bulkhead. Two gleaming white urinals almost look as if they were installed only yesterday, although as with the WC bases their heavy backs are badly damaged, providing additional evidence, as if it were needed, of the stern's likely forceful impact on the seabed.

Moving further into the wreck, it was impossible to miss a fallen iron bar gate, balanced precariously over part of the doorway leading into the second-class entrance. The current location of this heavy gate, originally mounted just inside the shell door, probably owes more to decades of corrosion rather than damage caused during the sinking process, but of more concern was the gaping hole in the aft bulkhead of the hitherto mystery compartment. Much of the dividing wall has now disappeared completely, but on the other hand this unwelcome opening not only made entry into the area that much easier, but it also quickly revealed the ultimate use of the room. Almost immediately, a large mechanical device could be seen lying on top of another badly deteriorated bulkhead, balancing precariously above a stairwell, the prominent manual treadle at its base leaving little doubt that it was a manually operated printing press. The bolts securing the press to the steel deck had clearly failed long ago, but although largely intact, the advanced state of corrosion to the iron frame and mechanical parts suggest that considerable restoration work would be required if the press mechanism was ever to be restored to a working condition.

In practical terms, the printing process used in the *Britannic* would have been little

Above: The broken WCs of the third-class men's toilets, immediately to the right as the dive team entered the hull. The cleaned area of the floor's surface indicates that the ceramic tiles are identical to those used in the forecastle crew accommodations.

THE UPPER AND MIDDLE DECKS

Above: The base of the fallen Arab printing press resting against a badly corroded internal dividing wall.

different from the technique pioneered by Johannes Gutenberg in 15th-century Germany, using type blocks arranged by a compositor; the only real difference would have been that Gutenberg's system was more labour intensive, unlike the *Britannic*'s Arab Anglo-American press, which in this case was operated by a simple treadle. Large deposits of .918-inch lead typeface blocks also lie scattered over what remains of the badly corroded bulkhead directly above the stairwell, suggesting that if a retrieval of the printing press was ever to be contemplated, then such an operation would need to be carried out sooner rather than later, before this bulkhead gives way altogether. As to how much further the printing press might fall cannot be ascertained with any great certainty; the wall of the potato locker might still have enough integrity to arrest its downward journey, albeit temporarily, but in view of the proximity to the open shell door, the thinner metal in this area of the interior does appear to be corroding at an accelerated rate, effectively

Top: The printer's type face blocks lying scattered on top of the bulkhead next to the printing press, still in as good a condition as they were on the day the ship sank.
Above: A control switch for the store hoist.

casting doubt on the overall ability of the weakened internal structure to support as heavy an item as the printing press indefinitely.

Back in the working passage, there was only one direction of travel, which was forward and towards the bow. All the existing GA plans indicated that the route to the watertight door in bulkhead K, a mere 150 feet (46m) away, would be relatively open, and certainly wide enough that any experienced wreck diver would be able to take it in their stride, but while much of the imagery would retain a certain feeling of familiarity about it, at the same time everything seemed completely different. Inside the working passage is a world turned almost but not quite completely on its side, the former deck effectively transformed into the left side wall, while the pipes and trunking originally fixed to the ceiling are seemingly attached to a bulkhead to the right

The thinner steel walls of the second-class WCs and bathrooms now comprise what has effectively become the floor surface, and are covered in thick deposits of silt, which can be easily stirred up if the diver moves too quickly or gets too close to the surface. Numerous holes in the steel dividing walls between frames 62A and 63A provide glimpses of some of the otherwise well-preserved second-class bathrooms and WCs, while, hanging overhead,

Below: The space once occupied by the engineers' mess. Most of the iron table and chair supports remain attached to the steel deck, but most of the red linoleum tiles have detached

the equally corroded walls between frames 56A and 64A provide relatively easy access to the now open space of what would have been the engineers' mess, where many of the iron supports for the mess tables remain firmly in situ. The wooden tabletops themselves are long gone, but once again fragments of the original red and white linoleum tiles on the floor surface remain in place, providing a visual clue as to the standard of accommodation to which the White Star engineering officers in the Olympic class liners would have been accustomed.

Even though the standard of the steel preservation in this area of the ship had become a cause for concern, the general lack of remaining fabric inside the *Britannic* was more than offset by the fact that not only were we about to locate our first evidence of any surviving material inside the working passage, but also that it would be so well preserved. As the divers continued to move forward along the passage, a number of indistinct obstacles gradually began to appear ahead of them. These obstacles didn't present any great hazard in terms of blocking the way, but what was curious was that not only did the pile seem to resemble a jumble of mattress-like objects, but that the tightly woven mattress fabric (usually made from linen or cotton), and the tufting studs inserted through the layers of the mattress in order to keep the internal stuffing from moving or shifting, showed no sign whatsoever of any damage or deterioration. Later analysis would reveal that they were collision mats, specifically intended for damage control purposes. These mats were filled with kapok, known for its hydrophobic qualities, and would have been stored near vulnerable areas of the ship, such as the cargo holds and, so it would seem, the engine room spaces. Prior to the loss of the *Titanic*, collision mats were not supplied in merchant vessels, largely due to the additional training required for their effective use. They would have been held in place by timber baulking, most likely made from pine as large reserves of this relatively inexpensive wood were always retained in the shipyard's timber store, but while these mats would have sufficed for minor hull cracks or split plates, they would have been of no use in the case of major damage caused by a mine or torpedo. The more immediate question, however, is what were collision mats doing in a non-critical area some 15 feet (4.6m) above the load line?

We would soon have the answer. As the dive team continued to move forward, gradually the number of hanging obstructions began to increase, but although progress was still possible, it quickly became apparent why the overall level of damage was becoming so much more extensive than anticipated. Where the structure of the aft bulkhead of the reciprocating engine room should have been, instead there was only an open void. Looking up in the direction of the small suite of rooms that would have served as the quarters of Chief Engineer Robert Fleming – relocated from their original location one deck lower and on the starboard side in the *Olympic* and *Titanic* – the way forward was partially blocked by a large section of the devastated transverse metal bulkhead, which had previously served as the

Above: An unexpected pile of collision mats in the aft working passage provided the first indication of any fabrics having been preserved, either on or inside the wreck itself.

rear bulkhead of the reciprocating engine casing on that deck at frame 53A. Unlike the damage already observed further aft in the working passage, however, whatever had happened here was clearly not the result of any long-term corrosion. If anything, the scale of the destruction and the nature of the twisted angle of the blown-out bulkhead provided compelling evidence as to the speed and force of the seawater flowing into the previously un-flooded aft compartments in the ship, so great that it was strong enough to tear through the lighter metal wall structures in this area.

Without a closer examination of the damage, there was little possibility of making any further progress along this section of the working passage, but, on the other hand, while the damage had effectively halted the way forward to the watertight door, by default it had, if anything, made the way into the reciprocating engine room compartment that much easier.

Lateral thinking

What I came to refer to as 'Point X', located at the bottom of the forward main entrance staircase on the E deck landing, served as an ideal jumping-off point for two potential

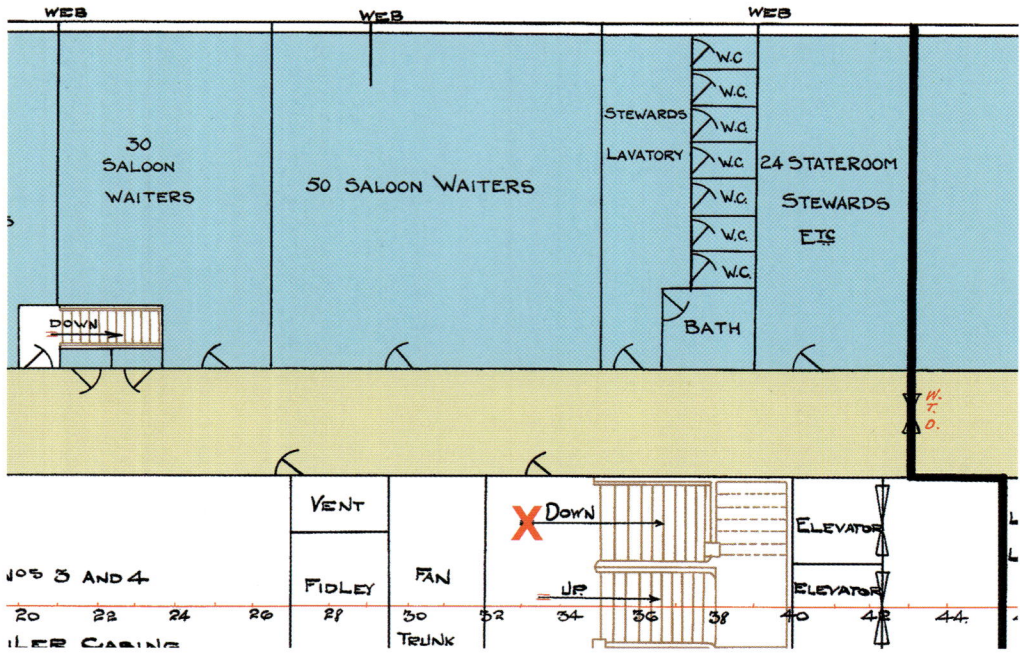

Above: Point X, at the top of the E deck landing, would provide the ideal jumping off point for the survey of the Turkish bath, and the mid-section of Scotland Road.

penetrations. On the one hand it was located right at the top of the small stairwell leading down to the Turkish bath on F deck, while an open doorway immediately above the diver's head led directly into the midship section of the main Scotland Road working passage. Once inside this area, a diver has the option to turn right and head forward, until reaching the watertight door in bulkhead F – a journey of little more than 30 feet (9m) – or they could instead turn left and head aft, potentially as far as the watertight door in bulkhead K, a journey of approximately 180 feet (55m).

I had fully expected each of these penetrations to be relatively straightforward surveys of the areas in question, although the notion of entering the Turkish bath was one I had been toying with for 18 years, ever since James Cameron had obtained his remarkable imagery from inside *Titanic*'s cooling room in 2005. My hope was that we would find an equally colourful interior inside the *Britannic*, and while much of the wood panelling throughout the ship had not been installed, the fact that there was no known reference to the sale of the Pilkington tiles in the post-war auction of the *Britannic*'s fittings suggested that maybe – just maybe – there would be a pleasant surprise awaiting us. In neither case, however, had it ever occurred to me that within a few hours the resulting imagery would also provide a totally different dynamic as to how and why the *Britannic* may have sunk.

The date was 1 October 2023, our final day

of diving on the 2023 expedition. Divers Perry Brandes and Barry McGill had been tasked with a final survey of the stokehold crew's quarters and cargo hold 1 in the forecastle, Stewie Andrews and Katy Kohler were headed for some additional imagery of the gymnasium and first-class lounge, while Evan Kovacs and Richie Kohler had the prize of entering the Turkish bath cooling room. I also asked them to make a detour on the return journey, if time permitted, for a quick look at the forward watertight door in Scotland Road. With the infamous Meltemi wind threatening once again to stir up the Kea Channel, potentially wreaking havoc on the divers' proposed in-water decompression schedule, I always knew this was no small thing to be asking, but if they encountered no unexpected problems in the cooling room then I was confident that they would get the job done.

After a quarter of a century analysing *Britannic* wreck footage, there are always a number of penetrations that will stand out in the memory, and Rich Stevenson's 2003 penetration of the forward pipe tunnel and the first images of the two open watertight

Above: The top of the E deck landing, leading down to the Turkish bath one deck below.

doors leading into the forward stokehold of boiler room 6 will forever be one of my highlights in the annals of *Britannic* exploration, even if the available lighting and Mini DV tapes of 20 years earlier lack the resolution of today's modern 4K digital cameras. The available diving and imaging technology may have come on in leaps and bounds over the last 20 years, but even then it means little if divers do not know where they are going, or what to look for. On this, their seventh expedition to the wreck, Evan and Richie knew exactly what I needed, and they knew exactly how to get there. Video logs tend to be rather detached records, with few of the 150 words below conveying anything like the excitement at what I was seeing on my laptop screen at the time, but when analysing the final day's footage from the 2023 expedition, the results would be totally unexpected:

00:00: At level of boat deck, near shot line.
01.30: Enter through window into main entrance.
02.20: Begin staircase descent.
02.55: At level of D deck (Marconi tuner resting on beam).
05.05: Reach E deck landing.
05.26: At door to Turkish bath (partially obscured by debris, but enough room to get past).
05.43: Enter Turkish bath door (vestibule gone, so straight into the cooling room). Wood and tiles visible, and a few fallen light fittings. (Many tiles have now fallen, but the pattern is very different from tiles in Ken's 2005 *Titanic* mosaic.) Long rusticle...
10.34: Exit Turkish bath, back into area at the bottom of the F deck staircase. WTD partially open. Heading back up.
11:57: Cross threshold and up into Scotland Road (caulking very evident again). Turn towards WTD.
12:30: Arrive at WTD (Open).
13:20: Turn back.
15:20: Back in staircase at level of promenade deck when camera cuts.

While the large number of fallen tiles in the Turkish bath was a disappointment, the fact that fairly substantial sections of the tiling were still intact, and that so much colour was still visible, provided a welcome relief to the monotony of bare metal walls and red Veitchi flooring that permeate much of the wreck's interior. The chances are that the tiles on the lower starboard side will be much better preserved, although some silt would still need to be excavated in order to reveal them, but the option for future investigation of the Turkish bath's steam, hot and temperate rooms is now also a distinct possibility. In that the decoration in the cooling room was largely complete, with the exception of the floor where there is no evidence of any tiles having

Top right: The layout of the *Britannic*'s Turkish bath was practically identical to that in the *Titanic*, but differed considerably to the original concept in the *Olympic*. (Harland & Wolff)
Bottom right: The concept drawings indicated that the decorative style in the *Britannic*'s cooling room would be considerably different from the earlier ships. (Harland & Wolff)

THE UPPER AND MIDDLE DECKS

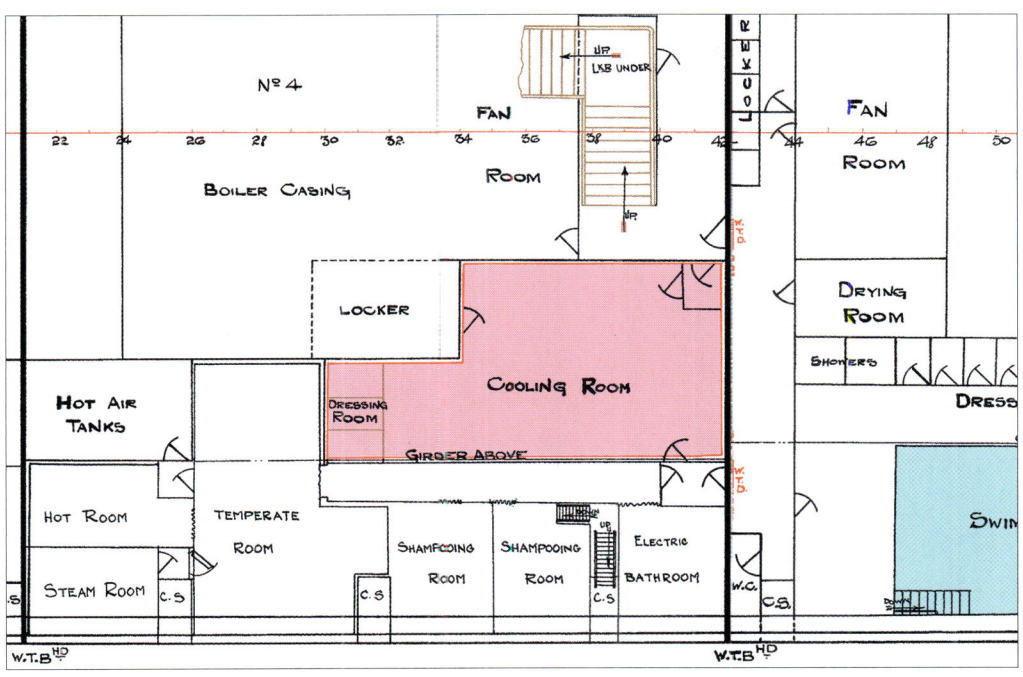

This page and opposite: The surviving tiling in the cooling room confirms that these spaces were totally different when compared to the 2005 *Titanic* images.

Above: Moving aft along Scotland Road, the casing of boiler rooms 3 & 4 now supports much of the as yet unidentified debris in this section of the working passage.

been laid, there remains the distinct possibility that all three of these other spaces might also have been in an advanced stage of completion.

Aside from the imagery of the cooling room tiles, however, the last 15 minutes of the 2023 footage also contained something completely unexpected, and something that would turn many of my previous beliefs on their head.

In the space of two minutes, between 10.34 and 12.30 minutes into the footage, we imaged two of the *Britannic*'s forward watertight doors. This comes as no great surprise, as the route into the Turkish bath passed directly next to a watertight door leading into the passageway that led straight to the ship's swimming pool on the lower starboard side. Similarly, the watertight door in Scotland Road was a target that we had purposefully set out to image on this last dive of the expedition. I had fully expected to see both doors in the closed position, and yet when viewing the imagery I was staggered to see that not only was the door in Scotland Road completely unsecured, but the watertight door outside the Turkish bath was only partially closed. Both of these watertight doors were an integral part of bulkhead F, which, crucially, is the sixth bulkhead from the ship's bow. The fact that the two vertical drop-down watertight doors leading from the forward pipe tunnel into boiler room 6 had failed to close, as well as the watertight door between boiler rooms 6 and 5, had been acknowledged in the original report of the naval inquiry into the sinking, but,

Right: An open space where the door leading to the boiler rooms below once stood.

crucially, paragraph 7 of that same report had stated: 'We are confident that no water penetrated abaft No. 5 stokehold in the lower part of the ship.'

Much has been made in the history books of the *Britannic*'s increased watertight subdivision following the *Titanic* disaster, leading many to speculate as to how and why she sank at all. If Harland & Wolff's claim that the *Britannic* could float with all six of her forward compartments flooded was true then she ought to have survived the mine explosion, even with the two forward boiler rooms flooded. It is clear that this claim was not just marketing hyperbole on the part of the shipbuilder. The White Star Line was certainly confident that they had resolved all the deficiencies highlighted in the loss of the *Titanic*, and that the *Britannic* would have been able to survive the scale of damage inflicted by the iceberg on her unfortunate sibling; and for proof positive we need look no further than an official letter written on 28 September 1915 by Harold Sanderson, then White Star chairman, to the Director of Transports at the Admiralty. The rationale behind Sanderson's letter was to request that the Admiralty revise their first cost valuation of the SS *Olympic* for wartime insurance purposes, so that the additional £156,501 incurred in augmenting the ship's powers of flotation following the company's 'unfortunate experience with the *Titanic*' could be factored into the first cost calculations, on which the depreciated insurance value of the ship would be fixed:

'The object of these alterations is, of course, to increase the ship's powers of flotation, the result attained being that at her designed draft the bulkhead arrangements alone will enable her to float with six compartments open to the sea. I doubt very much if any other ship in existence, with the exception of her sister the new *Britannic*, has powers of flotation equal to this.'

As to why these two doors are open, we can only speculate. The watertight door outside the Turkish bath is at least partially closed, a gap of approximately 6 inches (15cm) suggesting that its failure to close may also be linked to the issue of a twisted bulkhead or runner, even though the watertight door in bulkhead F at the level of the tank top between boiler rooms 5 and 4, according to the report, was still able to close. As for the watertight door in Scotland Road, it still hangs in the same open position that it has assumed for more than a century. Unlike heavier conventional watertight doors fitted in areas at a high risk of flooding, which were operated either vertically or horizontally by a ratchet and cog system and when closed effectively became a key part of the bulkhead structure, these lighter doors were not classed by Lloyd's as being either fully watertight or fire resistant; consequently they were fitted in locations well above the freeboard waterline, and would have played little part in the structural integrity of the actual bulkhead. Even so, the sight of the open watertight door was not at all what I had expected to see, the door's current attitude suggesting that it probably swung free from its open position due to the *Britannic*'s

Above: The watertight door in bulkhead F. Imaging this door had always been on the list, but finding it to be open, on the very last day of the 2023 expedition, was totally unexpected.

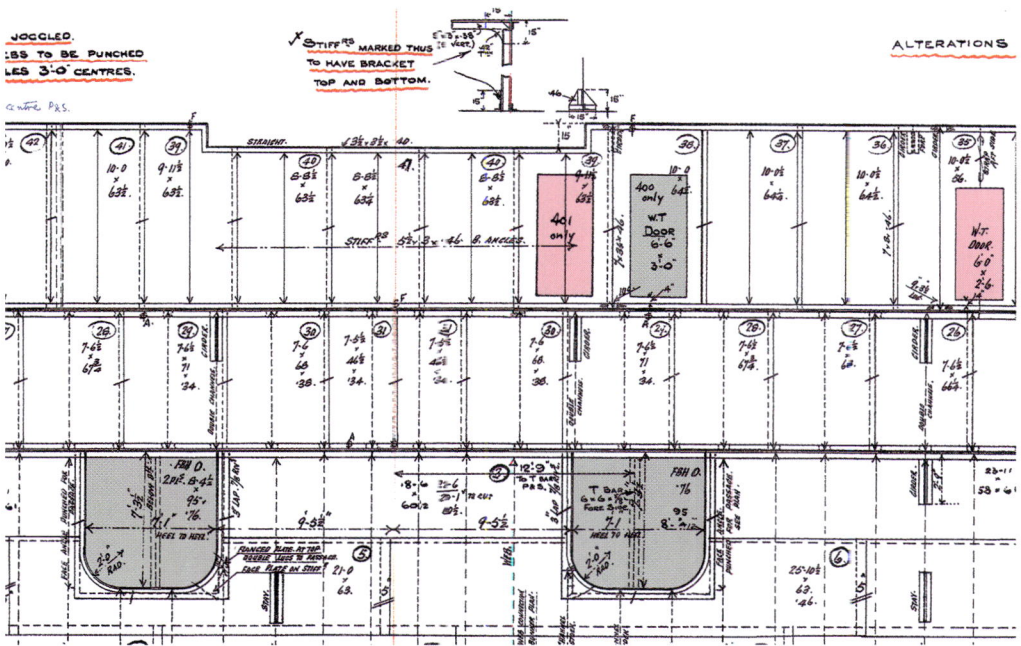

Above: Bulkhead F, detailing the watertight door arrangements at the level of F deck in all three ships. (Harland & Wolff)

THE UPPER AND MIDDLE DECKS

Above: A closer view of the opening in the inboard F deck watertight door, estimated to be in the region of 6 inches (15cm).
Left: A closer view of the debris against the doorway leading into the cooling room of the Turkish bath.

increasingly heavy list to starboard.

The fact that these two doors are open at all suggests that it was very likely that the additional water ingress into the crucial seventh compartment at the level of the upper and middle decks may well have been a decisive factor in undermining the *Britannic*'s ability to survive the mine explosion. Despite the White Star Line's confidence in September 1915 that the *Olympic* and *Britannic*, on paper at least, were still considered to be practically unsinkable, the inescapable fact is that all the strengthened bulkheads and increased watertight subdivision in the world means nothing if the watertight doors cannot be closed. As a result of what we have now found inside the *Britannic*, while bulkhead F may well have extended as high as the underside of the bridge deck, it would seem that the ship's margin of survival on the morning of 21 November 1916 would have been little different from that of the *Titanic* a little over four years earlier.

11

THE TANK TOP

Although the torpedo theory is now largely debunked, there is little doubt as to the ultimate cause of death in the case of the *Britannic*. At 08.12 hrs, on the morning of Tuesday 21 November 1916, she steamed into a minefield, laid some three weeks earlier in the Kea Channel by the German submarine *U73*, and sank 55 minutes later after succumbing to the injuries sustained in the attack. Case closed.

Insofar as the basics are concerned, perhaps the case is closed, but as with any investigation it is generally the post-mortem that fills in the all-important gaps in the overall picture. In the case of the *Britannic*, we may now know what caused the fatal injury, but it is only recently that we have been able to reflect more meaningfully on the nature of the damage caused to the hull itself. As with any autopsy, the investigation involves examining the vital areas of the body, usually starting with the initial wound, and in this respect even after a hundred years the wreck still provides us with an obvious starting point. Not only that, but the British naval inquiry into the loss of the *Britannic* clearly records the detail of the circumstances immediately following the explosion:

1. There was one explosion only, low down on the starboard side in the vicinity of the bulkhead between holds 2 and 3.
2. The bulkhead between holds 2 and 3 was damaged, allowing both compartments to flood.
3. The bulkhead between holds 1 and 2 was also damaged, and water found its way into hold 1.
4. The bulkhead between hold 3 and boiler room 6 appeared to be undamaged, but water gained free access through the open watertight doors between the forward stokehold and the tunnel, which had not closed.
5. Water also had free access to stokehold 5 via the watertight door between boiler rooms 6 and 5, this door being only 'partly closed' at best.

Left: One of the *Britannic*'s two turbine sluice valves, photographed at Belfast by Robert Welch during construction. It is interesting to compare this image with the photograph taken in September 2023, on page 223. (Harland & Wolff)

Based on the information contained within the report, there can be no doubt that at least five of the *Britannic*'s forward compartments were open to the sea – probably even all six. This scale of damage seems largely to tally with the length of the damage inflicted on the *Titanic*'s hull by the iceberg, and yet, despite the increased safety modifications, the *Britannic* sank three times faster than her elder sibling, with the apparent failure of the watertight doors to close pointing to an issue that had not been a factor in the loss of the *Titanic*.

While the question inevitably arises as to why these additional built-in safety features had failed so catastrophically, we need to keep in mind that the Olympic class design, in common with most mercantile vessels, made little or no allowance for such hazards as mines or torpedoes. Indeed, the *Britannic* was by no means the only mercantile vessel to experience this problem. In March 1917 the damage inflicted by a single torpedo on the stern of the hospital ship *Asturias*, another Harland & Wolff vessel of a similar vintage to the *Britannic*, was so extensive that because the bulkheads and framework in the vicinity of the explosion were so distorted, the watertight doors in the aft pipe tunnel had failed to close completely. The hospital ship *Dover Castle* was also torpedoed, in May 1917, and this ship's second engineer would later testify that one of the engine room watertight doors would not move after the ship was struck, while the report into the torpedoing of the ambulance transport *Warilda*, in August 1918, also includes a reference to one of the bulkheads immediately above the location of the explosion having been so warped by the concussion that the watertight door could not be fully closed. With the issue of a mercantile ship's framework or bulkheads being so vulnerable to the shock loading following an in-water explosion, the notion of looking for some careless design flaw therefore seemed pointless. A closer inspection of the watertight doors' closing mechanisms would certainly be the best option, but the only way to do that would be to get inside the forward boiler rooms, and the most direct path to achieve that goal would be to take the exact same route used by the *Britannic*'s stokehold crew.

The firemen's tunnel

The damaged hull structure beneath the forward well deck may seem outwardly daunting, but without question the break in the forward hull at the location of bulkhead C still provided relatively straightforward access into the firemen's tunnel. The tunnel had originally extended over a length of a little over 100 feet (30m), between bulkheads B and D (frames 114F to 78F), but, despite the jumble of twisted steel, the nature of the break in the lower part of the hull seems to be remarkably clean. The opening where the watertight tunnel passes through bulkhead C can be quickly located, with the reasonably intact aft section of the tunnel, extending for a further length of 51 feet (15.5m), leading directly to boiler room 6. Despite the devastation to holds 2 and 3, the aft section of the tunnel retains much of its structural

THE TANK TOP

Above: The two forward watertight doors, at either end of the vestibule leading to boiler room 6.

integrity, with the raised walkway still in place, guiding a diver to the first of the vertical dropping watertight doors in frame 78F; the second watertight door, in frame 75F, is barely 10 feet (3m) further aft, no more than the width of the transverse coal bunkers located on either side of the vestibule.

At first glance, everything appears to be in a reasonably intact condition. The bulkheads show no immediate sign of any potential warping, although it has to be said that the necessary engineering tolerances required in an efficiently functioning watertight door would probably have been extremely tight, meaning that even the smallest damage to the frames or door guides, invisible to the naked eye, could have had a significant effect. The problem may be due to the fact that the hull frames or bulkheads close to the explosion were warped by the initial blast, although with the three doors also being the furthest forward from the mid-point of the hull, they were perhaps more susceptible to the violent vibrations and more extensive hull movement that may have occurred in the forward part of the ship immediately afterwards. The phenomenon is more commonly referred to as a hull whipping response, resulting in the rapid flexing of the hull girder following an impact in the flat bottom of a ship with anything from a wave to an underwater explosion, the net result being increased vertical bending moments and shear forces.

Aside from the potential warping of the guides into which the watertight doors dropped, there was also another potential cause taken into consideration at Belfast. After the *Britannic* had been lost, there were a number of discussions at the Board of Trade regarding the possibility of side pressure, caused by a head of water on one side of a watertight door, holding it open after release. At some stage, Harland & Wolff were also asked to carry out tests to ascertain the amount of side pressure that would be necessary to prevent a watertight door from closing, although for reasons unknown those tests were apparently never carried out. Then again, following the *Olympic*'s post-war reconstruction and conversion of the dropping watertight doors to a type that could be opened and closed by electrical power, by that stage the tests would probably have been less pertinent anyway. One thing, however, is very clear from even the most cursory visual inspection: there is no evidence whatsoever to suggest that any of the three doors had been prevented from closing through the jamming of unidentified pieces of wreckage or other obstructions in the door openings. Not only is there no significant debris in the vestibule itself, but the fact that neither of the two watertight doors are even partially closed seems to confirm that, most likely, one of the aforementioned structural issues resulted in their failure to close.

Boiler rooms 6 and 5

Despite the passage of time, the frustration of the 2006 expedition coming so close to reaching the third watertight door remained an open wound. The way forward was clear,

Above: To the left, one of the illuminated boiler room telegraphs manufactured by Evershed & Vignoles of London; to the right, a Kilroy stoking indicator, each covered in silt but otherwise as well preserved as the day the ship sank.

and, crucially, the data within the *Britannic*'s specification book confirmed that while it would be a tight squeeze, it could be done:

> 'The Boiler seats to be of the built type, the plates having lightening holes and stiffened by large double angles on the edges; these stools to be connected to the tank top by large fore and aft brackets. Two stools to be fitted in each S.E. Boiler and four to each D.E. Boiler. The centre Boilers to be kept 2'6" clear above the tank top, and the wing boilers 2'0".'

Fate unfortunately decreed that a single fallen wheelbarrow would frustrate our efforts in 2006, but in June 2015 another opportunity would arise, and the resulting imagery of the two forward boiler rooms would be a revelation.

Moving aft of the vestibule and into stokehold 11, the immediate sight of the four huge Scotch marine boilers, still firmly planted on their individual stools, confirmed that there was no indication of any significant movement having occurred over the 12-year interval since they had first been observed. All the boilers, along with their uptakes and associated steam piping, seemingly remained as firmly fixed as they were on the day the ship sank, while a closer visual analysis of these two compartments has so far revealed no evidence of any significant internal damage being sustained during the sinking. Even the gleaming faces of the boiler room telegraphs and stoking indicators display few signs of any noticeable deterioration, save for the occasional rusticle hanging down towards the lower starboard side.

At first glance they are very different from the forests of rusticles that have completely overrun the exterior of the *Titanic*, or, come to that, the larger and more robust-looking rusticles on the deeper sections of the *Britannic*'s exterior, the enclosed and pitch-black environment of the boiler rooms having instead resulted in a significant number of elongated and incredibly fragile-looking structures. Presumably this is due to the almost total lack of any current in these sealed spaces, or of any light-sensitive marine life finding its way into the darkened bowels of the ship. If we were ever looking for an anaerobic interior inside the *Britannic*, then this is surely it.

Suddenly, elements of the *Britannic*'s human story were also starting to come into clearer focus. The trimmer's wheelbarrow from 2006 had been a less cheery reminder of the men who had originally toiled in the heat and filthy boiler room spaces, but there were other indications of the firemen and trimmers who had been on duty on the morning the ship was sunk. The damper handles were still fixed firmly in their original positions, but perhaps the most telling evidence of the men who had once worked in this compartment was the sight of a single fireman's shovel, still buried in the ashes of one of the Morison-type boiler furnaces. Even after more than a century on the seabed, this shovel is a forceful reminder of the moment the water came flooding into the compartment, forcing the stokehold crew to abandon their posts, according to the

Above: One of the furnaces in boiler room 5, with a stoker's shovel still buried in the ashes after more than a hundred years.

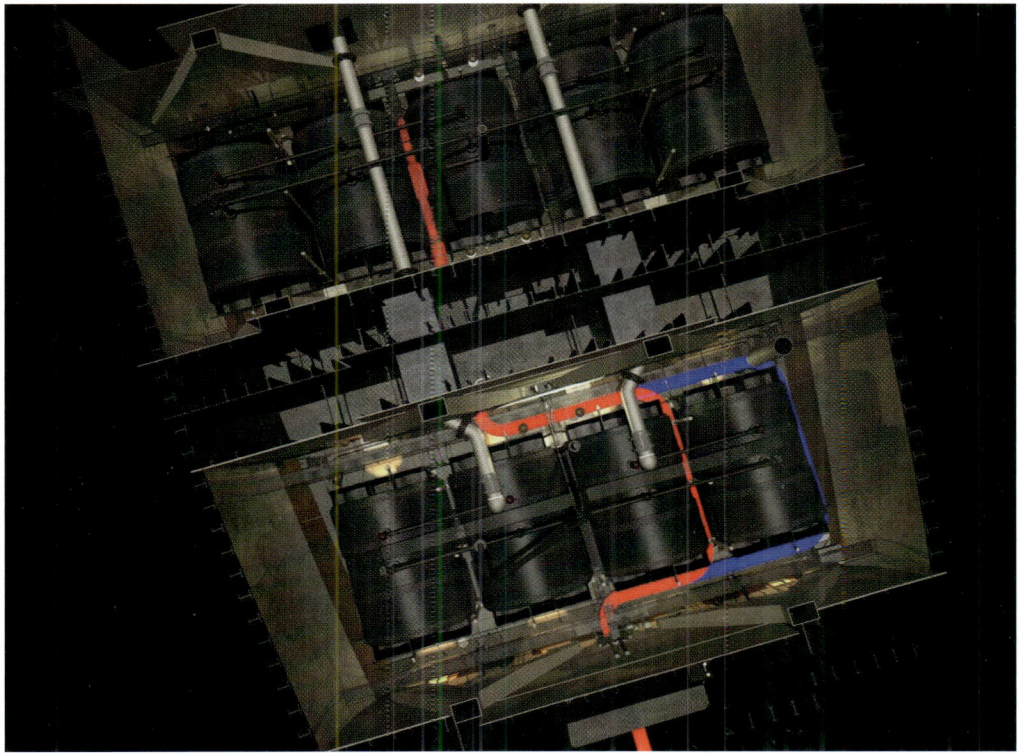

Above: The diver's route beneath the boilers to the third watertight door. (Parks Stephenson)

official report, within a couple of minutes.

Planning a way further aft, the tank top itself appeared to be in an equally robust condition, its surface composed of the same chequered steel plate found in the structure of the walking platform in the forward pipe tunnel. Standing some 5 feet 3 inches (1.6m) above the keel, the surface carries out from the centreline to each side of the compartment, but with thicker plating throughout the engineering spaces and with additional stiffening beneath the boiler bearers. Even so, the next stage was by no means a task for the faint-hearted. Boiler room 6 is barely 54 feet (16.5m) in length, but the passage to the next compartment could only be undertaken by squeezing between – or, more accurately, beneath – one of the 105-ton boilers, and while the structure may have looked substantially intact, the divers would still need to display additional caution when wedged into such an enclosed space, particularly with an unwieldy rebreather strapped to their back.

The confined area itself extended no more than the overall length of the 21-foot (6.4m) boilers, and immediately upon entering the more open space of what would have been stokehold 10, a curious grid-like opening in

Above and opposite right: The grate and pump machinery for the Stone's ash expeller, as opposed to the See's ash expellers fitted in the *Olympic* and *Titanic*.

the tank top came into view. This grate represented another of the internal design modifications in the improved *Britannic*. Whereas the *Olympic* and *Titanic* were equipped with See's ash ejectors, whereby the boiler ash was fed into a water jet and pumped up an inclined pipe until being discharged from the side of the ship near the surface, the *Britannic* was instead fitted with Stone's ash ejectors. The ash was still fed into a discharge hopper, but instead of being pumped towards the surface, it was instead discharged directly through the ship's double bottom. This ejector,

along with the pump located in a small recess directly behind it, remains completely intact, with only the layers of silt or the occasional rusticle giving any indication of it having lain dormant for over a century. More importantly, the recess where the pump was located also marked the forward extent of the compartment's aft port-side coal bunker. This transverse bunker was divided in two by the watertight bulkhead separating boiler rooms 6 and 5, meaning we were finally on the verge of imaging the crucial watertight door into boiler room 5. Although the evidence contained within the report clearly stated that this third watertight door had failed to close, the sight that greeted us was not at all what had been expected. The naval inquiry into the sinking had noted that there was some evidence to suggest it may have been at least 'partially closed', yet the resulting footage indicated that the opening was in fact as wide open as the previous two watertight doors in the forward vestibule. Once again, there was no evidence of any debris having obstructed the opening, but nor was there any evidence of the door having closed to even the slightest degree. More importantly, the open space of stokehold 9, at the forward end of boiler room 5, provided even more room to obtain better images of parts of the door itself, which were less visible in the forward vestibule, including the lowering mechanism and the keyway, where a detachable handle would have been used to manually operate the door itself. Sadly, there was no sign of the handle in the keyway, but perhaps it lies nearby...

In reaching bulkhead E, we had finally obtained images of the crucial watertight

Top: The frozen mechanism of the watertight door between boiler rooms 6 and 5.
Above: The manual control for lowering the watertight door. The detachable key to operate the mechanism has not yet been found.

door, which, prior to 2003, I had thought to be all but impossible. I even remember timing the exit time from the third watertight door to the original entry point in the forward tunnel, a swim that took marginally under six minutes and yet represented the work of four separate expeditions, spread over a 12-year period. The question of the third watertight door had finally been resolved, yet others remained. Even with the two forward boiler rooms flooded, the water should still have been sufficiently contained for the *Britannic*, supposedly capable of floating with her forward six compartments open to the sea, to remain afloat. So what had gone wrong?

It is here that the laws of physics take on a more telling role in the story. As a result of the forward three watertight doors' failure to work, not only had two additional spaces equating to approximately 9,500 square feet (882 sq m) been subjected to flooding, but the influx of such a large volume of moving liquid in the partially filled compartments would have resulted in significant dynamic forces acting against the righting effect of the ship. This movement of water is known as a 'free surface effect', and it is more than likely that this internal motion would have been the primary cause of the *Britannic*'s initial starboard list, which ultimately led to the ship's capsize. In heavier seas, this movement can result in a virtual positive feedback loop, with each roll becoming more and more extreme to the point where a vessel ultimately capsizes, as happened with the *Herald of Free Enterprise*, a roll-on/roll-off ferry that departed from Zeebrugge on 6 March 1987 with the bow doors in the open position. The *Britannic*'s transverse watertight bulkheads had at least helped to partially contain the flooding, with the result that the ship took almost an hour before losing the last vestiges of stability, whereas the *Herald*'s undivided car deck allowed the water to flow unimpeded from one end of the vessel to the other, before rolling over and capsizing to port in barely 90 seconds.

There can be no comparison between the actions taken by Captain Bartlett on the *Britannic* with the shortcomings displayed by the key personnel when the *Herald* sank, but where the two cases are similar is the manner of the flooding. Not only did the *Britannic*'s boiler rooms straddle the centreline of the ship, extending the full width of the hull, but as the list to starboard gradually increased, just as it did in the *Normandie*, which capsized to port in a single continuous roll as the weight of seawater from the New York fireboats overwhelmed the stability of the ship, this gradual roll instigated a chain of events from which the *Britannic* would never recover. As a result, within 15 minutes of the explosion the forward scuttles on the lower starboard side of E deck were awash, at which point the *Britannic*'s remaining time above the surface could be counted in minutes.

Despite the similarities in the sinking of the *Britannic*, the *Normandie* and the *Herald of Free Enterprise*, we can at least be practically certain of one thing. If any one of the *Britannic*'s three forward watertight doors had been properly closed, the ship would not now be lying at the bottom of the Kea Channel.

The reciprocating engine room

On 7 December 1915, 18-year-old Richard Lee, an apprentice at Harland & Wolff, had been appointed 'pupil in charge' of the tug *Herculaneum* at Queen's Island to attend the steam trials of the *Britannic*. Lee was so excited by the honour that the night before the trials he took home the White Star house flag, which would be flown from the tug's masthead, lying awake for most of the night before boarding the tug at 8.30 the following morning. Like any impressionable teenager, he never forgot the sight of the five tugs starting to move the gleaming white hull of the *Britannic*, with her yellow funnels, green hull band and red crosses, and he later wrote of feeling that the *Britannic* had far better proportions and balance than the *Olympic* or *Titanic*; from any angle, she was what he could only describe as 'aristocratic'. Later that day, however, this seemingly beautiful creature would cause him no end of grief.

By the time *Herculaneum* arrived off Bangor to escort the *Britannic* back up Belfast Lough, it was 5.30pm, the light was fading fast and the sea conditions were far from ideal. To make matters worse, as a light fog began to rise, the tug's hard-bitten skipper was urging the inexperienced youngster to order the return to Belfast. Not one to be pressured, for a while Lee stood his ground, but by 7:30pm the fog was thickening and the tug skipper remained convinced that no captain would take a ship the size of the *Britannic* into the Lough at night in fog like that. By this time, Lee was beginning to wish he had never even heard the name *Britannic*, and he seemed to be getting no help whatsoever from the tug skipper, who refused to put him ashore at Bangor in order to phone Harland & Wolff for instructions. Then, all of a sudden, the deep pulsations of three large chime whistles sounded over their heads; as the skipper snapped the tugs telegraph to 'full astern', the *Britannic*'s huge white hull suddenly appeared out of the fog, towering over the *Herculaneum*'s masthead.

Within minutes, the tug had made fast to the liner's starboard side, as Lee clambered up a shipyard ladder on his way to the bridge. As soon as he had delivered the dispatches to Captain Ranson, he quickly made his way down to the engine room doors to collect a number of engine room officers whom he was to convey back to Belfast, recording the impressions of his one and only visit into the *Britannic*'s engine rooms:

> 'I looked into a cathedral of steel; pink-tinted arc lights softly lit the two *gigantic* reciprocating engines' (the largest ever made) polished steel, brass and copper work and through it all the weird soft wails of the feed pumps, puffing auxiliaries and sitting on the cylinder tops and the steel stanchion rails some sixty E.R.A.s in brown boiler suits singing, 'We Are Here Because We Are Here'. Never shall I forget that scene of power and beauty in the heart of a lovely vessel.'

While Richard Lee might never have forgotten his impressions of the *Britannic*'s engine rooms, when entering this part of the

Above: The *Britannic*'s reciprocating engine room during fitting out, taken from the location of the forward low-pressure cylinder on the port side. (Harland & Wolff)

ship I had few illusions of finding a pristine environment to rival his memories of that glorious day. There was every possibility that after more than a century lying on their sides, the massive engine bedplates would have broken free from the tank top itself, leaving little more than a pile of broken and twisted machinery in the lower reaches of the starboard side. On the other hand, there was always the hope that maybe – just maybe – things might not be quite so bad.

It was only in 2015 that a closer submersible inspection of the skylight above the reciprocating engine room indicated that the way into this compartment may not have been as complicated as originally thought. Parts of the skylight were undoubtedly still intact, but looking along and into the cavernous opening it was clear that despite the tangle of fallen lifeboat gantries, a large enough path existed for a team of divers to enter what is almost certainly the most fascinating compartment of the wreck.

It's strange to think that, after years of trying to plan a single route into the reciprocating engine compartment, by the end of the 2021 expedition we had actually mapped out three. The successful penetration

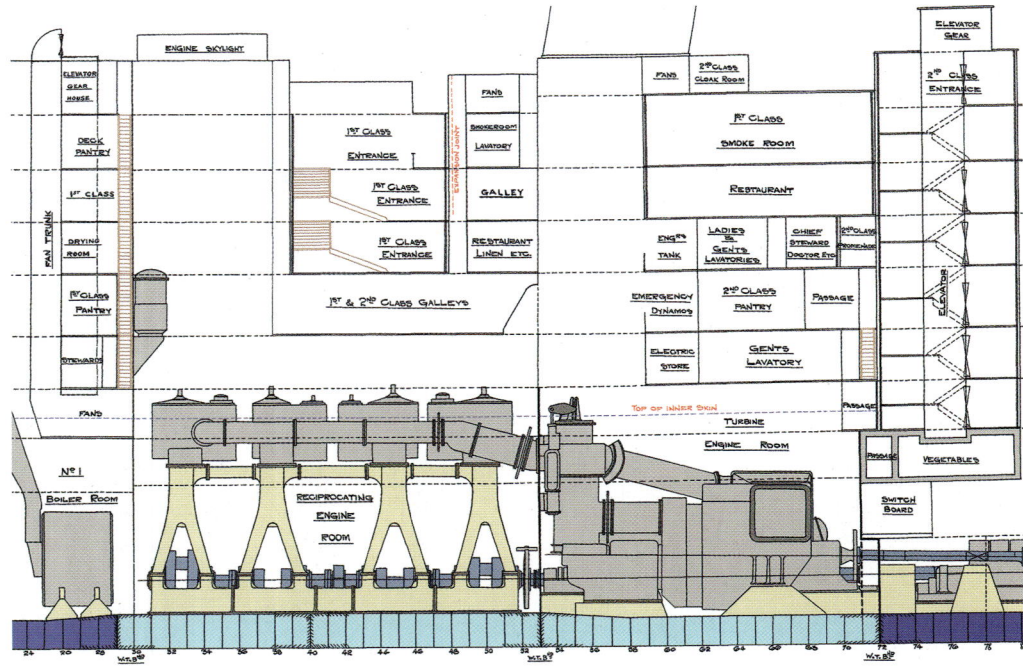

Above: Elevation of the reciprocating and turbine engine rooms. (Harland & Wolff)

along the E deck working passage and into the reciprocating engine room via the collapsed casing wall was a particular highlight, but while that damage is a cause for some anxiety, of more concern is the partial collapse observed of the compartment's forward bulkhead (K) at the approximate level of E deck. During a penetration from the first-class lounge pantry on the promenade deck into the compartments directly beneath, when moving along the opening left by the internal crew stairwell the dive team suddenly and unexpectedly found themselves back in the engine room. Going by the original Harland & Wolff GA plans, the watertight bulkhead, extending to the underside of the bridge deck, should have made this route all but impossible.

One thing we were learning on the 2021 survey was that a number of the internal bulkheads were in an undeniably advanced state of decay, including the area between the first-class restaurant galley and the B deck staterooms, as well as the aft casing wall of the reciprocating engine room on E deck. This, however, was different. The previous areas had mostly been thinner, internal dividing walls, playing little or no appreciable role in maintaining the *Britannic*'s overall structural integrity, whereas bulkhead K, delineating the forward extent of the reciprocating engine room, also served as one of the ship's main transverse bulkheads, which not only restricted the ingress of any floodwater but also provided crucial structural support for

THE TANK TOP

Top left: The forward low-pressure cylinder on the starboard side, along with the overhead mechanism used when maintaining the engines.
Top right: The top of the intermediate pressure cylinder on the higher port engine. The insulation and lagging seem to be in as good a condition as the day the ship entered service, with the stencilling still perfectly legible.
Above: The prize: the Harland & Wolff maker's plate still proudly attached to the pillar in the reciprocating engine room.

Above: The boiler room telegraph transmitters mounted on the support pillar closest to the starting platform, used to communicate any orders to the individual stokeholds.
Left: The eduction pipe of the port reciprocating engine, still with its well-preserved insulation, next to the stairwell leading directly to the tank top.

the hull. Even so, despite the apparent strength of this structural member, there was no mistaking the torn riveted seam and twisted plating, which seems to have been unzipped and peeled back like paper, due to the force of the incoming water.

I was never expecting to find any great surprises in the general arrangement of the reciprocating engine compartment. Broadly speaking, the *Britannic*'s propelling machinery was arranged pretty much on the same lines as the engines in the *Olympic* and *Titanic*, with the twin four-cylinder triple expansion reciprocating engines, each 63 feet (19.2m) long, surrounded by the usual feed, sanitary and bilge pumps, as well as the customary auxiliary machinery that would be found in any ship's engine room. There was, however, one principal difference in the *Britannic* as opposed to the two earlier ships, in the form of the gravitation filters on the discharge side of the feed pumps, which necessitated a slight rearrangement in the positioning of the main feed pumps and other auxiliaries. As for the actual engines, all the moving parts were made from forged steel, save for the connecting and piston rods, which were made from high-tension steel. The crank shafts were actually built in four pieces, but in addition to the eight bearings in the original design – two for each crank pin – the *Britannic*'s engines contained an additional bearing in the centre of the engine that helped to further 'steady' the shaft. It was a relatively small modification, and certainly not one that would be apparent in any of the resulting imagery, but the overall result was the same, with each engine driving a 23-foot 9-inch (7.2m) diameter triple-bladed manganese bronze propeller, the two engines indicating collectively 32,000 horsepower when running at 77 revolutions per minute.

So much for the technobabble, but from this point onwards the issue was not so much one of engineering minutiae, but rather one of seeing what remained of the engines themselves. Initial expectations were not optimistic, with good reason to fear that the mountings would by now have given way after 105 years lying almost perpendicular to the seabed, resulting in the two engines, each 40 feet (12m) high and weighing significantly in excess of 700 tons, detaching from the tank top and crashing to the lower starboard side. Had this occurred then the chances are that many of the compartment's load-bearing supports would also have been seriously damaged in the process, making this an even more hazardous penetration. In a worst-case scenario, apart from a few remaining pieces of auxiliary machinery on the higher port side, there would be little prospect of finding anything more than a huge pile of twisted machinery.

In the end, none of this appears to have come to pass. My first view of the compartment, literally as the dive team passed into the aft

Above: The aft low-pressure cylinder of the port reciprocating engine, showing how the catwalks were sculpted around the individual cylinder chests.

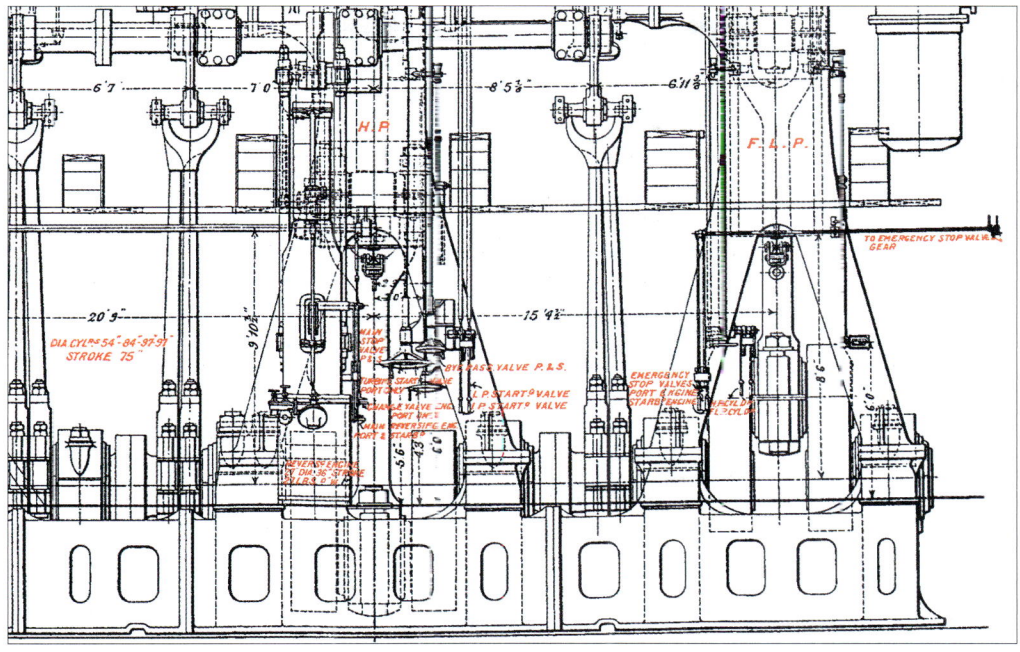

Above: Schematic of the engineers' starting platform. (Harland & Wolff)

end of the engine room via the collapsed casing wall in the E deck working passage, was the top of the almost completely intact port-side reciprocating engine. Studying the four huge engine cylinders as they gradually appeared into the gloom towards the forward end of the compartment, I realised it was more than I could ever have hoped for. At first glance the engine itself seemed to be largely unaffected by its 100-year-plus immersion, displaying fewer rusticles than had been observed in the forward boiler rooms. This may have been due to the fact that the more exposed skylight opening had resulted in a higher flow rate of water through the compartment, as opposed to the smaller and less exposed entrance into the forward pipe tunnel, but it quickly became evident that any scrutiny and identification of the engine room compartment was going to be considerably more straightforward than originally thought.

As luck would have it, the location of the initial penetration could not have worked better. The port reciprocating engine was always going to be the key starting point in this compartment, even though the two engines were practically mirror images of each other, because they differed in one key respect. Nestling at the base of the port engine's high-pressure cylinder was a work station, known as the 'starting platform', where the engines would be controlled by the senior engineers on duty. The reciprocating engines themselves were operated by opening a valve that controlled the supply steam to the engine, while the direction of the engine was

Above: The control levers of the reciprocating and turbine engines, clearly indicating the engine settings as the *Britannic* sank.
Right: The engineers' starting platform, located at the base of the port-side high-pressure cylinder.

effectively controlled the ship. If there was ever any question as to the settings prior to the engineers abandoning their posts, they were answered at a single stroke: the lever for the reciprocating was set midway between the 'Ahead' and 'Astern' settings, while the lever controlling the turbine had been pushed all the way forward to the 'Shut' position, leaving no doubt that before the engine room was evacuated, the engines had unquestionably been stopped.

As for the engines themselves, all the crank shafts, which continued to turn until the last minutes of the *Britannic*'s all-too-brief life, remain locked in position, almost frozen in time, and yet all is not quite perfect. From a structural point of view, the engines may have withstood the sinking, but some of the less robust catwalks surrounding them have not fared so well. In addition, twisted beams and heaps of scattered machinery bear visual testimony to the violence with which this compartment was so suddenly overwhelmed during the final stages of the sinking. It was probably little different from the sudden deluge of water in the aft first-class staircase as the weather cover imploded, except that while the lighter fixtures and fittings in the entrance were most likely swept further into the hull, potentially ending up anywhere along the aft sections of C deck, the combination of the enclosed engine compartment and heavier machinery meant that there was practically nowhere for the debris to go, except to the lower starboard side. Even so, one or two fragments of lighter debris still managed to escape the confines of the reciprocating engine

controlled by the simple action of moving a lever to the 'ahead' or 'astern' setting. The turbine engine was also controlled from this station, but the crucial point was that while Captain Bartlett's orders came from the bridge, it was in this exact spot that Chief Engineer Robert Fleming and his staff

Above: A fish-eye photograph taken inside the space leading into the reciprocating engine room.

times be just as easily influenced as Richard Lee, the impressionable 18-year-old Harland & Wolff apprentice who took the *Britannic* out on her trials over a hundred years earlier. It was probably one of the best – if not *the* best – dive of their lives.

The turbine engine room

A preliminary visual inspection carried out by the dive team on the September 2003 expedition had already indicated that the turbine engine was also largely intact, but it was only after the success of the 2021 penetration of the marine reciprocating engine room that I was ready to focus more fully on this compartment.

As in the earlier ships, the *Britannic*'s turbine was designed to take steam direct from the two reciprocating engines, but although essentially similar in design to the low-pressure Parsons turbines fitted in the *Olympic* and *Titanic*, it was in many ways substantially different. As a result of the higher pressure, which was exhausted from the reciprocating engines at a pressure of about 10lb absolute, the *Britannic*'s turbine could develop about 18,000 shaft horsepower when running at 170 revolutions per minute, making it substantially more powerful than the two preceding turbines, even though the arrangement was practically identical to the earlier ships. The change valves at the forward end of the turbine engine compartment served exactly the same purpose, namely directing the exhaust steam from the reciprocating engines

room, bursting through the now collapsed aft casing at the level of E deck, only to end up in an untidy heap midway along the aft section of the working passage.

I can't imagine what must have been going through the dive team's minds as they sat though their customary four-hour in-water decompression, but I will probably never forget the excited looks on their faces that day as they clambered back aboard our dive platform, the *Nicolakis*. As I quietly stood back and listened to their excited chatter, describing what they had seen to each other in incredible detail, it occurred to me that despite the passage of years, these old campaigners, who had probably seen and done practically everything in their diving careers, could at

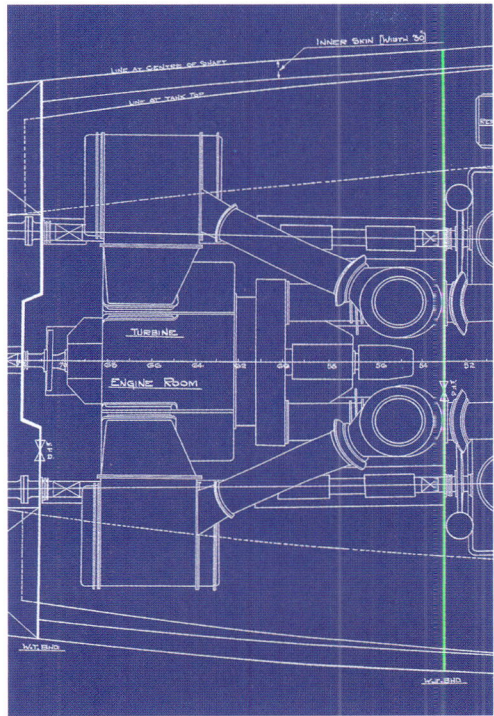

Above: Blueprint of the *Britannic*'s turbine engine arrangement. (Harland & Wolff)

into the turbine, or directly into either of the two condensers mounted on each side of the turbine, while sluice valves between the turbine and each of the two condensers enabled either condenser to be shut off in order to carry out any maintenance or repairs.

Moving aft, the huge cast-iron turbine casing, ribbed both circumferentially and longitudinally, displayed one of the important differences with *Britannic*'s turbine in that it was manufactured in the Harland & Wolff foundry at Belfast, whereas the casings for the two earlier ships had been manufactured by John Brown & Co. As before, the rotor drum, formed from two pieces of forged steel in the longitudinal line, was manufactured at the Atlas Works of John Brown & Co. in Sheffield, with the rotor blades built up on the rosary system in segments, with two binding strips for the shorter blades, and four for the longer ones. The blades varied from between 16 inches (40cm) and 26½ inches (67cm) in length, and when complete the fully bladed rotor accounted for approximately 150 tons of the turbine's overall weight of 490 tons; in practical terms, this made the *Britannic*'s marine turbine the largest built up to the date she entered service, if not necessarily the most powerful.

Accessing this space was, or so I thought, always going to be relatively straightforward when compared to the reciprocating engine room spaces. With the fourth funnel having detached completely from the wreck, now lying several hundred feet to the north and right next to funnel 3, the open engine casing between frames 53A and 59A seemingly provided the ideal route, directly to the top of the change valve between the reciprocating and turbine engines. The structural condition of the turbine engine machinery was expected to be as robust as that of the two reciprocating engines, and based on our previous experience within the other engine and boiler room spaces this was not an unreasonable assumption. Very quickly it became apparent that accessing this space was not going to be quite as simple as we had hoped.

The first indications of a potential problem came while accessing the reciprocating engine room, via our already established working passage route on E deck. Pausing to look through the access door to the turbine engine casing at frame 58A, it became evident that the force of the water flooding the ship's hitherto dry aft compartments during the last seconds afloat had been so great that large deposits of unidentified wreckage, torn violently from its mountings, lay piled on top of the change valves and seemed to be impeding our ability to safely access the further reaches of the turbine engine room. Returning to our original stratagem of accessing the compartment through the fourth funnel casing, sadly, did not improve the situation.

The divers were able to pass through the top six decks with little difficulty, passing the engineers' tanks on C deck, the seemingly open void on D deck where the emergency dynamos would have been installed, and the electric store at the level of E deck, but while parts of the funnel casing still looked to be in a reasonably robust condition, the thinner steel walls in other places had not fared so well. In fact, the steel bulkhead at the aft end of the first- and second-class galley is now so deteriorated that large areas of the non-slip kitchen tiling could be clearly seen. The condition of this part of the bulkhead was so poor that I recall making a mental note to use this route as a possible alternative and perhaps altogether easier way of accessing the galley on future expeditions. But despite the wealth of structural information that was being gathered at these deck levels, the reality was that the obstacles caused by the mounds of debris were significant enough that it prevented a manned diver with a limited bottom time from proceeding any further without a more considered dive plan.

Above: A less cluttered section of the turbine engine compartment.

Top: Although still largely intact, much of the turbine machinery is now covered with heavy debris, torn loose during the sinking.
Above: The space at the level of D deck, where the *Britannic*'s emergency dynamos would have been mounted.

INSIDE THE BRITANNIC

There can be no denying that this was a major disappointment. Had the way been clear then there is every chance that we might have progressed as far as the electric engines and, conceivably, even to the electric switchboard gallery. Even so, it had by no means been a wasted journey, and despite the evident devastation significant parts of the turbine engine machinery are at least visible, confirming that the engine itself is still largely undamaged. The eduction pipes running between the change valves and the condensers also appear to be substantially intact, and we were still able to observe sections of the huge cast-iron turbine casing beneath the wreckage, even though it lacks the more intricate close-up detail of the engines in the reciprocating engine room. Without doubt, the most noticeable highlight of this particular penetration was locating the port sluice valve between the turbine casing and the condenser; but for a few rusticles, even after more than a century it still looks as if it could have been installed yesterday.

Undoubtedly, there is a way through the obstructing debris, and in time we will find it, but for the time being diver safety means that the machinery in the lower reaches of the turbine engine room, including the propeller shafts, the thrust blocks, and closer detail of the associated pumps and feed tanks, all remain tantalisingly just beyond our reach.

Below: Exiting the turbine room via the casing leading up through the dummy fourth funnel.

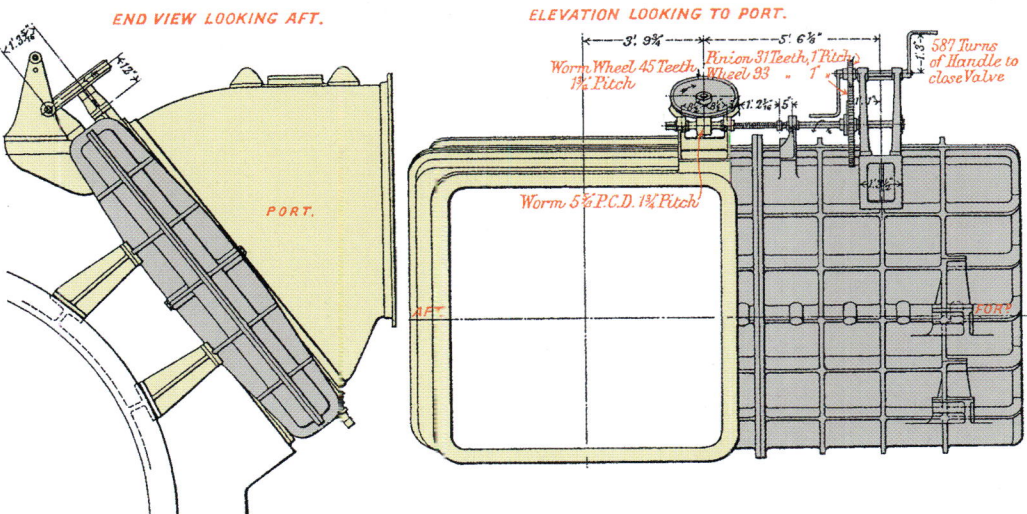

Above: Schematic showing the workings of the sluice valve. (Harland & Wolff)

Above: The sluice valve in September 2023, still firmly mounted between the turbine and the port condenser.

12

THE STERN

One of the main external differences between the *Britannic* and her two sisters was the more lofty stern construction. This was in no small part down to the additional strengthening required to support the heavier weight of the two Armstrong davits, intended to service no fewer than 14 of the *Britannic*'s increased complement of lifeboats, but the redesign of the stern also provided Harland & Wolff with the opportunity to rearrange some of the internal layouts in several other parts of the ship.

In the original design, the aft shelter deck between frames 123A and 138A had incorporated two third-class public rooms; on the starboard side of the centreline was the third-class general room, while to port was the smoking room, each space a virtual mirror image of the other in terms of area, if not quite in layout. Aft of frame 138A was the steering gear compartment, accessed through an inboard door in the aft corner of the third-class general room, although the layout in the *Britannic* was slightly different, with an additional entrance via an enclosed stairwell on the starboard side of the poop.

The lifeboat tiers on the stern had necessitated the inclusion of an additional shade deck, directly above the poop, which in turn had created an additional covered space directly beneath. As a result, Harland & Wolff incorporated an additional deckhouse into this area, which would serve as the third-class smoking room; the original space intended for that purpose would instead be used to house the ship's hospital. In the *Olympic* and *Titanic*, the ship's hospital had been located on the starboard side of D deck, between frames 52A and 71A, placing it immediately aft of the first- and second-class galley – very handy for feeding the patients, even if the practice of housing sick people so close to an area where food was being prepared might nowadays be considered questionable. In turn, the area

Right: The modified design of the *Britannic*'s poop needed to be significantly larger and stronger, in order to accommodate the Armstrong davits that served 14 third-class lifeboats.

DOCKING BRIDGE

SHADE DECK

POOP DECK.

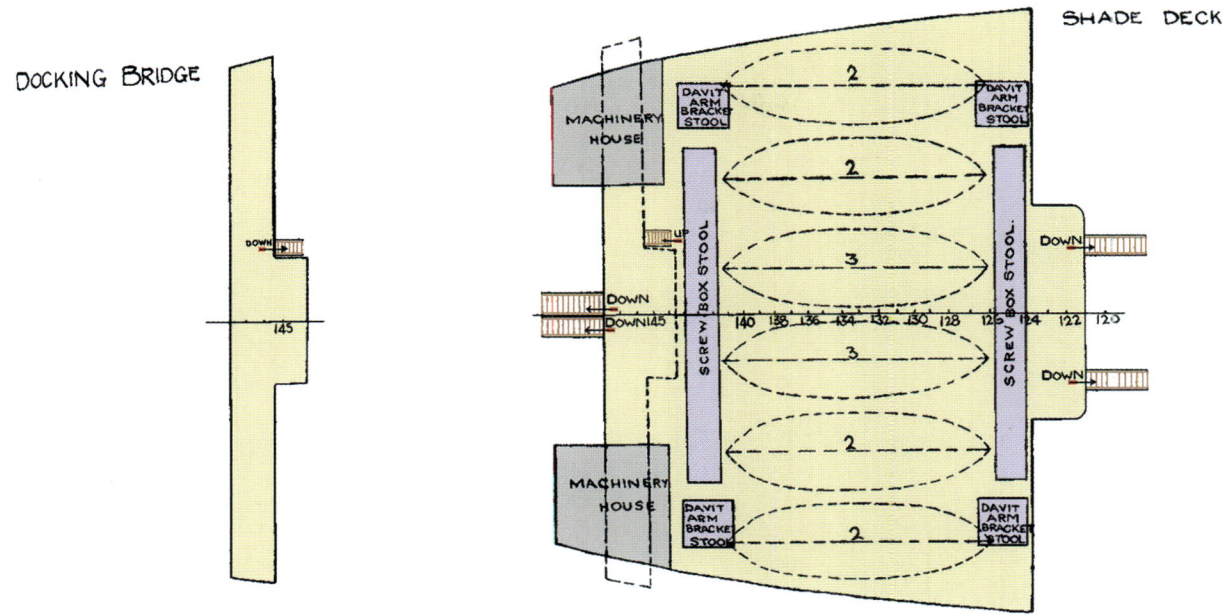

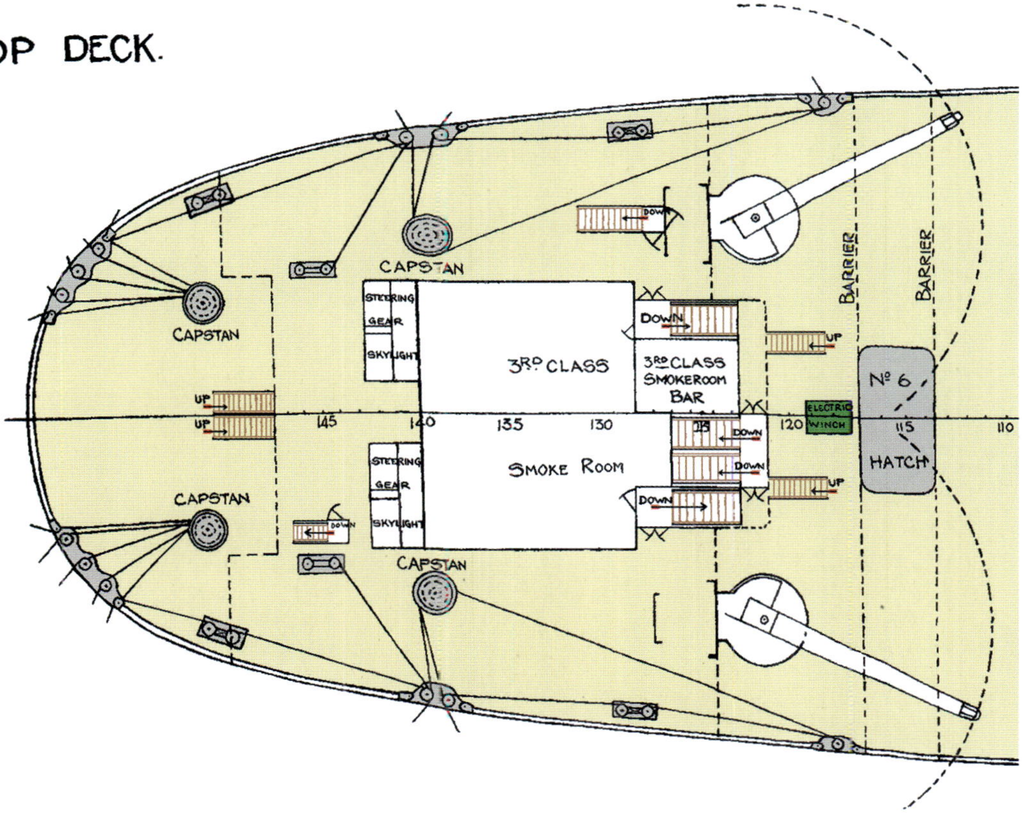

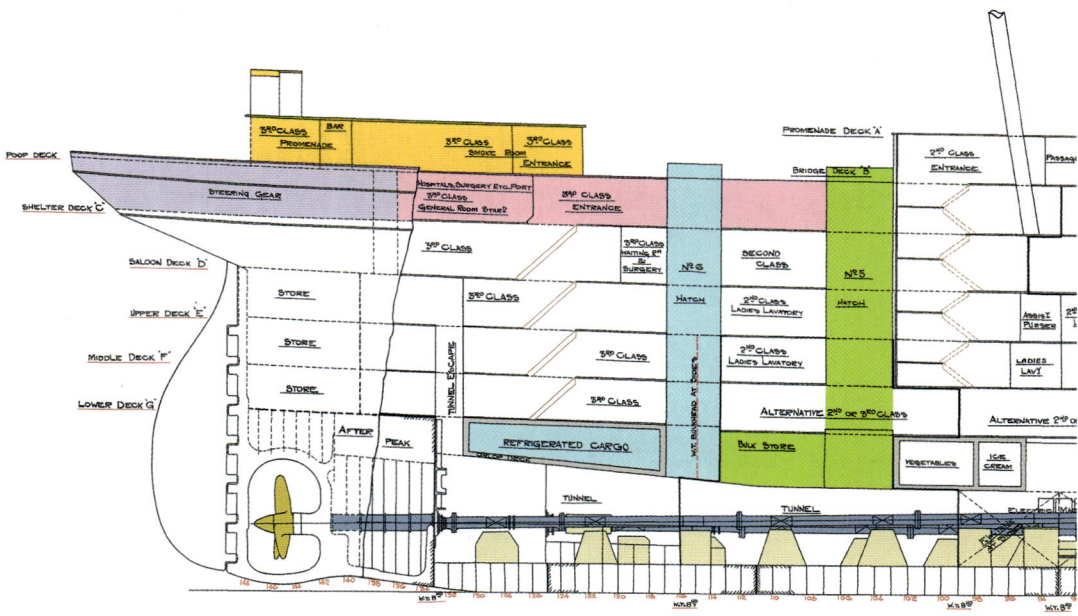

Above: Elevation of the *Britannic*'s stern. (Harland & Wolff)

vacated by the hospital would be taken up by the maids' and valets' dining saloon, along with a smaller dining area for the postal officials and Marconi operators, while the original location of this room, on C deck, would instead be given over to three additional revenue-generating first-class cabins.

The redesign of the stern had also resulted in an additional area of open deck space, meaning that the *Britannic*'s bridge deck now extended all the way from the forward superstructure to the stern, effectively dispensing with the aft well deck in the original design. Broadly speaking, the additional open deck space would be split between the second- and third-class passengers, while the now enclosed shelter deck below would be given over almost entirely to the third-class passengers, who would in effect have their own sheltered promenade. The only area of the enclosed well deck to be allocated to the second-class passengers would be their own gymnasium, located at the forward end of the now enclosed space on the starboard side.

While the additional expenditure incurred by the revised design would have been considerable, the new deck arrangement did at least enable White Star to make a not inconsiderable saving elsewhere. By mounting the two cargo cranes originally located in the well deck at frame 100A one deck higher, it

Right: The shade deck, still firmly attached to the poop. Note the stool supports on the roof, intended to support the worm gear of the Armstrong davits originally intended for this area.

THE STERN

meant that they could service both holds 4 and 5, thus doing away with the two smaller 30cwt cranes utilised for hold 4 in the two earlier ships. Insofar as the layouts of the aft holds were concerned, the now continuous bridge deck above the enclosed well deck meant that the height of the cargo hatch covers also needed to be raised by one deck. Other than that, the general arrangement was more or less identical, with hold 5 given over to bulk stores – in other words, cargo or stores that are shipped loosely and unpackaged – while hold 6 continued to be used for transporting any refrigerated cargo.

Crucially, however, the aft cargo and third-class spaces would be of particular interest in the exploration of the *Britannic*, as, despite the aforementioned differences in layout when compared to the *Titanic*, the fact that the *Titanic*'s stern has been practically torn apart by the combination of the ship's breakup and the heavy impact with the seabed 12,500 feet (3,810m) below means the *Titanic*'s stern is now little more than a devastated pile of twisted and tortured steel. The reciprocating engines are still upright and just about accessible, albeit with each of the forward low-pressure cylinders torn from their original mounting, but entombed inside the remaining debris are the remains of the ship's turbine engine, the second-class library and smoking room, the third-class general and smoking

Above: The lower starboard side of the third-class smoking room, which remains almost completely intact.

rooms, and the aft cargo holds. Inside the *Britannic*, however, all these spaces are still completely intact.

Not surprisingly, the investigation of the aft section began with a look at the easiest structures to access on the stern, namely the ship's mortuary and the third-class smoking room. The mortuary was the curious box-like structure located at the aft end of the poop and occupying most of the ship's counter overhanging the rudder directly beneath. This structure does not appear in any of the *Britannic*'s pre-1915 plans, confirming that it was always intended as a temporary measure, hence the materials used were probably not as robust as those used in the existing deckhouse beneath the shade deck. The temporary nature of its fabrication probably explains why there is no evidence whatsoever of it ever having existed, and if there were any traces on the pine deck where it was once mounted then they are now lying on the seabed, buried in the accumulated mass of saddle oysters that have completely overrun the stern. In places, the layers of saddle oysters are so thick that even the aft deck railings have taken on the appearance of an apparently solid bulkhead.

Forward of the docking bridge, directly beneath the shade deck, the structure of the third-class smoking room has fared somewhat better, partly protected by the structure of the deck above even if the imploded windows have left the interior completely exposed to the marine organisms. When in military service, this room had in fact served the same purpose for which it was originally intended, although instead of being used by third-class passengers, it was, according to Private Percy Tyler, utilised by the medical officers as their smoking room.

The disappointment of the reasonably bare interior of the smoking room came as no great surprise, but the key areas of interest in the stern were always going to be the enclosed well deck, the third-class entrance and general room, the ship's hospital, and, if the bulkhead doors permitted, access to the ultimate prize – the steering compartment. As wreck penetrations go, accessing the *Britannic*'s enclosed well deck, even in 90 metres (295ft) of seawater, is about as easy as it gets. Aside from the six supporting stanchions, with the two central supports close together on either side of the aft expansion joint, the open sides along the shelter deck between frames 99A and 116A offer ample space and no obstruction whatsoever. Descending into the covered third-class promenade immediately brought the team into the area utilised by the RAMC orderlies as their parade ground, the enclosed sides of the hatches to cargo holds 5 and 6 partially reducing the width of the space along the centreline of the ship, before once again opening up to reveal what was then, and indeed still is, a largely open expanse of deck area. In common with the rest of the wreck, practically no trace of the pine decking remains, the only indication of it ever being

Below: The enclosed aft well deck. The pine decking is long gone, but the ridges of caulking and a few remaining fragments of wood can still be clearly seen.

there at all once again being the visible ridges of caulking, made from oakum, impregnated with tar and wax.

The enclosed shafts provided no access point into the cargo holds from the shelter deck, but a closer look inside these compartments was always going to be essential, if only to lay to rest once and for all any lingering doubts regarding an illicit cargo of munitions. Despite the shortcomings of the 1976 exploration of the wreck, at the end of his programme Cousteau had at least acknowledged that nothing suspicious had been found inside *Britannic*'s cargo holds, effectively cleansing the ship's previously tarnished reputation, but with his divers' bottom time so limited, based on the available diving technology at that time, questions inevitably remained as to how thorough any search by a manned diver in the late seventies might have been. The Board of Trade shipping casualty report had also specifically noted that the *Britannic* carried no cargo on her final voyage, but although hold 1 had revealed no evidence of anything on those lines, to say nothing of the complete lack of any evidence in the debris of what was once holds 2 and 3, the lingering controversy could not be fully laid to rest until the two aft compartments had also been searched.

The access point to the two aft holds is located at the level of the bridge deck, and the

Above: The lower starboard opening of the enclosed well deck, some 374ft (114m) below the surface. The seabed does not appear to have been disturbed since 21 November 1916.

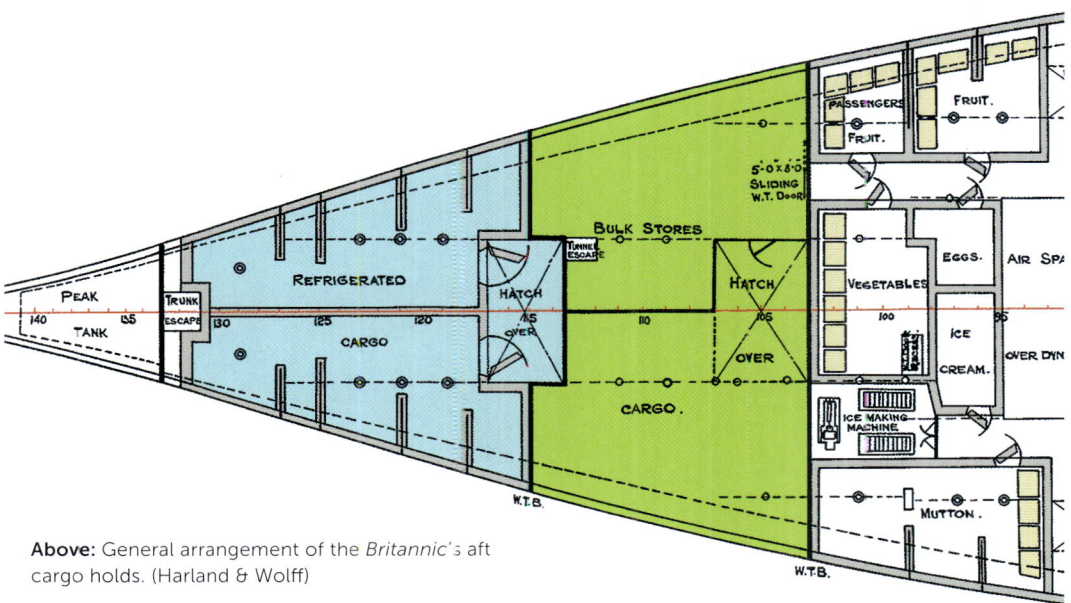

Above: General arrangement of the *Britannic*'s aft cargo holds. (Harland & Wolff)

route could not have been simpler. The wooden covers atop each of the two holds had rotted away decades earlier, and the two gaping openings, each leading deep within the wreck's aft section, could only help to make each penetration reasonably straightforward. Unlike the forward holds, where there was a clear expanse of relatively open deck area all the way down to the level of the cargo spaces beneath the lower deck, the narrower shafts leading into the aft holds passed through five decks, before opening up into the more open expanse of the aft orlop deck, where, like her sisters, the *Britannic* would carry a combination of bulk stores and refrigerated cargo.

The *Britannic*'s refrigerating plant consisted of two large horizontal duplex CO_2 machines, manufactured by J. and E. Hall Ltd. of Dartford, both of which were situated on the tank top at the port side of the reciprocating engine room. The evaporators were placed in an insulated space on the orlop deck, directly above this machinery, where three brine pumps were also fitted. The ship actually only needed half of this refrigerating installation capacity to ensure that the individual provision rooms and refrigerated holds could maintain the desired temperatures, not to mention the drinking water and two large ice-making tanks, while the various refrigerated provision rooms and cargo spaces were fitted with electrically welded galvanised brine grids, each kept at a moderate length and thoroughly interlaced to ensure an equal distribution of cooling throughout the circuit.

Based on the survey, both holds remain completely intact, the only evidence of any 'hazardous' cargo – if it can be called that – in hold 5 coming in the form of the hundreds of

Top: Entering hold 5, the support struts for the weather cover still firmly attached.
Above: A ladder still fixed in position at the top of cargo hold 6, beckons the dive team into the final unexplored cargo hold.

beer and wine bottles that lie scattered around the compartment in the now heavy deposits of silt. From a visual standpoint, however, hold 6 is undoubtedly the more interesting of the two, as it was always intended as a space for refrigerated items. Unlike the bare walls of the other cargo spaces, the walls in hold 6 are still covered with hundreds of refrigeration pipes, of which nearly all remain in situ. A few of these pipes – but not many – have detached and fallen away, but perhaps more surprising is the fact that there is still evidence of some well-preserved wood in what appears to be an otherwise almost completely intact compartment. The only thing that was conspicuous by its absence was evidence of any illicit munitions being stored in the aft parts of the ship, confirming that to date nothing has been observed in any of the internal hull spaces to suggest that the *Britannic* was carrying anything other than legitimate stores or medical supplies.

Above: The empty beer and wine bottles stored in the bulk stores section of cargo hold 5, suggest that the *Britannic* must have been a happy ship.

Top: A rusting bulkhead indicates the level of deterioration in this more open area of the ship.
Above: Part of a collapsed bulkhead, where the riveted seam has literally been ripped open, although the effect has been somewhat exaggerated by the wide-angle lens.

Top: Despite the reasonably easy access, the sight of some well-preserved wood on the way to the orlop deck was a pleasant surprise.
Above: Nearly all the brine refrigeration piping remains firmly in situ, having suffered little degradation after more than a century on the seabed.

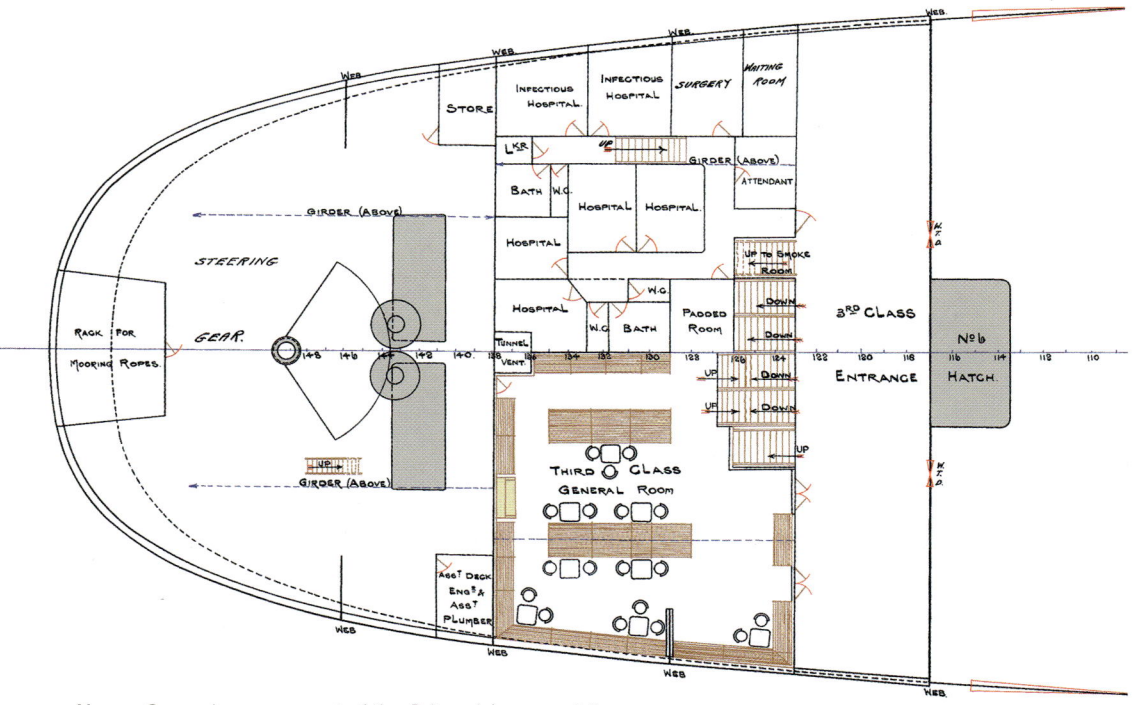

Above: General arrangement of the *Britannic*'s poop at the level of the shelter deck. (Harland & Wolff)

With the last of the cargo holds finally ticked off the list, the focus once again turned to the four remaining spaces in the aftermost part of the wreck, which still needed to be recorded: the third-class entrance and general room, the ship's hospital and the steering compartment.

Another useful pointer in Percy Tyler's journal was the location of the *Britannic*'s isolation wards, and being situated on the higher port side of the shelter deck, it was also the easiest space to access in the poop. Passing through the open watertight door into the third-class entrance, this space is now almost completely open, although in common with all the staircases observed to date, the metal structure of the third-class stairwell remains completely intact. Not surprisingly, the wooden steps had also been eaten away decades earlier, and although time has not yet allowed for a more extensive survey of the lower reaches of the stairwell, all the indications are that it almost certainly provides a direct and open route into what would have been the aft third-class accommodations on all four of the decks below.

Interestingly, the *Britannic*'s hospital is one of the few working areas inside the ship utilised for its original intended purpose. The hospital berths were originally intended to be arranged three to a room, mostly with two of

Above: The open watertight door leading into the aft third class entrance.

the berths being arranged in the standard upper and lower configuration, while the third was a single bed 2 feet 6 inches (76cm) wide. The surveys to date provide telling images of crumbling medical cots and disintegrating internal metal bulkheads dividing the individual rooms, with much of the surgical equipment now most likely buried in the silt, although the sight of the well-preserved flooring has provided one of the more pleasant discoveries in this part of the wreck. The entire compartment is still extensively covered with large expanses of the original well-preserved 3-inch (7.6cm) white octagon and black dot encaustic ceramic tiles, making a pleasant change to the all-too-familiar faded red colour of the Veitchi flooring that seems to permeate throughout most of the ship.

Returning to the third-class entrance and descending towards the lower starboard side, the opening that once housed the set of double doors leading into the third-class general room would prove even less of an obstruction than the single door of the hospital. The same featureless Veitchi flooring provides a visual testament to the customarily functional and utilitarian areas of a hospital ship, the only identifiable item in the scattered debris being the remains of a fallen third-class basin water reservoir, while the relatively open expanse of the general room itself, aside from the heaps of unidentified debris piled up on the bulkhead

This page, opposite and overleaf: The well-preserved tiled flooring inside the *Britannic*'s hospital, which served as the ship's isolation wards, undoubtedly makes this one of the more attractive areas inside the ship.

below, has so far revealed little evidence of the use to which that space was put. It might have been another ward but, equally, being so close to the RAMC parade ground, it might easily have served as a barrack room for the medical orderlies.

The steering compartment

Visualising the steering gear associated with the Olympic class liners is actually not difficult, as several photographs taken at Harland & Wolff by Robert Welch during the *Britannic*'s construction indicate that the manoeuvring gear was exactly the same as that of the *Olympic* and *Titanic*.

The ship's steering was controlled from the bridge wheelhouse by a telemotor, built by Brown Brothers & Co. of Edinburgh, with the pipes of the telemotor transmitter in the wheelhouse connecting it to the motor cylinders in the aft steering gear compartment. The steering engines were of the well-established Harland & Wolff design, incorporating a spring quadrant on the rudder stock that engaged with a wheel and pinion driven by either of the two steering engines, ensuring that there was always a standby in the event of any mechanical failure.

The quadrant itself was designed to minimise any shocks due to heavy seas, and when the *Britannic* was launched it was

Top: A fallen and badly rusted water reservoir is one of the few identifiable items to be found in the third-class entrance area so far.
Above: The *Britannic*'s steering engines, under construction at Belfast. (Harland & Wolff)

confidently claimed in the technical journals of the day that the steering gear had a complete record of immunity from breakdown in the many large Belfast ships in which it had been fitted. Unfortunately, this impressive record would be dented somewhat on 21 November 1916, when Captain Bartlett reported that due to an apparent failure of the steering gear following the explosion, it was only possible to turn the *Britannic* towards land using the engines. To be fair, the steering engines had never been intended for use in a warship, having been originally designed more with a view to working efficiently in the stormy waters of the North Atlantic rather than having to deal with the initial force of the explosion of a mine or torpedo, so the resulting shock loading as the ensuing destructive vibrations were introduced into the system throughout the entire ship was by no means the norm. Whether or not we would find any indication as to why this mechanical failure occurred was always going to be a long shot, but even the opportunity of just imaging the steering engines themselves would have made the trip worthwhile.

The open expanse of the general room would ultimately prove to be no great obstacle, leaving the route to the steering compartment wide open. As the aft bulkhead at frame 138F slowly emerged from the gloom, just off the centreline, next to the aft tunnel vent, the

Above: The doorway leading from the third-class general room into the steering compartment.

darkened outline of the doorway opening into the steering compartment gradually began to take shape. Almost immediately there is a visible difference in the flooring, with the familiar red of the Veitchi surface suddenly being replaced by the surprisingly well-preserved remains of the teak wood decking in the steering compartment, just before the unmistakeable outline of the starboard steering engine comes into view. The passage is a little tight for a diver wearing a rebreather and carrying a couple of bailout tanks, but there would have been more than enough space for the unencumbered crew to access the aft compartment itself.

Beyond the steering engines lies the aft warping gear, consisting of four separate 18 inch x 14 inch (46cm x 36cm) double-cylinder engines, driving the four capstans fitted through spur and bevel gear on the deck above. Time has not yet permitted a more extensive examination of these windlass machines, but a preliminary inspection of the wheel and pinion mechanism driving the powerful three-cylinder steering engines, which engaged with a spring quadrant attached to the rudder stock, has so far revealed no visible sign of any major damage. Like the engines in the reciprocating and turbine engine rooms, those in the steering compartment also remain firmly attached to their mountings, the smashed glass face of an otherwise pristine engine telegraph seemingly the only visible evidence of the stern's heavy impact with the seabed.

Although I didn't realise it at the time, in many ways the final penetration of the steering

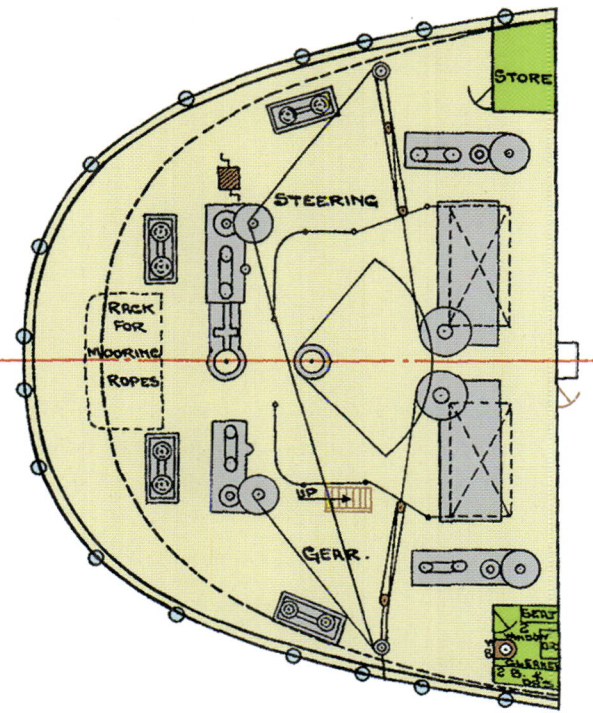

Above: General arrangement of the Olympic class steering compartment. (Harland & Wolff)

gear compartment has come to mark the end of this part of the journey. For years I had been co-ordinating the exploration of the *Britannic*'s interiors, but it was only on 24 September 2023 that I could finally tell myself that we had, at long last, covered the wreck from end to end. None of this means that the task is now finished – or, come to that, anywhere near to being finished; on an intact wreck some 883 feet (269m) in length, there will always be things left to do and places still to see, but somehow this particular achievement served as a personal milestone as to just how far we had finally come.

THE STERN

Above: A close-up view of the steering engine mechanism, linking the engines to the steering quadrant.
Left: The *Britannic*'s starboard-side steering engine, still completely intact and seemingly undamaged.

13

A TALE OF TWO SISTERS

The 2021 and 2023 surveys have not only resulted in a giant leap forward in the field of *Britannic* research, but also marked an important milestone in the field of *Titanic* wreck investigation, as the *Britannic*'s previously unexplored interiors shed new light on the story of the Olympic class as a whole. A detailed comparison of the two wrecks is beyond the scope of this book, but with both wrecks now extensively surveyed inside and out, we can, perhaps, start to make a more meaningful comparison.

In the *Britannic*'s case, the outlook following the 2021 and 2023 expeditions has been changed beyond all comprehension. True, many of the conspiracy theories had already been settled long before commencing the 2021 survey, with the 1976 and 2003 expeditions confirming that the forward cargo holds were empty, while not one of the divers on the 11 expeditions that I have supported over a 23-year period has ever reported seeing any evidence of an illicit cargo of munitions in the collapsed structure of holds 2 and 3. The secondary explosion theory, be it caused by either the aforementioned munitions or as a result of a coal dust explosion, has also gone the way of the dodo, while the mine v. torpedo theory has been largely resolved with the sonar scan of the minefield in September 2003. For

Above: Taken at Vourkari, Kea, on 20th September 2021, the first day of the internal survey. The White Star burgee has been used in every team photo since 2003.
Left: The nurses and some of the medical officers photographed outside the Aktaion Hotel, Piraeus, in November 1916. (Angus & Jonathan Mitchell)

the few remaining holdouts, when a large fragment of an exploded German mine casing was finally visualised in August 2008, the last of the conspiracy theories were effectively staked through the heart, although I sometimes wonder if they are truly dead and buried in some quarters. The task now was to revisit the evidence that has stood the test of time, while at the same time introducing the new data into the mix for a more forensic approach.

For the 107 years that the *Britannic* had lain at the bottom of the Kea Channel, pretty much everything in the British naval records had been taken at face value, the ship's fate having been more or less decided by the combination of events laid out in the report of 24 November 1916 by Captain Hugh Heard and Commander George Staer. Compared to the 18 days taken by Senator William Alden Smith's *Titanic* investigation in America, or the 36 days of the British Wreck Commissioner's *Titanic* inquiry in London, the two days allotted to Heard and Staer seem almost paltry. Nevertheless, their final 726-word summary [Appendix II] laid out the available information in as much detail as was reasonably possible, considering the logistical and political situation existing in Athens at the time, and despite these limiting factors it still provided a concise and plausible summary of the known evidence. Unlike a newspaper column, their report didn't seek to over-sensationalise the events for the sake of extra sales, but merely listed, in a characteristic military fashion, the information they believed to be relevant to the loss of the ship. As a result, researchers have for decades known all about the single explosion, the watertight doors for the two forward boiler rooms failing to close, and the open portholes. All these factors combined present a wholly plausible summary as to why the *Britannic* sank, and yet it would now seem that even this didn't tell the whole story.

To be fair, Heard and Staer did include two important caveats in order to cover their backs, neither of which seem to have been given very much attention until now, simply because there had been no particular reason – or, come to that, evidence – to question it. The first observation came in the report's very first paragraph, when Captain Heard noted: 'It must be premised that the enquiry was necessarily incomplete owing to the shortness of time at our disposal and the difficulty of finding witnesses scattered over the whole fleet.' Such a caveat is actually not unusual in a good many reports into the sinking of a number of First World War vessels, but it may have helped to sow a degree of doubt in the less charitable minds of any conspiracy theorists who remained sceptical as to why there was never an official inquiry into the ship's loss, or even why the survivors had apparently been shipped home with such unseemly haste. In his own summary, Rear Admiral Arthur Hayes-Sadler, commanding the British Mediterranean Squadron at Mudros, wrote that he had assumed there would be a more formal investigation once the survivors had returned to Britain, but there was actually another more pressing motive for the British naval authorities in Athens to repatriate the *Britannic* survivors as quickly as possible.

In many ways, the survivors had already

Above: The British war cemetery at Paramo, Piraeus, where four of the five recovered *Britannic* casualties are now buried.

been given an unwelcome taste of what was to come. Nurse Sheila Macbeth recalled in her diary that after they had been landed at Piraeus, the nurses were billeted in the Aktaion hotel at Phaleron, where the owner was sympathetic to the Allied cause; the medical officers, on the other hand, were not so fortunate, and had been quartered in a hotel whose owner was more sympathetic to the Greek king, Constantine I. The stage was already set for what is now known in Greece as the 'Noemvriana', or the 'November events', on account of the fighting that took place in Athens on 1 December – a quirky historical anomaly, due to the fact that in 1916 Greece still used the old Julian calendar, only adopting the Gregorian calendar in 1923.

The background to the Noemvriana has, up until now, been largely overlooked in its link to the *Britannic* story, and yet in many ways it may be crucial to understanding the apparent haste with which the *Britannic* survivors were evacuated from Athens. Although still officially neutral, by November 1916 Greece was politically divided between the Greek monarchists, with Constantine seemingly favouring the Central Powers, and the provisional government of Greek prime minister Eleftherios Venizelos, based in Salonika, who was more sympathetic to the Allied cause. By November 1916 the already tense political situation in Athens was on the verge of exploding, just as the *Britannic* survivors were being landed at Salamis, and it would only be a matter of days before those tensions would be transformed into open warfare.

The ensuing fighting in Athens came barely three days after the last of *Britannic*'s medical staff had been evacuated, and would actually result in something of a military setback for the Allies, so much so that by the time the dust had settled, ten servicemen from the British battleships HMS *Duncan* and HMS *Exmouth* had been laid to rest in the same Piraeus graveyard where, less than two weeks earlier, *Britannic* casualties Arthur Binks, Joseph Brown, George Honeycott and Charles Phillips had also been buried. In one important respect, however, the fighting had finally resolved the thorny diplomatic issue, when, on 2 December 1916, the Allies formally recognised the Venizelos government in Salonika; within days, the provisional government had declared war on the Central Powers, but it would not be until after the king's abdication in June that a reunified Greece would properly enter the war on the Allied side. Seen in this light, it can be reasonably argued that the prospect of the fighting in Athens in December 1916 more than justified the apparent haste demonstrated by the British naval authorities in signing off the report into the *Britannic*'s loss and repatriating the survivors. Then again, it still begs the question that if Heard and Staer had been given the luxury of more time to conduct their inquiry, might certain other important factors have come to light any sooner?

The second observation, in paragraph 7 of the report, is more interesting, where it notes,

'We are confident that no water penetrated abaft No. 5 stokehold in the lower part of the ship.' It is the last seven words of this paragraph that have suddenly become so crucial.

One of the great surprises on the 2015 expedition was the extent to which the watertight door between boiler rooms 6 and 5 was found to be open. Heard and Staer had gone out of their way to note that there was evidence to suggest that this door might have been 'partially closed', yet closer examination of the door itself had shown no evidence whatsoever to support this assertion, leading to the inevitable question as to where this evidence might have come from. It was not until 1 October 2023, when the dive team tasked with penetrating the cooling room observed that the sliding watertight door immediately outside the entrance to the Turkish bath was partially open, that a possible answer may have been found. Might this watertight door have been the door to which Heard and Staer were actually referring?

If the watertight door between boiler rooms 5 and 4 is indeed closed, as the report states with absolute certainty, then the scale of the internal flooding, according to the White Star Line correspondence with the Admiralty in September 1915, should have been within the *Britannic*'s designed margin of safety. Up until now the evidence has effectively maintained that it was the increasing list to starboard, exacerbated by the combination of open portholes, that ultimately led to the *Britannic*'s capsize, but while this loss of stability would almost certainly have been a crucial factor in the sinking, the available evidence meant that at no time prior to the 2023 exploration had any serious consideration been given to the possibility of any other crucial watertight doors also being left open.

With the loss of boiler rooms 6 and 5, the upward flooding of E deck became inevitable, but while the *Britannic*'s F bulkhead extended all the way up to the underside of the bridge deck (B), the open watertight door in the crew's working passage would have effectively negated this modification. From this point aft, the water would have had unimpeded access along a 200-foot (61-metre) section of Scotland Road, at least as far aft as the watertight door in bulkhead K, in effect rendering the ship's watertight integrity on the morning she sank little better than that of the *Titanic* when she hit the iceberg. If anything, the partially open watertight door outside the Turkish bath, some four decks below the top of the watertight bulkhead, could actually have made the situation even worse.

To all intents and purposes, the arrangement of the F deck watertight doors in the *Britannic* was identical to those in the *Titanic*, other than the watertight door outside the *Olympic*'s Turkish bath being slightly further to starboard. There were two sliding doors in this bulkhead, each needing to be closed manually, and we know from the testimony of Assistant Second Steward Joseph Wheat, at Lord Mersey's inquiry, that in the *Titanic*'s case each

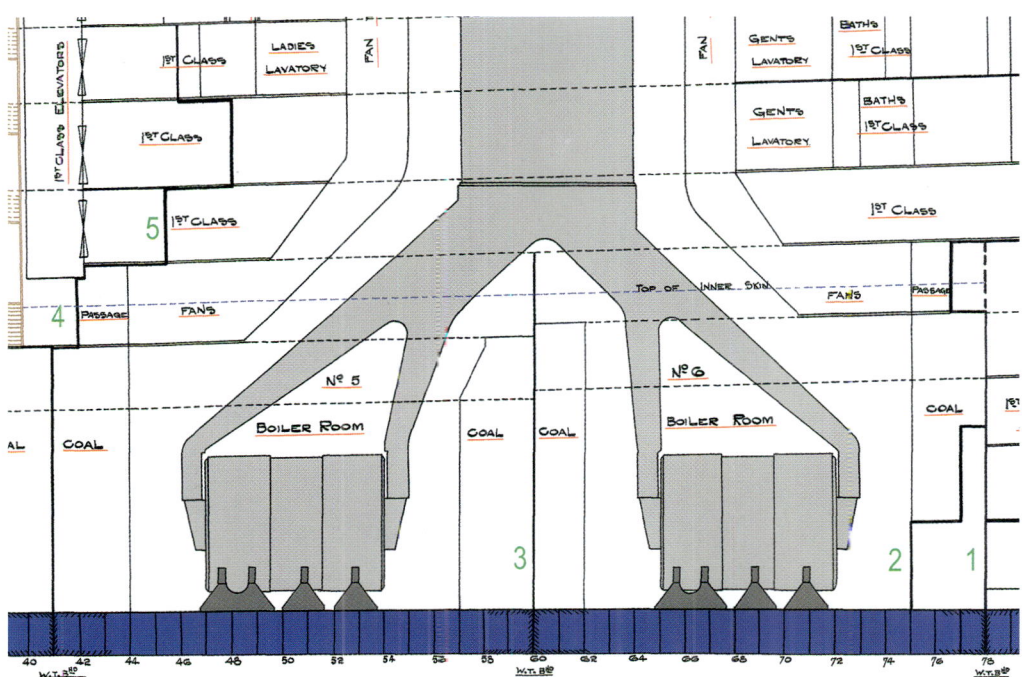

Above: Side elevation of the forward boiler rooms, indicating the location of the open watertight doors.

Above: The debris-obstructed entrance to the Turkish bath, with the partially open F deck watertight door to the left.

of these doors had been closed by the time the water reached them. After observing the rising water level in the mail room, on his own initiative Wheat had personally closed the watertight door next to the entrance to the Turkish bath, and then, using a key from E deck, was assisted in closing the second door, further to starboard – opposite the entrance to the swimming pool – by Second Steward George Dodd and John Crosbie, the Turkish bath attendant. All three of these men occupied cabins on F deck, directly across from the entrance to the Turkish bath. As the *Britannic*'s layout was almost identical in this part of the ship, perhaps it is not unreasonable to speculate that the ship's second steward and second assistant steward, J. Reed and L. Bristow, might have performed the same role in the *Britannic*. However, while Wheat, Dodd and Crosbie were able to successfully close the *Titanic*'s watertight doors, the attempt to close the same doors in the *Britannic*'s case were evidently only partially successful; as a result, a critical watertight door, four decks beneath the height of the bulkhead itself, remained partially open. The opening is not large – about 6 inches (15cm) – but it still equates to an overall area of approximately 3 square feet (0.23 sq m), which could have added considerably to the extent of the flooding aft of bulkhead F on the lower starboard side.

Exactly why the *Britannic*'s F deck watertight door could not be closed is uncertain, although we do have a clue in the damage report of the salvage ship *Ranger*, when assessing the torpedo damage to the *Asturias*. They noted that the ship's stepped bulkheads – a design similar to those in the *Britannic* – had been a problem. Stepped bulkheads were not incorporated into warship designs, and in fairness to Harland & Wolff both the *Asturias* and *Britannic* had always been intended for commercial service, so while the design was not necessarily flawed, in a wartime situation there could indeed have been a weakness. It is also worth considering the fact that the thickness of the *Britannic*'s watertight bulkheads became progressively thinner towards the higher levels, and could therefore have been more prone to warping higher up than in the thicker plating lower down.

Considering the heavy gearing utilised by the sliding watertight doors, the possibility of the F deck watertight door being jarred open after the hull made contact with the seabed is remote at best, but it is interesting to consider that even the open watertight door in the working passage one deck higher may not actually have altered the final outcome. Bearing in mind the *Britannic*'s increasingly heavy list to starboard, it seems likely that by the time the working passage, located on the higher port side of the ship, had started to flood, the *Britannic* would have been beyond saving anyway. Either way, once the water level had risen to the height of D deck there could no stopping it, and it was at this point that Captain Bartlett, in his official report (Appendix III), finally accepted the inevitable and gave orders for everyone left on board to abandon ship.

It is, of course, all too easy to lay the blame for any disaster on an over-reliance on technology. The always unpredictable human element often plays a crucial role in any disaster, and inevitably this raises important questions as to the extent of the *Britannic*'s inadequate watertight stance while operating in an acknowledged danger zone. As in the *Olympic*, the *Britannic*'s best defence against any U-boat was considered to be her speed, although as a military hospital ship she was, unlike her sister, theoretically immune to the possibility of a deliberate attack. It also has to

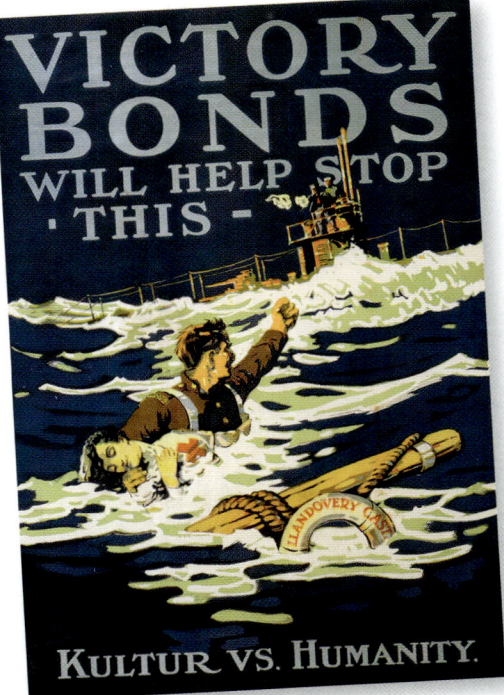

Above: Following the German reintroduction of unrestricted submarine warfare in February 1917, the torpedoing of *Llandovery Castle* would prove once and for all that hospital ships would no longer be considered as immune from attack.

be said that at this stage of the war the Germans were, for the most part, not in the habit of deliberately attacking passenger or hospital ships in the Mediterranean. The standing orders issued to the individual submarine commanders on 12 October 1916 leaves little room for doubt as to what was expected of them:

> 'The campaign against commerce in the Mediterranean should be conducted in accordance with the Prize Regulations. Enemy cargo steamers, the armament of which is recognisable beyond doubt, may be attacked submerged in the area west of Gibraltar and in the Mediterranean. Passenger steamers are not to be molested in any circumstances anywhere even if they are armed.'

As if that wasn't enough, the orders issued on 15 July that year also made it abundantly clear that the Kaiser was not inclined to accept any excuses if mistakes were made:

> 'Commanding officers are expressly informed that mistakes concerning the character of a vessel met with must not occur, and that if made, they will be held personally responsible.'

Despite this apparent restraint on the part of the Germans, however, it still begs the question as to whether the *Britannic*'s non-combatant status might possibly have engendered a subconscious false sense of security in the minds of the officers and crew on board. Even if there was the reduced threat of a torpedo attack, the risk of running into an altogether less discriminatory weapon, such as a sea mine, would have been no less than that of any other vessel. It can of course be reasonably argued that the watertight doors at the level of the tank top needed to be opened temporarily that morning, in order to assist with the change of the stokehold watch at 8am, and that it was just plain bad luck that the timing of the explosion occurred exactly when the watch was changing. But at the same time legitimate questions also need to be asked as to why – in light of what has now been observed inside the wreck, along with the well-known reference to the open portholes ('scuttles'), which Captain Heard had noted in his report was 'against orders' – the level of preparedness elsewhere was so lax.

The more forensic and archaeological approach taken by the 2021 and 2023 surveys of the *Britannic*'s interior has undoubtedly changed the emphasis in terms of how we assess the loss of the *Titanic*'s supposedly even more unsinkable sister ship. Certainly, the more colourful issues of mines, torpedoes, illicit munitions and political cover-ups have always been perfect for grabbing the headlines, but the more prosaic matter of the ship's lack of preparedness for operating in a war zone has somehow never really attracted the public interest. It has always been known that the watertight doors in boiler rooms 6 and 5 had failed to close, but the discovery of the open watertight door in Scotland Road, and the partially open door outside the Turkish bath, must now surely be seen as major factors as we reassess what might have been going on inside the *Britannic* prior to her loss.

For years, people have also tried to compare the wreck of the *Britannic* with that of the *Titanic*, and it is fair to say that at first glance we are indeed looking at two very similar wrecks, albeit in two very dissimilar settings. The problem, however, is that very often this

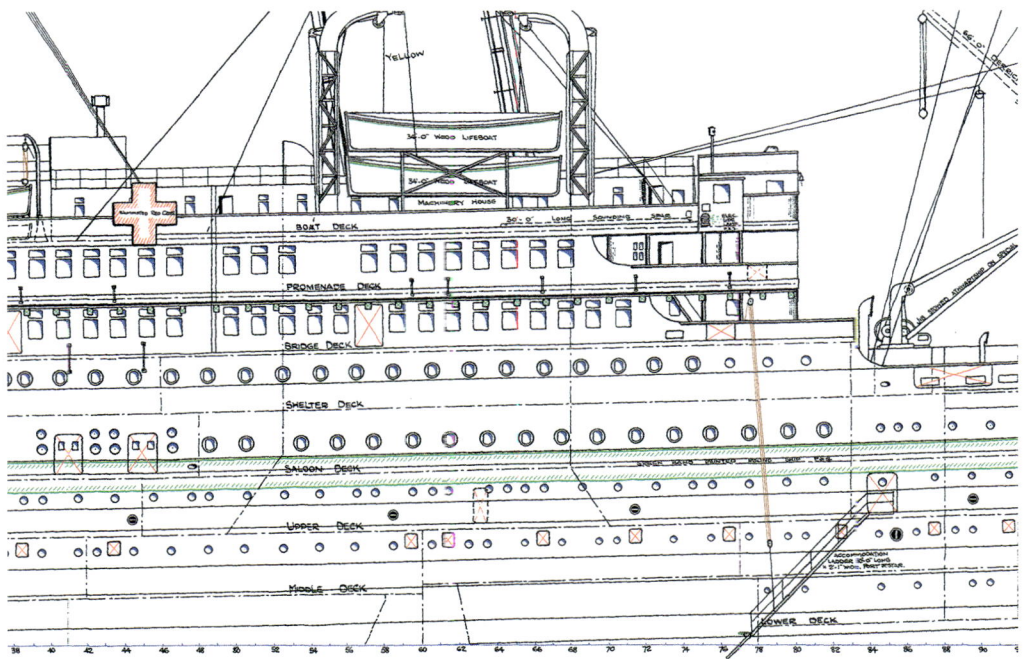

Above: The crucial portholes that may have doomed the *Britannic*. (Harland & Wolff)

Above: Launching the Mir 2 submersible in August 2005, for the two-hour drop to the wreck of the *Titanic*.

comparison is just too simplistic. The environments are very different, of course; but while on the surface the two ships seem to be practically identical, the internal differences are considerable. It is true that the *Britannic* was built largely to the same design as the *Olympic* and *Titanic*, but the internal modifications following the loss of the *Titanic* had resulted in a considerably stronger and stiffer structure in comparison to the original design. Additional questions as to whether the *Britannic* would have broken in half in the same manner as the *Titanic* also arise from time to time, but these can only really be addressed by a more detailed structural analysis, although the usefulness of any investigation along these lines is probably open to question. Certainly, each of the ships found their forward hull seriously compromised, albeit to a different extent. The *Titanic*'s brush with the iceberg resulted in six compartments being open to the sea, and while Edward Wilding's estimate was that the overall size of the damage amounted to little more than 12 square feet (1.1 sq m), it was still more than enough to overwhelm the safety features incorporated into the hull. The *Britannic*'s end was quicker, not to mention considerably more violent, but while the blast damage was more confined – largely focused in the area of holds 2 and 3 – the failure of the internal watertight doors to contain the resulting torrent of water ultimately meant that the scale of internal flooding in the *Britannic* was little different from that of the *Titanic*.

While the extent of the damage that sank the *Titanic* is known, that same information pertaining to the *Britannic* is more speculative. In their 1996 paper, Harland & Wolff marine architects Chris Hackett and John Bedford estimated that for the *Titanic* to capsize, it would have required something in the order of 38,000 tons of seawater to enter the hull before the last vestiges of stability would have been lost. In that the *Britannic* ultimately capsized to starboard, they calculated that if the time for the inflow of the 38,000 tons of water to cause capsize is reduced to 50 minutes, then the area of damage in the *Britannic*'s case would therefore be increased to about 32 square feet (3 sq m) – almost three times greater than that sustained by the *Titanic*. In that the *Britannic* heeled over quite quickly, with the flooding being augmented due to the E deck sidelights being open, and which were said to have been immersed after about 15 minutes, if that estimated area of the damage was reduced to 26 square feet (2.4 sq m) – twice that of the *Titanic* – then the remaining 23,000 tons of floodwater would have entered the hull over a period of about 35 minutes, equating to a total area of approximately 40 square feet (3.7 sq m). While these calculations are admittedly theoretical, on the basis of the initial damage being no more than twice the area of that of the *Titanic*, it is therefore not difficult to explain the rapid capsize and sinking of the *Britannic*.

The *Titanic*'s angle of heel, on the other hand, remained relatively stable throughout the sinking process, at first taking a slight list to starboard, and then a list to port before foundering. This point was not lost on Lord Mersey at the official inquiry into the sinking,

Above: Launching Perry Tritech's ROV *Voyager*, during the 1995 external survey.

but Edward Wilding was able to theorise as to how the angle of heel might have been slightly affected. The initial list to starboard suggested that the post and baggage rooms were flooded in hold 3 at an early stage, but because of the non-watertight partition bulkheads on G deck, the water would have been temporarily restrained from entering the space on the port side, which was taken up by third-class cabins.

Above: Extending more than 500 feet (152m) from end to end, the Scotland Road working passage fades into the gloomy darkness...

This restriction in flow resulted in a noticeable list to starboard, until, once the level had risen to the height of E deck, the Scotland Road working passage would have offered a much easier route for the water to flow aft, aided and abetted by the several stairways in the forward boiler casing, which would also help the rising water levels to progress further along the much wider working passage.

The *Britannic*, however, never had the opportunity to return to an even keel, as she took on a relentless heel to starboard until the last vestiges of stability had gone. Even so, bulkhead F was seemingly always going to be crucial in any investigation of the sinking, and while the *Titanic* was effectively doomed as soon as the iceberg damage progressed aft of bulkhead D, the *Britannic's* additional safety features should have sufficed to keep the ship afloat, even though the six forward compartments were flooding. Based on the figures in the 1996 paper, it would seem that in addition to the resulting loss of stability caused by a free surface effect of the water and the open portholes, we can now add the partially open watertight door on F deck, all of which combined to inflict the final coup de grace. Moreover, had the *Britannic* sunk on a more even keel then it is likely that the open watertight door in the working passage would have played a more significant role in the sinking, with bulkhead F effectively having at least two open watertight doors, three and four decks beneath the height of the bulkhead itself.

In the end, though, it seems probable that the *Britannic*'s starboard heel finished the ship before the working passage would have played any significant role in the internal flooding. Once again, it is *Titanic* steward Joseph Wheat who provides us with a clue as to what might have happened in the *Britannic*'s case, when he noted that about 90 minutes after the *Titanic* hit the iceberg, water started to run down the staircase from E deck to the Turkish bath on F deck. Wheat was in no doubt that the water was actually making its way aft via the first-class starboard passage on E deck, and that at that time Scotland Road was still dry, in which case if the heel was still significant enough to channel the water along the *Titanic*'s starboard side some 90 minutes after the ship hit the iceberg, then we have to consider that a similar effect would have been even more pronounced in the *Britannic*'s case.

An additional factor that needs to be taken into account is the movements of both ships immediately after their respective encounters with the iceberg and the mine. The *Titanic* did briefly resume a westerly heading for a few minutes after the collision, after which the ship remained motionless for the rest of the night, while the *Britannic*, in accordance with naval procedure, stopped immediately after the explosion while the damage was assessed. Once the ship began to head towards land, the forward movement almost certainly increased the rate of flooding, and the force of the water entering the hull may have caused further structural damage in the forward spaces. It was only when Captain Bartlett heard that the forward holds were filling rapidly and that water was reported in boiler rooms 5 and 6 that he eventually gave the order for the ship to be stopped, and for the lifeboats to be sent away.

Either way, both ships began to settle by the head, the *Britannic* the more quickly of the two, although during the 20 or so minutes that the ship lay stopped when lowering her lifeboats, Captain Bartlett also noted that the ship seemed to be settling more slowly. With the stern by that time so high in the water, it is questionable as to whether the rudder would have been of any great use in steering the vessel, to say nothing of the fact that the propellers, by now working above the surface, would have lost much of their efficiency, but even so he made one last attempt to work the *Britannic* toward the nearby shore. In the end it was a forlorn hope, and when it was reported that the water had risen inside the ship to the level of the saloon deck, he finally gave the order for the engineers to come topside, and to abandon ship.

The *Titanic*'s end was more drawn out as the forward compartments gradually filled with water, slowly pulling the bow deeper as the water inside the hull flowed over the internal bulkheads dividing the boiler rooms, one by one. The ship's post-collision stability may also have been helped by the fact that her engines had been stopped, while the elaborate internal subdivision provided by the wooden partitions between the various staterooms would also have inhibited any potential transverse shift of floodwater, to the point where it may have significantly lessened any potential free surface effect. As the minutes ticked by, however, the *Titanic*'s structural problems increasingly lay elsewhere. Over the next two and a half hours, as the ship's bow sank deeper into the cold North Atlantic water, the hogging effect to the hull resulted in a major stress concentration at the upper edge of the ship's strength deck in the region of funnel 3, and a smaller one at the rise in the tank top floor near boiler room 1. Finally, at 2.18am, the hull, by now listing at an approximate angle of 11 degrees to port and possibly down by as much as 23 degrees by the head, could withstand no more, breaking in half as the pent-up energy stored within the increasingly strained structure was finally released.

By comparison, the *Britannic*'s rapid heel to starboard left little time for the same internal

Above: Detail of the double bottom, indicating the final point where the *Titanic*'s hull appeared to separate. (Lone Wolf Media)

Above: The *Titanic*'s broken double bottom, lying upside down in two sections at the bottom of the Atlantic. (Lone Wolf Media)

forces to build up, although other factors, including her marginally greater beam, stronger hull, increased number of expansion joints, starboard heel and the fact that she sank in much shallower water, preventing her from attaining the same angle as the *Titanic*, may have combined to ensure that she did not break apart like her sister.

The two sisters' individual journeys to the seabed were also considerably different. During the *Titanic*'s two-and-a-half-mile (4km) descent, the hull sections reached an estimated speed of between 25 and 30 knots, the bow section sinking at a relatively shallow angle but still with enough momentum for the forward section of the wreck to bury itself in the mud up to 60 feet (18m) deep; the heavier stern section, on the other hand, sank straight down, slowly rotating as the force of the water practically tore away the poop itself. The stern's impact with the seabed was considerably less graceful than that of the bow, instead coming to a jarring halt approximately 2,400 feet (732m) further to the south and hitting the seabed with so much force that the rudder is now buried in something like 50 feet (15m) of mud. The force of the impact was so great that even the wing propeller shafts have been forced upwards, while the upper decks have collapsed and compressed on top of each

INSIDE THE BRITANNIC

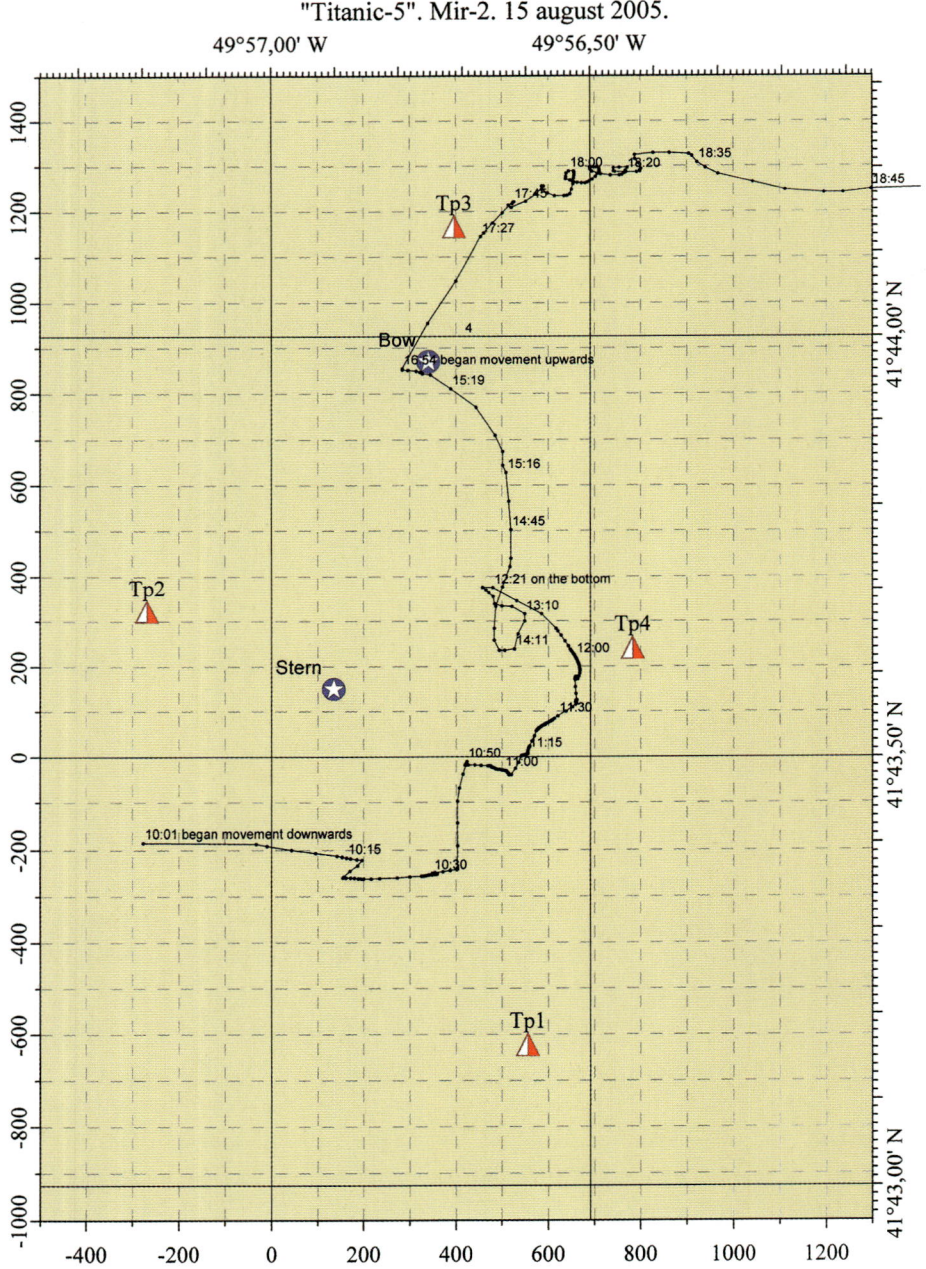

Above: Submersible track of Mir 2 on the *Titanic* wreck in August 2005. (Lone Wolf Media)

other, effectively bursting the hull. As for the *Titanic*'s midship section, everything between frames 13A and 36A, accounting for some 70 feet (21m) of the keel, lies just to the east of the stern, broken and scattered across the seabed.

The *Britannic*'s hull clearly fared somewhat better in her final moments above the surface, although, lying at an overall depth of between 344 and 374ft (105 and 114m), the final contact would certainly have been something of a soft landing when compared to the *Titanic*'s. The most visible damage to the hull lies directly beneath the forward well deck, while most of the keel remains completely intact. Unlike the *Titanic*, however, the *Britannic*'s wreck site has practically no debris field, the intact structure effectively containing everything inside the hull, as opposed to the many thousands of items that spilled out of the *Titanic*'s broken hull on its journey to the seabed. The only real debris, if it can be called that, to be found around the *Britannic*'s hull at the bottom of the Kea Channel are the four funnels lying just to the north, largely intact but having all partially collapsed under their own weight, and retaining little sign of their original oval shape.

The net result is not only two very different wreck sites, but also the need for very different technologies to investigate them. At a depth of 2.4 miles (3.9km), the pressure on the *Titanic* equates to approximately 380 atmospheres, meaning that the only way to access the wreck is with a suitably equipped submersible capable of withstanding the pressure, or with autonomous underwater vehicles (AUVs) and

Above: The *Britannic*'s bow impacting with the seabed. (Anton Logvynenko)

ROVs controlled from the surface but also capable of withstanding the huge pressures. The *Titanic* also requires an array of lighting to be able to see anything at all, whereas the *Britannic* is considerably less challenging, with warmer water and daylight resulting in an altogether different environment. Nevertheless, even at 374 feet (114m) the technical diving equipment and expertise required to explore the wreck safely is considerable, and the hazards involved can be life-threatening. News of the *Titan* submersible's catastrophic implosion over the *Titanic* wreck site on 18 June 2023 and the loss of its five passengers went around the world in minutes; and although less in the public eye, to date the *Britannic* has sadly also claimed the lives of two divers, proof positive that the risks that come with deep-water exploration or marine tourism should never be discounted or taken for granted.

14

TAKING STOCK

Despite the huge amount of progress resulting from our two successful seasons inside the *Britannic*, the autumn of 2023 left little time for any self-congratulation. Our final day of diving, 1 October 2023, was also the starting gun for the one-month's grace I had been granted by the Greek Ephorate of Marine Antiquities before having to deliver copies of the survey footage to the Ministry of Culture in Athens. The more generous six-month span granted in 2021, even if it was much longer than I really needed, had allowed much more time to view the footage and to include a detailed analysis, but even just glancing at the latest images as they were being transferred made me realise that even though I had attained practically every target I had set for the dive team that year, I still wanted more. Far from being the end of my personal Greek odyssey, if the conclusions of the 2023 survey have taught me anything, it is that on a wreck the size of the *Britannic* there is still much work to be carried out before reaching my own Ithaca.

Even so, it had been quite a journey. Cousteau and Ballard had undoubtedly blazed a trail for me to follow, but there could never be any accounting for how their resulting imagery would be interpreted by the *Titanic* faithful. To some, the structure appeared to be so robust that very quickly a distinct impression began to prevail that the *Britannic* might possibly be raised, restored and put back into service. This thinking may always have been more than a touch fanciful, but it has to be conceded that externally the hull did at least look to be in remarkably good condition. Crucially, however, the 1995 permit from the Greek Ministry of Culture, in common with any permission granted even today, did not allow us to explore any parts of the interior, the net result being that one year later, once the UK government title had been transferred to me, the task of resolving the many mysteries of the *Britannic* would instead become mine.

We have probably always known that the clock is ticking. The microbiological research carried out by Droycon Bioconcepts between

TAKING STOCK

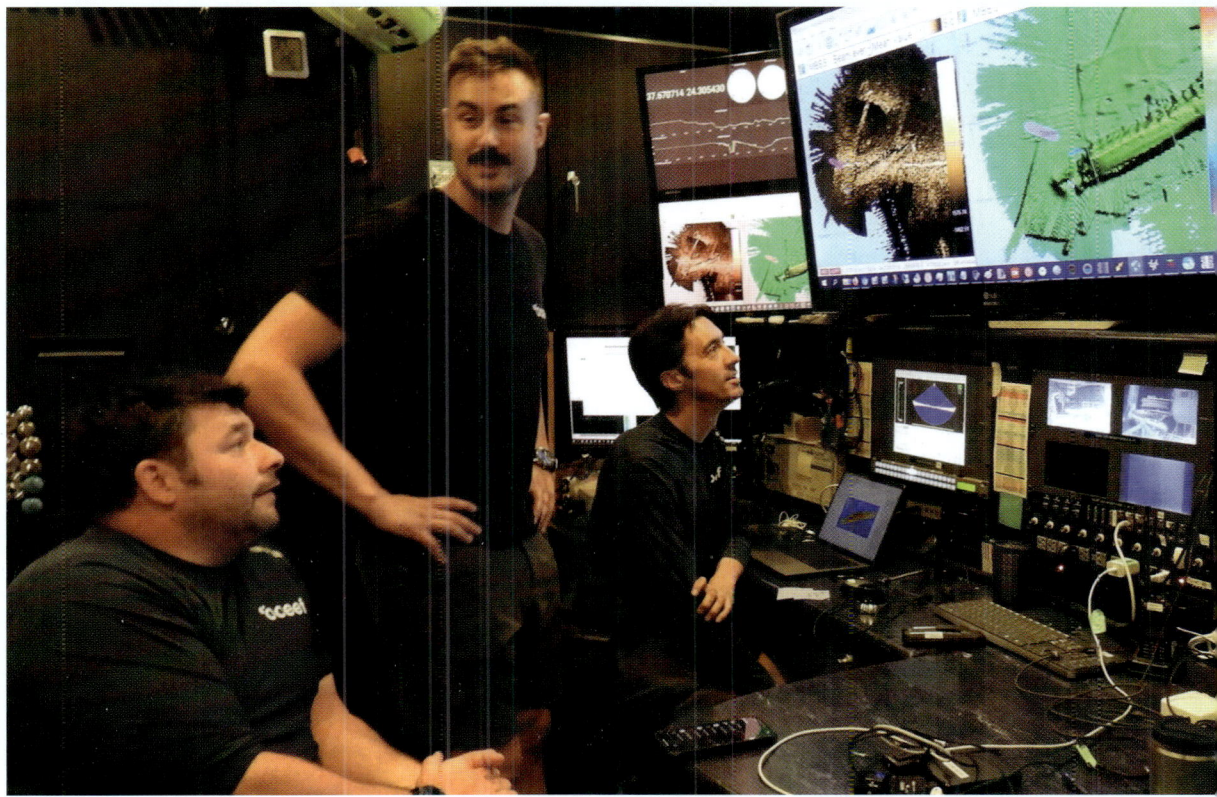

Above: Mission control aboard the RV *Odyssey*, taken during the August 2022 multibeam sonar survey of the wreck site, when the wreck of the HMS *Louvain* was also relocated.

2003 and 2009 clearly indicates that the *Britannic*, like any steel shipwreck in a saltwater environment, is living on borrowed time. It was never a question of *if* the wreck is going to collapse, but rather an issue of *when*; but while I had already come to terms with this reality 20 years ago, even now it is still not possible to predict an accurate timeframe before the inevitable structural collapse occurs. It may not happen for years, or it could happen tomorrow. In a region noted for its seismic activity, the possibility of an undersea tremor unexpectedly rendering the coup de grace cannot be ruled out either, but based on the work to date it seems likely that when the collapse does eventually take place, it will probably happen very quickly. One has only to study the deteriorating internal divisional bulkheads along Scotland Road, or in the turbine engine casing, to observe nature doing its work, as the iron-eating bacteria and marine biomass combine to gradually eat away at the structure to the point where it can no longer support its own weight. Once the collapse is

Above: The *Britannic*'s aft starboard superstructure, hanging unsupported above the seabed. At these greater and darker depths there is much less sea life, so the rusticles have gained a greater foothold.

initiated, the wreck may start to deteriorate even more quickly.

Taking into consideration what we have seen to date, we can at least start to speculate on where that initial collapse will take place. The *Britannic* lies on her starboard side, but while the main body of the hull is in contact with the seabed, the superstructure is most likely to be the wreck's Achilles' heel. The hull is not perpendicular to the seabed, instead lying at an approximate angle of 77 degrees to the surrounding seabed, and as a result, the lighter, more exposed and unsupported superstructure is already showing extensive signs of deterioration. Nor is this idle speculation, as a similar collapse has already been observed on the wreck of the *Andrea Doria* in the North Atlantic, although the combination of the *Britannic*'s location in deeper Mediterranean waters, being less susceptible to tidal movements and being constructed of steel, rather than the lighter aluminium superstructure of the Italian ship, has at least helped ensure that the wreck remains in a more robust condition. That said, the superstructure – being of a generally lighter construction and also more exposed to the marine environment – is where we have found evidence of the greatest deterioration of the exterior. The side bulwarks of the boat deck all rotted away decades ago, with significant perforations having also been observed in the sides of the forward deckhouses. Perhaps most concerning of all is the fact that the dive teams were able to access internal areas of B deck by means of two reasonably large holes in the A deck aft portside promenade. That cannot be good.

One key factor in how long the wreck's structural integrity can be maintained might well be influenced by the nature of the hull's impact on the seabed. Unlike the *Titanic*'s drawn out final minutes afloat, the *Britannic* sank relatively quickly – 55 minutes as opposed to the *Titanic*'s 160 – with the result that the stresses that gradually built up in the *Titanic*'s hull and superstructure did not affect the *Britannic*'s stronger and wider hull in quite the same way. Moreover, the *Britannic*'s marked heel to starboard may well have helped to dissipate the unseen forces that ultimately overwhelmed the structural integrity of her sister. By sinking in much shallower water, the final movements of the stern would also have been very different. As she capsized to starboard, once the bow had come into contact with the seabed the *Britannic*'s now restricted hull movement essentially pivoted on a point

Above: Part of the forward third-class entrance, still dangling precariously over the huge chasm once occupied by the *Britannic*'s forward well deck. (Derk Remmers)

Top: A twisted stanchion at the forward end of the firemen's accommodation in the forecastle.
Above: Another badly deformed stanchion, this one much further aft in the first-class à la carte restaurant.

that, based on the extent of the structural collapse, would have been located in the area directly beneath the remains of what were once cargo holds 2 and 3.

Compared to the *Titanic*, the *Britannic*'s final contact with the seabed can be looked upon as something of a soft landing, but at the same time the nature of the internal flooding would also have been completely different. While the *Britannic*'s forward compartments would have filled relatively slowly, the flooding of the undamaged aft compartments clearly happened far more quickly and violently, as the relatively light weather covers and skylights above the aft first-class staircase, reciprocating and turbine engine rooms were each overwhelmed by the differential in the internal and external pressures. Based on the visual evidence, there is little doubt that the incoming seawater tore through the aft compartments with an incomparably more violent scale of ferocity. Moreover, as the aft section of the hull would have been pivoting that much faster than the mid-section, those sections located further towards the stern would have hit the seabed with considerably greater force, which may explain why there is less evidence of any deformation to the internal support stanchions in the mid-ship areas of the structure, as opposed to those further aft. The forward first-class entrance and staircase supports show no sign of any deformation, whereas a number of deformed and broken support stanchions aft on B deck bear visible testimony to the forces being exerted inside this part of the structure. The deformation even further aft becomes increasingly noticeable, particularly in some of the supporting members at the base of the aft first-class main entrance on the shelter deck, but it is to some of the stanchions within the first-class à la carte restaurant where the damage is most pronounced. It is not yet possible to suggest that this damage may have been caused by the dislocation of the upper decks as the stern section impacted with the seabed, but there can be little doubt that significant internal structural damage has occurred inside the aft section of the hull, which may well have been further extended as the wreck settled into its current posture on the seabed.

While the long-term outlook is undoubtedly concerning, there is still much encouragement to be taken from some areas deeper within the hull. It was the goal of the 2021 and 2023 surveys to carry out a detailed internal recording of the wreck with a view to taking the first steps to properly assess and formulate the opportunities and requirements for conservation. Strictly speaking, an ongoing observation of the *Britannic*'s condition has already been underway since the summer of 1995, with the external imagery of no fewer than ten expeditions between 1995 and 2023 contributing to our understanding of exactly what is happening at the bottom of the Kea Channel, and how the wreck has adapted to its marine environment. Because of the *Britannic*'s legal status as a monument in Greece, permission will not be granted for any internal penetrations by recreational divers, and in fact it is only my status as holder of the UK government's former legal title to the wreck that has allowed me to occasionally sidestep this restriction. Even then, in view of the wreck's additional sensitivity as the symbolic grave of 30 British servicemen killed in the First World War, applications to carry out surveys of the interior will be few and far between. Only five permits for internal work have been requested between 2003 and 2023, but as a result of a carefully planned and clearly defined strategy, we can at least say that over this 20-year period we have now properly addressed the really important questions with regard to what is happening inside the wreck, and of the potential effect that this will most likely have on its future structural integrity.

As with most shipwrecks, the *Britannic* is full of contradictions. On the one hand, you can enter the forward main entrance where the extent of preservation is such that there does not appear to be any suggestion of an imminent major structural collapse, while the noticeable deterioration of the dividing walls along the aft sections of the Scotland Road working passage provide undeniable evidence of the ongoing deterioration that must surely be undermining the entire structure. For the most part, this deterioration seems to be limited to the thinner metal divisions inside the hull, while the more important load-bearing structural members appear to be holding their own, for the time being at least. Then again, we have also found evidence of a

Above: The badly rotted bulkhead leading into the printing room is a telling sign of the ship's deterioration.

Above: The aft end of the first-class galley, now accessible from the turbine engine casing as a result of the extensive deterioration of the bulkhead.

partial collapse in some of the more substantial structural bulkheads. Bulkhead K (frame 30A), which extended as high as the underside of the bridge deck, is displaying noticeable deterioration at the approximate level of E deck, so much so that in 2021 a dive team was unexpectedly able to access the forward end of the reciprocating engines via the crew staircase at the aft end of the first-class galley. Such a penetration should not have been possible through the solid watertight bulkhead, but it remains unclear as to whether this partial collapse, undoubtedly initiated during the sinking process by the force of water, has been further extended by the subsequent deterioration of the structure over the ensuing years. Even so, we can be certain of one thing: bulkhead K remains an important structural entity of the wreck, and any further deterioration in this area will need more regular and careful monitoring in the coming years.

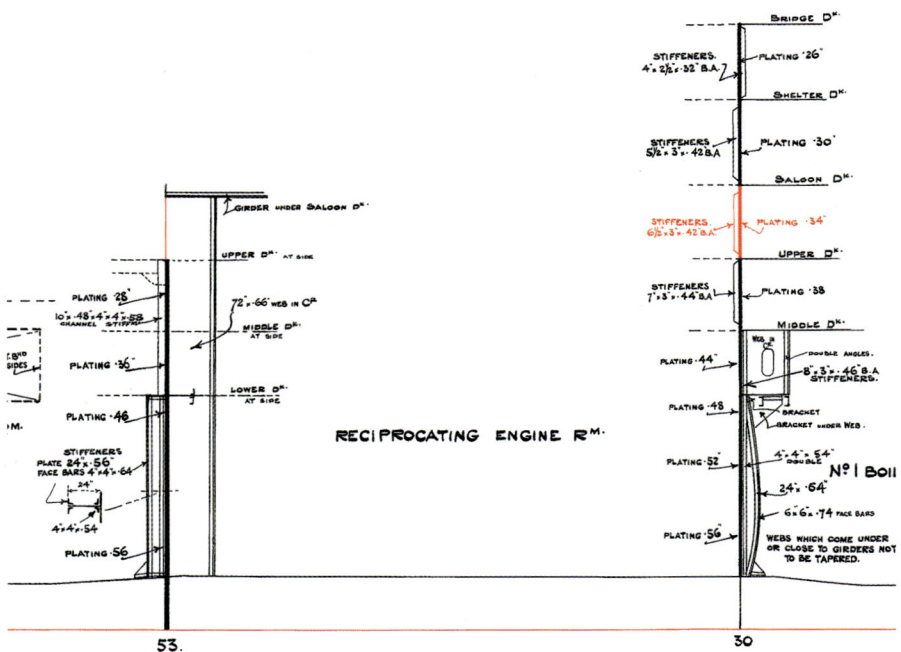

Above: Detail of bulkhead stiffening in the reciprocating engine room, the red section highlighting the areas significantly damaged during the sinking process.

Notwithstanding these areas of concern, however, there are also signs of hope. The sight of both reciprocating engines, still intact and firmly attached to their bedplates after more than a hundred years on their side, the intact turbine engine one compartment further aft, and the nine double-ended Scotch marine boilers of boiler rooms 6 and 5 still sitting in their cradles, all provide significant evidence that parts of the structure seemingly remain as robust as ever. Despite the perennial speculation as to the quality of materials and workmanship in the *Titanic*, all I can say is that what I have seen inside her sister ship is a phenomenal testament to the quality and skill of the Harland & Wolff workforce.

After more than a century lying on the Aegean seabed, the *Britannic* has to all intents and purposes become a man-made reef. As a former coal-burning vessel, the wreck presents no conceivable hazard from leaking oil to the marine environment, and this environmental stability has resulted in a thriving and unique marine ecosystem. Nor has this factor been lost on the Greek Ministry of Culture. On 10 June 2022, the Kea Channel became a designated marine park, allowing divers to access not just the *Britannic* but also the French liner *Burdigala* and the SS *Patris*, a Greek paddler sunk off the island in 1868. Each of the areas surrounding these wrecks measure something in the region of 360 acres, creating zones where all fishing is effectively prohibited, but allowing suitably qualified

Above: Close-up detail of the damaged forward bulkhead, the riveted seam having failed completely.

recreational diving to the wrecks in question. Not only does this effectively protect the wreck from the hazards of carelessly discarded fishing nets – by far the biggest problem in the past – but it will hopefully guarantee an appropriate degree of control from human interference. As the UK owner of the wreck, this is an arrangement that I can quite easily live with, as it essentially mirrors the 'look but don't touch' policy taken by the British Ministry of Defence when divers access British naval vessels lost to enemy action, particularly when loss of life is involved.

Ultimately, though, the *Britannic* is not just about divers; nor should it be. The footage resulting from the 2021 and 2023 surveys has already generated literally hours of invaluable data, with a view to formulating the conservation project, but regardless of the huge amount of additional information at our disposal, many of our discoveries have still ended up raising almost as many questions as we have answered. Naturally, I am looking to return to the site in due course to continue where we left off, but it also has to be said that the internal survey work to date, carried out in collaboration with the National Museum of the Royal Navy and the Greek Ministry of

Above: The blown-out bulkhead leading from the aft working passage into the reciprocating engine room.

Culture, is hopefully just the first step as we move to discuss not only the wreck's conservation, but also the possible retrieval of a representative number of artefacts for conservation and public display.

After a quarter of a century toiling in the Kea Channel, it is only now that we are finally beginning to understand exactly what is happening inside the *Britannic*, but if there is one thing the 2021 and 2023 surveys have conclusively proved it is that it is impossible to anticipate exactly how long we will be able to look upon the wreck as a recognisable entity. That she will eventually collapse is beyond doubt, but even when that happens the project will not end there. The *Britannic* will not simply cease to exist as a shipwreck; she will just be a different kind of shipwreck, and I think I can live with that.

Above: 1 October 2023, after the final day of diving during the second stage of the survey. Despite the huge amount of data resulting from the two expeditions, perhaps it is still too early to finally say "job done."

APPENDIX I

Details from Section A of the Harland & Wolff specification book for Yard No. 433

GENERAL DESIGN.

a) PRINCIPAL DIMENSIONS.

Length overall	...	about 883' 0"
Length between perpendiculars	...	850' 0"
Breadth moulded	...	93' 6"
Depth from top of keel to top of Shelter Deck beams at lowest point	...	64' 6"
Depth moulded to Shelter Deck at lowest point	...	64' 3"

b) HEIGHT OF 'TWEEN DECKS.

Lower Orlop to Orlop	...	8' 0"
Orlop to Lowe (11' 0" in No.2 Hold)	...	forward 8' 0" aft. about 9' 6"
Lower to Middle	...	8' 0"
Middle to Upper	...	8' 6"
Upper to Saloon	...	9' 0"
Saloon to Shelter	...	10' 6" forward 9' 0"
Shelter to Bridge, Poop and Forecastle	...	9' 0"
Bridge to Promenade	...	9' 6"
Promenade to Boat	...	9' 6"
After Boat Deck	...	9' 0"
After Docking Bridge	...	8' 0"

c) SHEER.

Forward	...	about 12' 0"
Aft	...	about 4' 0"

CAMBER.   Decks to be cambered 3" in full width of vessel.

d) HEIGHT OF HOUSES AND PUBLIC ROOMS, ETC.

Chart and Wheelhouse	...	8' 3"
Captain and Officers' Mess	...	8' 3"
Elevator Gear House	...	7' 6"
Engine and Boiler Casings	...	9' 6"
Engineers' Smokeroom, &c	...	8' 3"
First Class Entrance (Boat Dk.)	...	9' 6"
Second Class Entrance	...	9' 6"
Raised Roof over after First-Class Entrance	...	5' 3"
Raised Roof over forward First-Class Entrance	...	6' 0"
First Class Lounge	...	12' 3"
First Class Reading & Writing Room	...	12' 3"
First Class Smokeroom	...	12' 3"
First Class Dining Saloon	...	10' 6"
First Class Reception Room	...	10' 6"
First Class Gymnasium	...	9' 6"
Children's Playroom	...	9' 6"
First Class Veranda and Palm Court	...	9' 6"
Restaurant	...	9' 6"
Restaurant Reception Room	...	9' 6"
Squash Racquet Court	...	16' 6"
Second Class Dining Saloon	...	10' 6"
Second Class Library and Entrance	...	9' 0"
Second Class Smokeroom and Entrance	...	9' 6"
Second Class Gymnasium	...	9' 0"
Third Class Smokeroom & Entrance	...	9' 0"
Third Class General Room	...	9' 0"
Third Class Dining Saloon	...	8' 6"
Hospitals	...	8' 0"

e) NOTATION OF DECKS.

Promenade Deck	...	'A'
Bridge Deck	...	'B'
Shelter Deck	...	'C'
Saloon Deck	...	'D'
Upper Deck	...	'E'
Middle Deck	...	'F'
Lower Deck	...	'G'
Orlop		

APPENDIX II

Report into the loss of the HMHS *Britannic* **by Captain Hugh Heard and Commander George Staer (UK National Archives File No: ADM 137/2171):**

H.M.S. 'Duncan',

24th November 1916.

Sir,

Having enquired into the circumstances attending the loss of the Hospital Ship 'Britannic', we have the honour to make the following report. It must be premised that the enquiry was necessarily incomplete owing to the shortness of time at our disposal and the difficulty of finding witnesses scattered over the whole fleet.

2. The following is a brief description of structure of 'Britannic' in the region of the explosion. Rough sketches are attached. Forward of Bridge were situated the Fore Peak and Nos 1, 2 & 3 holds, No 3 hold being a reserve coal Bunker, Water tight bulkheads separating these compartments. No 6 Boiler Room was immediately under Fore Bridge & No 5 Boiler Room being immediately abaft No 6. A W.T. tunnel ran from forward bulkhead of No 6 and under Nos 3 & 2 holds to No 1 hold, compartments over which were situated Firemans quarters.

Unless therefore the W.T doors in this tunnel were closed the boiler rooms were in free communication with Nos 1, 2 & 3 holds in the event of Tunnel being damaged.

The Watertight doors were automatic in action and could also be closed by means of handles abaft doors or from deck plates on E deck.

3. There was one explosion only. This took place on Starboard side low down and in the vicinity of the bulkhead between 2 and 3 holds, breaking this bulkhead and thus filling Nos. 2 & 3 holds. Whether the bulkhead between Nos 1 & 2 holds was broken is not certain, but it is probable. Anyway No. 1 hold also filled either in this way or through the tunnel.

4. It appears that the bulkhead between No. 3 hold & No. 6 Stokehold was not broken, but water from the holds gained free access through the W.T. door between stokehold and tunnel which was not closed, the tunnel having been broken.

5. Water also had free access to No. 5 Stokehold through the W.T. door between 5 and 6. It is clear that this door was not wholly, although there is evidence to show that it may have been partly, closed.

6. There seems to have been a period of 1 to 2 minutes from the time of the explosion until the water in the stokeholds was too deep for work to be performed, when these doors might have been closed. This

would have secured the two boiler rooms, measuring about 35' x 90' in area, from incursion by water. This might have saved the ship, but without plans of the whole structure it is impossible to offer an opinion.

7. We are confident that no water penetrated abaft No. 5 stokehold in the lower part of the ship.

8. A further means for the admission of water was by side scuttles. The W.T doors before the stokehold seem to have been closed except in the tunnel. The scuttles on F deck should not have been open as it was contrary to orders at that time, but there is evidence that these orders were occasionally disobeyed. Many of the scuttles on E deck were open.

The ship taking a list of about 25 degrees to starboard and getting down by the bows would quickly bring these under water. Direct evidence shows that about 15 minutes after the explosion, the scuttles on E Deck (normally 25' out of water) on a line between the foremost funnels were awash, and water was coming along this deck from forward.

9. Question of mine or torpedo. The water was deep, probably over 100 fathoms and there is a current through the Zea Channel. This against the mine theory.

Three persons gave good evidence of having seen

(a) A Periscope

(b) The wake of a torpedo immediately before the explosion and in its direction. This man F. Walters, Deck Steward having been an Officers Steward in the Navy had seen torpedo practice. He did not pretend to have seen the torpedo.

(c) The wake of a torpedo on port side apparently missing aft. It is to be noted that the sea was glassy smooth.

On other hand there is no evidence of a column of water having been thrown up outside the ship.

The effects of the explosion might have been due to either a mine or a torpedo. The probability seems to be a mine.

    We have the honour to be,
    Sir,
    Your Obedient Servants,
    H. H. Heard.
    Captain.
    G. H. Starr.
    Engineer Commander.

Due to a typographical error, Commander Staer's name was incorrectly recorded at the bottom of the page.

APPENDIX III

Report into the loss of HMHS Britannic by Captain Charles Alfred Bartlett (PRO File No: ADM137/1229):

H.M.T. ROYAL GEORGE

AT SEA.

November 30th 1916.

To the Director of Transports, Admiralty

Sir

It is with great regret that I have to report the sinking of H.M. Hospital Ship Britannic No. G608 by an enemy mine or torpedo, on the morning of the 21st. November at a position in Zea Channel, near the Gulf of Athens, Port St. Nikolo Lighthouse bore S. 48 E (Mag) distance 3 miles at the time of the explosion.

The ship at the time was steaming 20 knots, weather fine and the sea smooth, bound to Mudros to embark sick and wounded and was painted and carrying all the signals, in strict accordance with the Geneva convention.

We had on board a crew numbering 673 all told and in addition carried a Medical Staff comprising 22 Surgeons, 3 Chaplains, 77 Nurses and 290 Orderlies of the R.A.M.C.

No passengers were carried whatever.

We left Naples on the evening of the 19th. inst. and proceeded on the direct route for the Port bound to.

At 7.52 A.M. on the 21st we passed Angarlestro Point on the Island of Makio Nisi, distant 4 miles and set a course N. 48" E (mag) to pass through Zea Channel.

At 8.12 A.M. when in the position above mentioned a tremendous but muffled explosion occurred, the ship trembling and vibrating most violently fore and aft, continuing for some time; the ship fell off about 3 points from her course. Emergency Quarters were sounded on all Alarms throughout the ship, the engines stopped, and orders rung below to close water tight doors, at the same time sending out the S.O.S. signal by wireless.

My first impression was that we had struck a mine and would probably be safe. I gave orders to clear away all boats and have all possible ready to be sent away. After an interval, steering gear appeared to have failed, I turned the ship around to port to head for land by the engines, but the forward holds filled rapidly and water was reported in Nos. 5 & 6 boiler rooms, so I stopped the engines and ordered all boats possible to be sent away, but to stand by near the ship.

The ship seemed to stop settling a little and I passed word to stop lowering boats and again attempted to work ship toward the land, but she again started to settle rapidly and water being reported on 'D' deck, I gave the order for all to leave the ship, passing word to the engine room and blowing on the whistle for the last alarm.

The ship was sinking very quickly then, going by the head and listing to starboard and soon the water came to the bridge and Assistant Commander Dyke having reported to me that all had left, I told him to go and shortly after followed myself, walking into the water by the forward boat gantry on Starboard side, the third funnel falling a few minutes later. I was picked up about 30 minutes later by the motor boat.

Whilst in the water I saw the ship sink, having listed well to Starboard and when finally disappearing her stern was almost perpendicular, the time being given by those in the boats as 9.7 A.M.

When rescued by the motor boat I was informed that some boats had fouled the propeller on Port side and a number of men had been thrown into the water and injured, the two motor boats picking them up, so after a thorough examination of the vicinity I ordered both motor boats to proceed to Port St. Nikolo with the injured, passing word for all the other boats to follow. Whilst on the way we could see the H.M.S. Heroic and the Destroyer 'Scourge' making for the scene, they did splendid work in picking up the boats and then proceeded to Piraeus with the rescued.

Having landed with most of the injured at Port St. Nikolo, where we were well received and the injured men taken to shelter, the arrangements being superintended by the French Consul, I sent a telegram through him to the French Legation at Athens, also one to S.N.O. Mudros.

In all about 160 persons landed at St. Nikolo and later the Destroyer 'Foxhound' arriving we were all embarked and reached Piraeus about 5.30 P.M. when every care and attention was given us by the Rear Admiral, his Officers and men on the 'Duncan' also by the French warships in port.

After a careful roll call it was found that in all 1 Officer and 28 men were missing, the Officer and 7 men being of the R.A.M.C. the remainder being crew.

This loss I deplore as in my opinion it was caused by the wrecking of the boats as I feel confident all hands left the ship.

I have nothing but praise for the cool and orderly way all Officers, men and boys behaved throughout, there not being any sign of excitement or panic at any time. Lt. Col. Anderson R.A.M.C. the S.M.O. and his staff did splendidly not only at the sinking of the ship but afterwards in their great care of the injured, Surgeons using the Kapok from life jackets for dressings.

A number of Nursing Sisters pluckily came from boat to boat to aid the injured, finally landing with them at Port St. Nikolo to care for them.

Twenty eight Life Boats were lowered and two Motor Boats, the latter doing excellent service in quickly searching the scene and picking up many from the water especially those injured.

APPENDIX III

TORPEDO or MINE

The explosion occurred whilst '*Britannic*' was in about 65 Fathoms of water, and a mine might have been the cause, but there is good evidence that the tracks of two Torpedoes were seen, one of which struck the ship starboard side forward, the other missing the ship from the port side aft. Also two men declare they saw an object which they took to be a Submarine twenty minutes after the explosion just off the starboard side.

The damage was most extensive, probably the whole of the fore part of the ship's bottom being destroyed and in my opinion penetrating to No. 6 boiler room. Water was seen to be thrown up to 'E' or 'D' deck forward at the time of the explosion, and a cloud of black smoke was seen, the fumes for some time being suffocating.

In conclusion I am anxious to express my grateful thanks to Vice Admiral Sir Cecil Thursby K.C.M.G., Rear Admiral Hayes Sadler C.S.I. and the French Admiral for their promptness in sending rescue ships to us, also for the great comfort and care given to one and all, and for gifts of clothing which we received from the Officers and men of both fleets.

I would add that the Captain and Officers of H.M.T. Ermine and H.M.T. Royal George deserve thanks for their care of us whilst on their ships proceeding home.

I have the honour to be, Sir

Your obedient Servant

Charles A. Bartlett
MASTER

The Britannic's official number was actually G618.

For some reason, the name of 40213 Pte. Leonard T Smith was not listed along with the other casualties in Britannic's log, though his name does appear on the British war memorial at Mikra on the southern outskirts of Thessaloniki. This being the case, the final total of those killed on the occasion of the sinking of the Britannic comes to 21 crew, one officer and eight men of the RAMC.

BIBLIOGRAPHY AND SELECTED SOURCES

Ayrton, Rick (with Roberts, Scott): *Expedition Britannic: Diving Titanic's Sister Ship* (Dived Up Publications, 2021)

Beveridge, B, Andrews, S, Hall, S, Klistorner, D and Braunschweiger, A: *Titanic: The Ship Magnificent* (The History Press, 2016)

Fleming, Rev. John A: *The Last Voyage of His Majesty's Hospital Ship Britannic* (Wordsmith Publications, 1998)

Hutchings, David and de Kerbrech, Richard: *RMS Titanic: 1909-12 (Olympic Class) Owners' Workshop Manual* (Haynes Publishing, 2011)

Jessop, Violet: *Titanic Survivor* (Sheridan House, 1997)

Kohler, Richie (with Hudson, Charlie): *Mystery of the Last Olympian* (Best Publishing Company, 2016)

Macbeth, Sheila: *Pages from a Nursing Sister's Diary* (Unpublished diary, 1916)

Maxtone-Graham, John (ed): *Olympic & Titanic: Ocean Liners of the Past* (Patrick Stephens, 1988)

Mills, Simon: *Hostage to Fortune* (Wordsmith Publications, 2002)

Mills, Simon: *The Unseen Britannic* (The History Press, 2020)

Mills, Simon: *Exploring the Britannic* (Adlard Coles, 2019)

Mills, Simon: *Olympic Titanic Britannic: The Anatomy and Evolution of the Olympic Class* (Adlard Coles, 2022)

Thoctarides, Kostas and Bilalis, Aris: *Shipwrecks of the Greek Seas: Dive into their History.* (Aikaterini Laskaridis Foundation, 2015)

Tyler, Percy D: The Story of the Sinking of *HMHS Britannic* (Unpublished journal, 1916)

Engineering (27 February 1914)

The Shipbuilder magazine (February 1914)

The Titanic Commutator (Quarterly magazine of the Titanic Historical Society, Inc., PO Box 51053, Indian Orchard, Massachusetts 01151-0053, USA)

PAPERS

Bellou, N, Smith, C, Papathanassiou, E: '2008 HCMR *Britannic* Shipwreck Survey' (Elkethe, 2008)

Cullimore, R and Johnston, L 'Microbiological Evaluation of the Potential At-Site Corrosion of the Steels Used in the Construction of HMHS *Britannic*' (Droycon Bioconcepts, 27 August 2009)

Garzke, W, Mills, S. Dulin, RO, Bemis, FG, Ridder, D, Foecke, T and Brown, DK: 'The Saga of HMHS *Britannic*' (ASNE/SNAME Symposium Paper, September 1998)

Hackett, C and Bedford, JG: 'The Sinking of S.S. *Titanic* Investigated by Modern Techniques' (Royal Institution of Naval Architects, 1996)

Johnston, Lori: 'Final Report of the Scientific Examination of the HMHS *Britannic*' (Droycon Bioconcepts, 23 December 2003)

BIBLIOGRAPHY AND SELECTED SOURCES

Mills, Simon: 'Preliminary Findings of Explorations to the Wreck of HMHS *Britannic*, Kea Channel, Northern Aegean' (Marine Forensics Panel, 17 January 2000)

Mills, Simon: 'HMHS *Britannic* Expedition Summaries' (2003, 2021 and 2023)

Mullins, Cliff: 'Coal Analysis of Sample 137490' (Report for Marine Forensics Panel by Minton, Treharne & Davies Limited, 28 July 2000)

Stettler, JW and Thomas, BS: 'Flooding and Structural Forensic Analysis of the Sinking of the RMS *Titanic*' (International Marine Forensics Symposium, National Harbor, MD. April 2012)

ARCHIVAL SOURCES

Official records in UK National Archives

ADM 53/40400	Log of HMS *Duncan*
ADM 53/42159	Log of HMS *Foxhound*
ADM 53/57296	Log of HMS *Rattlesnake*
ADM 53/59512	Log of HMS *Scourge*
ADM 116/1395	German allegations of *Britannic* carrying troops (1915)
ADM 116/1586	Salvage of HMHS *Asturias*
ADM 137/1229	Loss of HMHS *Britannic*
ADM 137/2171	Loss of HMHS *Britannic*
ADM 156/117	HMHS *Braemar Castle*
BT 110/260	Registration documents of HMHS *Britannic*
BT 165/1569	Log of HMHS *Britannic* (1915-1916)
MT 23/443	Availability of Channel hospital ships
MT 23/461	Routine on board hospital ships
MT 23/476	Suggestion to embark patients at Naples
MT 23/540	Transfer of invalids at Italian ports
MT 23/541	Distinctive lights on hospital ships
MT 23/593	*Britannic* to convey stores and RAMC personnel
MT 23/596	Arrangement of hospital ships after loss of *Britannic*
MT 23/637	*Britannic* as a hospital ship and service details

ACKNOWLEDGEMENTS

It is no exaggeration to say that this book is the culmination of almost thirty years of work on a single shipwreck, during which time the contribution of a seemingly endless number of individuals from entirely different backgrounds has enabled me to collate the information now held within these 288 pages.

Starting in the historical world, I need to express particular gratitude to Ed & Karen Kamuda, David Hutchings, Richard de Kerbrech, Paul Louden-Brown, Ken Marschall, Tom McCluskie, Michail Michailakis, Captain Peter Starling RAMC and Parks Stephenson. I am also particularly grateful to Jennifer Clarke, Alasdair Fairbairn, John Fleming Jr., Ronald Goodman, John Harvey, Margaret & Mary Meehan, Angus & Jonathan Mitchell and Marion Sargeant, all descendants of *Britannic* veterans, who over the years have generously shared their time, memories and personal archives.

At the official level, a word of acknowledgment is also due to the Greek Ministry of Culture and the Ephorate of Marine Antiquities. Over the years I must have worked with no less than five Directors of Marine Antiquities, Dr. Eleni Banou, Dr. Katerina Dellaporta, Dr. Pari Kalamara, Dr. Dimitris Kourkoumelis and Dr. Angeliki Simosi, while particular thanks must go to Dr. George Koutsouflakis, the former Director of Underwater Archaeological Sites, Monuments & Research at the Ephorate of Marine Antiquities, for his assistance in helping me to navigate the minefield of official paperwork that made this project possible. At the UK end, I am also grateful to the Department for the Economy in Belfast, for their initial diplomatic support in instigating the conservation project, David McVeigh, the former marketing manager at Harland & Wolff, and also Professor Dominic Tweddle and Captain John Rees RN, OBE, formerly at the National Museum of the Royal Navy in Portsmouth.

Similarly, the support of Yannis Tzavelakos of Kea Divers, the office of the Mayor of Kea, the Hellenic Coastguard and the Hellenic Navy's Hydrographic Department also helped to ensure that our stays on Kea were not only a pleasure, but that our operations in the Kea Channel were carried out in absolute safety.

At the production level, this section would also not be complete without a word to Jenny Clark and Jonathan Eyers, my editors at Adlard Coles, for their enthusiastic support, to Jenni Davis for her fine-tuning of the manuscript, and to Nick Avery for the layout design. Nor should I overlook marine illustrators William Barney (who also designed our priceless expedition t-shirts), Cyril Codus, Anton Logvynenko and Ken Marschall.

Last, but by no means least, we come to the crucially important sharp end of the project. I may have been the one telling them where to go, but the reality is that none of the wreck imagery contained within this book would have been possible without the immense contribution of the several dive teams with whom I have worked since 2003, all of which helped lead to the phenomenal achievements of the 2021 and 2023 internal surveys. Available space doesn't permit me to list every expedition in the detail that they so richly deserve, but there is no denying that without the vital contribution of the dive teams, scientists and media personnel on the 2003, 2006, 2008, 2015, 2021, 2022 and 2023 internal surveys, this book would not have been possible. Listed in alphabetical order, they are:

ACKNOWLEDGEMENTS

Deep Diving Team: Stewie Andrews; Mike Barnette; Perry Brandes; Leigh Bishop; Christina Campbell; John Chatterton; Geraint Ffoulkes-Jones; Chris Hutchison; Katy Kohler; Richie Kohler; Evan Kovacs; Christian Malan; Barry McGill; Zaid al Obeidi; Antonello Paone; Martin Parker; Edoardo Pavia; Joe Pellegrino; Mike Pizzio; Kevin Pickering; Barry Smith; Carl Spencer; Rich Stevenson; Barry Smith; Teresa Telus; George Vandoros

Support Divers: Ed del Campo; Alex Frenzel; Heeth Grantham; Joe Porter

Submersible Pilots: Kostas Katsaros; Dmitry Tomashov; Kimly Do; Montana McKinnon

Support Vessels: MV *Commandant Fourcault*; RV *Aegaeo*; Kea Divers; MV *Loyal Watcher*; DV Nikolakis; RV *Odyssey* (OCEEF); MV *U-Boat Navigator*

Scientific Analysis: Dr. Roy Cullimore & Dr. Lori Johnston (Droycon Bioconcepts, Inc.); Bill Lange & Maryann Morin (Woods Hole Oceanographic Institution); Dr. Evangelos Papathanassiou (Hellenic Centre for Marine Research); Dr. Petar Denoble and Dr. Frauke Tillmans (Divers Alert Network)

Sonar & Digital Imaging: Bill Smith, Graeme Conagher & Alain Douglas (2003); Dr. George Papatheodorou (University of Patras, 2007); Richard Jeong (RV *Odyssey*); Leighton Rolley (REV Ocean); Evan Kovacs & David Ullman (Marine Imaging Technologies)

Media Support: Stamos Barsim (Olyvon Productions, Greece); Peter Davey (Carlton International); Mike McKimm (BBC Northern Ireland); Kelvin Murray (Eyos); Crispin Sadler (Mallinson Sadler Productions); Kirk Wolfinger (Lone Wolf Media); Channel 5 Television; Discovery Channel; The History Channel; National Geographic; The Explorers Club (New York); Tina Tavridou (Greek liaison)

Sadly there are two names in the above list who will never see the culmination of the work that they have helped to bring about. Anton Logvynenko was killed during a combat mission in the Kharkiv region of Ukraine on 27th November 2023, while the death of Carl Spencer, the dive team leader on the first internal survey in 2003, following an in-water decompression incident while returning from a dive to the *Britannic* on 24th May 2009, is still an open wound. Even after all these years his death remains an important reminder of the risks taken, and the price that is sometimes paid, in the name of exploration and science.

Much of the earlier wreck imagery in this book has been credited to the individual divers or photographers on the various expeditions between 2003 and 2019. Based on the abundance of material on which I could draw from the 2021 and 2023 surveys, however, it has often been all but impossible to prioritise one image over another, or identify the specific diver who may have taken the photograph in question. It is no exaggeration to say that Evan Kovacs, our dive team leader, assembled a team of deep divers who not only reached every target and attained every goal that I set for them, but returned with the imagery I needed to support what up until then had been just speculation. This book is as much their achievement as it is mine, and particular thanks (in alphabetical order) must go to: Stewie Andrews, Mike Barnette, Perry Brandes, Katy Kohler, Richie Kohler, Evan Kovacs, Barry McGill, Edoardo Pavia, Rich Stevenson and George Vandoros.

INDEX

À la Carte Restaurant 130–2, 269
À la Carte Restaurant Galley 137–43
Accumulator Room 126
Admiralty 19, 20, 21, 24, 39, 42, 93, 103, 107, 192, 250
Adriatic Sea 23
Adriatic (RMS) 12, 19
Aegean Sea 6, 23, 37, 60, 92, 272
Aegusa, HMY 24
Agia Triada (church) 5, 33
Aktaion Hotel 249
Aldam Heaton & Co. 107, 108
Aldershot 21
Anchors 67–70, 152
Anderson, Henry Stewart (Lieut-Col.) 29
Andrea Doria (SS) 76, 266
Andrews, Stewie 138, 185
Andrews, Thomas 10, 12
Andros (island) 26
Angalistros Point 27
Anglo-American Arab printing press 179, 181
Aquitania (RMS) 20, 23, 92, 109, 128, 165
Arizona (USS) 58
Armstrong, William Edward 16
Armstrong Davits 16–17, 29, 31, 77–8, 85, 91, 176, 90, 91, 130, 176, 224
Ash Ejectors 204
Asturias (HMHS) 96–7, 100, 198, 253
Athens 41, 44, 248, 249, 250, 264
Attica 5
Audacious (HMS) 96
Austria-Hungary 19, 39

Ballard, Robert D. (Dr.) 44, 46, 48, 52, 264
Baltic (RMS) 19
Bangor 208
Barber, Marjorie (nurse) 114, 117, 127
Barham (HMS) 21
BART platforms 54–6
Bartlett, Charles Alfred (Captain) 21, 23, 27, 28, 29, 30, 32, 33, 72, 94, 207, 216, 242, 253, 259
Bedford, John 88, 90, 257
Belfast 9, 12, 19, 20, 21, 93, 104, 112, 200
Belfast Lough 21, 208
Binks, Arthur (Private) 33, 250
Biscay, Bay of 24
Bismarck (SS) 109
Bismarck (KMS) 58
Bizerte (Tunisia) 24
Blabe Rocks 42
Board of Trade 12, 16, 77, 200, 230
Boiler Room 5 101, 190, 200–7, 250, 251, 259, 272
Boiler Room 6 100, 101, 186, 190, 198, 200–7, 250, 251, 259, 272
Boiler Room casings 84
Boiler Room vestibule 100
Boilers 16, 33, 63, 100, 201, 203, 272
Booth, Alfred 20
Bradford plate design 139–41
Braemar Castle (HMHS) 42
Brandes, Perry 185
Bridge 79–80
Bridge Engine Telegraphs 80
Bridge Steering Pedestal 80
Bristow, L (Second Assistant Steward) 253
British Mediterranean Squadron 248
Britannic, HMHS
    Coal dust explosion theory 48–50, 73, 247
    Construction 8, 12–19
    Final voyage and sinking 27–33
    Gigantic legend 36–7
    Inquiry into loss 94, 190–2, 197–8, 203, 205, 277–8
    Increased beam 34–6
    Launch 18
    Lifeboats 12, 16–17
    Mine theory 50–1
    Monument status 269–70, 272–3
    Munitions cargo theory 48–9, 156, 159, 230, 233, 247
    Service as hospital ship 23
    Stern redesign 224–7
    Torpedo theory 50, 197
Brittain, Vera (Nurse) 29, 92
Brown Bros. 80, 240
Brown, Joseph (Fireman) 33, 250
Burdigala (SS) 26–7, 38, 41, 73, 272

Cabins (B Deck) 144–5
Calypso (RV) 34, 38, 45, 52, 53
Calypso's Search for the Britannic (1977) 40
Cameron, James 161, 184
Capitol Cinema 93, 121
Cargo holds 49, 156–9, 198, 227, 229, 230, 231, 233, 247
Carlisle, Alexander Montgomery 10, 12
Cattaro 26
Celtic (RMS) 122
Central Powers 19, 40, 41, 250
Chapman, John (Sixth Officer) 31
Chatterton, John 101
Città di Tripoli (SS) 38
Children's Playroom 117
Cobh 122
Collision mats 182
Compasses 80
Compass Platform 82–4
Condensers 222
Constantine I (King) 249, 250
Cooling Room 186–90
Copeland Spode pottery 139
Costa Concordia (MV) 5
Cousteau, Jacques 34, 37, 38, 39, 40, 42, 44, 45, 46, 48, 60, 73, 80, 86, 112, 159, 230, 264
Crosbie, John (Turkish bath attendant) 252–3
Crow's Nest 71
Crownsin (trawler) 24
Cunard Line 12, 14, 20, 92, 109, 165
Cuxhaven 24

Danzig 24
Dardanelles 21
Demolition Ireland 121
Dining Saloon (First-Class) 167–73
Docking Bridge 228
Dodd, George (2nd Steward) 252–3
Doro Passage 5, 26, 27
Dover Castle (HMHS) 198
Dowse, Elizabeth Annie (Matron) 29
Droycon Bioconcepts 54, 57, 264
Dublin 93, 121, 122, 161
Duncan (HMS) 250
Dyke, Harry (Assistant Captain) 28, 32

Eckett, Thomas (Engineers' Writer) 41
Edinburgh 240
Edgerton, Harold (Dr.) 38, 52
Elevator (Aft First-Class) 84
Elevators (Forward First-Class) 82, 106–8
Elevator (Second-Class) 146–7
Emergency dynamos 220
Engineering (Magazine) 18
Engineers' Mess 181–2
English Channel 96
Ephorate of Marine Antiquities 133, 264
Etches, Henry (Baker) 41
Euboea (island) 26
Evaporators 231
Exmouth (HMS) 250
Expansion Joints 76–7, 80–2, 125–6
External survey 66–85

Farquharson, Richard (Captain RN) 26
Fearnhead, T (Captain, RAMC) 31
Fielding, Gordon (Fifth Officer) 28, 30, 31–2, 78
Firemen's staircases 155
Firemen's tunnel (Forward) 94–5, 98–100, 156, 185, 190, 198–200, 215
First World War 5, 248, 270

INDEX

Fleming, John Alexander (Rev.) 27, 32, 63–6, 127
Fleming, Robert (Chief Engineer) 32, 182, 216
Flooding Analysis (1996) 88–90
Forecastle 67–71, 151–7, 159
Foremast 71, 127
Foxhound (HMS) 33
Free Surface Effect 207, 259
Funnels 78–9

Galley (First- and Second-class) 220
Gallipoli 20, 23
General Room (Third-Class) 224, 229, 237–40, 242
Germany 19, 21, 37, 40, 41, 42, 96, 112, 254
Gialiskari 5
Gibraltar, Strait of 24
Gladstone graving dock 20, 21
Global Underwater Explorers 86
Goliath (tug) 33
Gurr, Kevin 47, 86
Gutenberg, Johannes 179
Gymnasium (First-Class) 114–17
Gymnasium (Second-Class) 226

Hackett, Chris 88, 90, 257
Hague Convention 41
Hall, J & E 231
Hamburg Amerika Line 109
Hampshire (HMS) 96
Hampton Court 126
Harland & Wolff 8, 10, 12, 16, 19, 21, 34, 77, 80, 88, 91, 96, 103, 104, 107, 110, 118, 122, 128, 167, 171, 174, 177, 192, 198, 200, 208, 218, 219, 224, 240, 253, 272
Haslar 10
Hawke (HMS) 36
Hayes-Sadler, Arthur (Rear-Admiral) 248
Heard, Hugh (Captain RN) 94, 248, 250, 255
Hellenic Centre for Marine Research 54, 58, 86
Hellenic Ministry of Culture 37, 264, 272, 273–4
Hellenic Navy 44, 53
Henry Wilson & Co. 141
Herald of Free Enterprise (MV) 207
Herculaneum (tug) 208
Heroic (HMT) 33
Herz Horn 51–2
Hexanite 52
Hillier, Thomas (Quartermaster) 42
History Channel 101
Holland 40
Honeycott, George (Lookout) 33, 250
Honeysuckle (HMS) 42
Hope, Nick 47
Hume, Robert (Chief Officer) 27
Hydrographic Office 38
Hynes, John 121–2

Imperator (SS) 109
Imperial War Museum 165
International Mercantile Marine (IMM) 19
Ioannis Point (Tenos) 42
Ioulis 5, 65
Irish Sea 21
Ismay, Joseph Bruce 128, 130
Italy 23

Jablonski, Jarrod (GUE) 47
Jessop, Violet (Stewardess) 30–1
John Brown & Co. 219
Jonquil (HMS) 42

Kaiser, The 254
Kaiserliche Werfte Shipyard 24
Kapok 182
Kea (island) 4, 6, 26, 28, 30, 32, 33, 53, 66
Kea Channel 5, 23, 25–6, 27, 33, 34, 38, 40, 41, 46, 47, 50, 52, 53, 54, 56, 57, 58, 60, 66, 73, 185, 197, 207, 248, 263, 269, 272, 274
Knorr (RV) 52, 53
Kohler, Katy 185
Kohler, Richie 101, 185, 186
Korissia 5
Kovacs, Evan 101, 185, 186

La Scala Theatre and Opera House 93, 121, 161
La Spezia 23
Lancaster, Claude (Purser) 32
Lapland (SS) 19
Laurentic (RMS) 14
Lavatory (third-class men) 176–8
Laws, Francis (Third Officer) 30
Laws, Frederick (Captain) 97
Lee, Richard 208, 218
Lisbon 24
Lemnos 21, 23
Library (Second-Class) 160–4
Liverpool 20, 21, 141
Livadi 5
Lloyd's 192
Lounge (First-Class) 82, 84, 120–3
Louvain (HMS) 38
Lusitania (RMS) 12, 14, 16
Luxor 39

Macbeth, Sheila (Nurse) 79, 249
Maids' & Valets' dining saloon 226
Main Entrance (Aft First-Class) 84–5, 125, 137, 269
Main Entrance (Forward First-Class) 82, 108–14, 183
Main Entrance (Second-Class) 85, 145–7, 160
Main Entrance (Aft Third-Class) 229, 236

Main Entrance (Forward Third-Class) 159–60
Mainmast 127
Mais, Ernest (Captain) 42
Makronisos (island) 27
Malta 39, 42, 92, 117
Marconi operators' dining saloon 226
Marconi Room 82, 105–6, 167
Marconi tuner 166–7
Marie Rose (trawler) 42
Massachusetts Institute of Technology 52
Mauretania (RMS) 12, 14, 20, 23
McGill, Barry 138, 185
Mediterranean Sea 20, 21, 23, 24, 25, 254, 266
Megantic (RMS) 14
Meltemi (wind) 5, 185
Mersey, Lord 10, 12, 251, 257
Messany, Adalbert Franz 39–40
Messina, Strait of 27
Metacentric Height 90–1
Millennium (MV) 92
Mine (EMA Type) 51–2
Minefield search 52–4
Ministry of Defence 273
Mondello Park Club House 121–2
Morris & Co. 122
Mortuary 228
Mudros 21, 23, 27, 33, 39, 40, 42, 248
Museum für Musikautomaten 112
Mykoni Channel 25, 42
Mykonos 26, 42

Napier Brothers Ltd 70, 151
Naples 23, 27
Nasturtium (HMS) 24
National Museum of the Royal Navy 273
Naval Engineering College (Devonport) 10
Naxos (island) 42
New York 207
Niemöller, Martin (Oberleutnant zur See) 54
Noemvriana 249–50
Normandie (SS) 207
North Atlantic 8, 14, 19, 23, 103, 266, 242
North Sea 21, 24
NR-1 (US Submarine) 44, 45

O'Brien, John "Bosco" 121–2
Officers' Mess 84
Officers' deck house 80, 104, 267
Oliver, George (First Officer) 31
Olympic (RMS) 10, 12, 14, 15, 18, 19, 20, 21, 23, 36, 69, 76, 77, 80, 84, 90, 91, 92, 95, 107, 109, 119, 120, 122, 126, 128, 130, 131, 148, 159, 160, 161, 171, 182, 195, 198, 200, 208, 213, 218, 224, 240, 251, 253, 256
Orientation of wreck 45, 66, 153, 266

Panelling 91–3
Pantry (First-Class) 172
Pantry (First-Class Lounge) 123
Paramo Cemetery 33, 250
Paramount Pictures 121
Parlour Suite (Port) 134
Patent Office 16, 139
Patras, University of 38
Patris (paddler) 272
Perman, George (Scout) 27, 31, 78
Phaleron 249
Philharmonie organ 109–12
Phillips, Charles (Trimmer) 33, 250
Phleva (island) 25, 33
Pilkington tiling 184
Piraeus 27, 33, 250
Pirrie, William (Lord) 10, 12, 36
Polyphemus (tug) 33
Port St. Nikolo 4, 26, 28, 38, 33, 53, 66
Potato wash room and locker 176, 179
Priestley, Harold (Major) 32
Printing Room 176, 178–80
Promenade (A Deck First Class) 117–8, 133
Promenade (B Deck First-Class) 133–6
Promenade (Second-Class) 160
Promenade (Third-Class) 229–30
Propellers 14, 15–16, 19, 28, 31, 32, 259
Psilas, Francesco 33
Public Record Office of Northern Ireland 36
Pustkuchen, Herbert (Oberleutnant zur See) 96

Queen Mary (RMS) 8, 18
Queen's Island 208

Ranger (Salvage vessel) 97, 100, 253
Ranson, Joseph (Captain) 21, 208
Rattlesnake (HMS) 26–7
Reading and Writing Room 82, 118–20
Rebreather technology (CCRs) 48, 94
Reception Room (First-Class) 164–7
Reciprocating Engines 15, 213–6, 218, 272
Reciprocating Engine Room 84, 182–3, 208–18, 231, 269
Red Star Line 19
Reed, J (Second Steward) 253
Refrigerating plant 231
Reserve Coal Bunker 49
Royal Army Medical Corps (RAMC) 21, 29, 30, 164, 229, 240
Royal Corps of Naval Constructors 10
Royal Mail Steam Packet Company 96
Royal Naval College (Greenwich) 10
Royal Naval Engineering College (Devonport) 10
Rudder 63, 228, 240, 243, 259
Russell (HMS) 24
Rusticles 56, 57, 186, 201, 202, 204, 215, 222, 266

Salamis 33, 249
Salcombe 97
Salonika 5, 26, 42, 249, 250
Sanderson, Harold 192
Saronic Gulf 25
Scotland Road 174–84, 185, 186, 190, 210, 220, 251, 255, 258, 259, 265, 270
Scourge (HMS) 33, 79
Shade Deck 224
Sharpe, William (Serjeant) 33
Shipbuilder, The 126
Ship's Hospital 224, 229, 236–7
Shrewsbury 93, 122
Siess, Gustav Johannes (Kapitänleutnant) 24, 25, 26, 73
Sluice valve 222–3
Smith, Albert (stoker) 100
Smith, Bill 53–4
Smith, Edward (Captain) 105
Smith, William Alden (Senator) 248
Smoking Room (First-Class) 125–6, 137
Smoking Room (Second-Class) 147–9, 160
Smoking Room (Third-Class) 224, 228, 229
Southampton 8, 27, 40
Sparti (SS) 33
Spickett, Daisy (Nurse) 92, 165, 167
Staer, George (Commander RN) 248, 250
Starehole Bay 97
Starfish Enterprise 86
Starting Platform 215–16
Steering Gear 224, 229, 236, 240–3
Stella (fishing vessel) 53
Stevenson, Rich 99, 185
Stoking Indicators 201
Stothert & Pitt cargo cranes 72, 160, 226–7
Superstructure 76–85, 118
Sunderland Forge & Engineering Co. 70
Swimming Bath 190
Syra (island) 33

Telemotor 80
Tenos (island) 26, 42
Thetis (HCMR submersible) 58, 60
Thompson graving dock 19
Thursby, Cecil (Vice-Admiral) 42
Titanic (RMS) 6, 8, 10, 12, 13, 14, 15, 28, 29, 30, 34, 36, 37, 40, 44, 48, 52, 54, 56, 58, 69, 76, 80, 82, 88, 90, 91, 92, 103, 104, 105, 107, 109, 114, 117, 118, 119, 120, 122, 126, 128, 130, 131, 134, 148, 153, 159, 160, 161, 165, 171, 174, 182, 184, 192, 195, 198, 202, 208, 213, 218, 224, 227, 240, 247, 251, 253, 255–63, 267, 272
Titanic Inquiries 10–12, 248, 251, 257
Titanic's Lost Sister (NOVA, 1996) 46, 47
Toilets (Third-Class) 176–7
Torbay (HM Submarine) 38
Toulon 26

Transport Division 20, 21, 192
Turbine Engine 15, 216, 218, 219
Turbine Engine Room 85, 215–22, 265, 269
Turkish Bath 184, 185–90, 250, 251, 252
Tyler, Percy (Private) 32, 161, 164, 228, 236

U73 23–6, 33, 38, 41, 42, 51, 54, 197
UC22 38
UC66 96
UK National Archives 38, 44
UK government title 46, 264, 269
Union Castle Line 42
Unrestricted Submarine Warfare 40, 254
US Navy 44

Valletta 24
Vaterland (SS) 109
Veitchi flooring 148, 186, 237, 243
Venizelos, Eleftherios 249, 250
Veranda Cafés 126–7
Vienna 40
Voluntary Aid Detachment (VAD) 92
Vourkari 5

Walters, Thomas (Steward) 41
Wandilla (HMHS) 39
Warilda (HMAT) 198
Watertight bulkheads 13–14, 28, 98, 100, 108, 152, 190, 192, 195, 204–5, 210–13, 250, 251, 253, 258, 259, 271
Watertight doors 95, 186, 190, 192–5, 198, 200, 205–7, 250, 251, 253, 259
Watertight double skin 11, 14, 28, 34–6, 91
Waygood-Otis Co. 107
Welch, Robert 140
Welin davits 29, 77
Welte & Söhne 109, 110, 112
Well Deck 72–6, 159–60
Wheat, Joseph (Assistant Second Steward) 251–3, 259
Wheelhouse 80
White Star Line 8, 12, 14, 18, 19, 20, 21, 36, 37, 109, 113, 128, 131, 138, 161, 164, 192, 195, 208, 250
White Swan Hotel (Alnwick) 92, 93
Wilding, Edward 10–12, 256, 257
Windlass gear 151–5, 243
Wreck deterioration 54–60
Wreck fauna and flora 60–1

Yarrow-Schlick-Tweedy system 15